Harriet M. Skidmore

Beside the Western Sea

A collection of poems

.

Harriet M. Skidmore

Beside the Western Sea
A collection of poems

ISBN/EAN: 9783741134890

Manufactured in Europe, USA, Canada, Australia, Japa

Cover: Foto ©Andreas Hilbeck / pixelio.de

Manufactured and distributed by brebook publishing software
(www.brebook.com)

Harriet M. Skidmore

Beside the Western Sea

BESIDE

THE

WESTERN SEA:

A COLLECTION OF POEMS.

BY

HARRIET M. SKIDMORE ("MARIE").

WITH AN INTRODUCTION BY THE MOST REV. J. S. ALEMANY, D. D.,
ARCHBISHOP OF SAN FRANCISCO.

SECOND EDITION.

NEW YORK:
P. O'SHEA, PUBLISHER,
37 BARCLAY STREET, AND 42 PARK PLACE.

———

1877.

DEDICATION.

To the greater glory of God, and the greater honor of His Immaculate Mother, IIis angels, and saints, those faithful ones whom the King Himself "delighteth to honor," this humble work is most earnestly and reverently dedicated.

"MARIE."

SAN FRANCISCO, CALIFORNIA.

PREFACE.

I FIND this preface necessary, as an apology for the unparalleled presumption of which I have been guilty, in collecting and publishing my poor rhymes and metrical attempts. And, in order to excuse myself, I am even fain to cast a portion of the blame on the too partial kindness of those revered friends who have suggested and encouraged the publication above referred to.

Most of the poems contained in this volume have been contributions to Catholic newspapers and periodicals; and that they have condescended to admit such productions into their columns, is another reason of my audacious attempt at bookmaking.

The only merit these humble rhymes possess is, the intention with which they were written, and which is stated in the dedication, viz.: "The greater glory of God, and the greater honor of His Immaculate Mother, His angels and saints." And as the simple weed blooming by the wayside, and the sparrow uttering its feeble chirp in the meadows, thus present their acceptable tributes of praise to "the dear All-Father," so may my humble verses be received as a like earnest, though infinitely less worthy, offering.

And if this, my poor mite, given to the cause of truth and virtue, find favor in His sight, then shall I even rejoice that I have sung my simple songs, and woven my garlands of wild verse-flowers, "Beside the Western Sea."

"MARIE."

San Francisco, California,
Feast of the Purification, February, 1877.

INTRODUCTION.

SEVERAL poetical pieces have appeared for some time past, in some public journals, under the signature "Marie," and they seem to have attracted more than ordinary attention. In common with others, I thought they were deservedly praised. Those which I happened to read, appeared to me to reveal the peculiar and, in our days, rare combination of poetical genius and Christian spirit. Hence I was glad to learn that the distinguished authoress consented to review and enlarge her poems, and offer them to the public in a single volume.

And although not born a poet, nor being very partial to poetical compositions, I take pleasure in using my name to introduce this volume, "Beside the Western Sea," for the following reasons: First, because the lovers of poetry will, in my humble opinion, possess in it a model of rare worth, to encourage them and guide their compositions; and, secondly, because a good poem, like an exquisite painting, when guided by a Christian spirit, is most interesting and beneficial to the reader. It presents the subjects in their true light, it gives them life and animation, it graces them with befitting beauty, engages the attention and admiration of the reader, refreshes his mind with vivid impressions of the true, and gladdens his heart with noble impulses, and a wish for the lovely.

 I frequently deem it a waste of time to read poetical compositions, because they frequently seem to contain but the repetition of one idea, without entertaining the imagination with any rhetorical flourish ; and so they might be called a sort of heavy, prosy poetry, tiresome without instructing. And the task is far more unendurable, when the object is an insidious encouragement to passion at the expense of morals. Such disguised attacks on truth and virtue should receive the frowns of all respectable persons. The case in the volume before us seems to be the very opposite ; for, while it presents but Christian subjects, refreshing the reader's mind with precious Christian recollections, it ornaments them with poetic beauty ; it breathes, while instructing, a chaste and pious spirit : it is, I believe, a precious offering to virtue and truth.

✠ JOSEPH S. ALEMANY, O. P.,

Archbishop of San Francisco.

SAN FRANCISCO,
FEAST OF ST. AGATHA, 1877.

CONTENTS.

x CONTENTS.

The Consecrated Months :

AD MAJOREM DEI GLORIAM.

I saw from the radiant East unrolled
　The curtain of cloud and gloom,
And the bright young monarch, in robe of gold,
　Arose from his riven tomb ;
And the shining hosts of his herald-rays
　Their limitless pathway trod,
And I read, in their glittering banners' blaze :
　"To the greater glory of God ! "

They hurled their lances of light adown,
　And the night-bound earth was free,
And jewels flashed in the mountains' crown,
　And gleamed on the golden sea.
They traced in the sheen of the purple hill,
　And wrote on the sparkling sod,
And the waves reflected, with joyous thrill :
　"To the greater glory of God ! "

In the dim old wood, and the bloomy bower,
　The gladdening splendor glows—
On the dewy cup of the forest flower,
　And the heart of the royal rose ;
And the tiny leaf, and the bloom most rare,
　That rise from the fragrant sod,
This legend fair on their brightness bear :
　"To the greater glory of God."

And earth awakens her grandest song,
　To welcome the kingly day ;
And soft are the notes of her insect throng,
　And sweet is her birdlings' lay.

And the echoes ring through the forest dim,
  Where the breeze-stirred branches nod,
The glad refrain of her ceaseless hymn:
  " To the greater glory of God."

So the countless voices of earth resound,
  While the sun's bright legions pass
Through the darksome caves of the deep profound,
  And over the bending grass;
Till far o'er mountain, and stream, and vale,
  Night stretcheth her mystic rod,
That song still sounds on the sighing gale:
  " To the greater glory of God."

Then the gladsome sounds of the daylight cease,
  And over a silver stair
The shining wings of the hosts of peace
  Float down through the dewy air.
And o'er that path of the moonbeams bright,
  That linketh the sky and sod,
They write, in letters of silvery light:
  " To the greater glory of God."

And an awestruck hush o'er the earth is spread,
  And the twilight murmurs die,
While the starry bands of the night-queen tread
  Their limitless realms on high;
And the silent heart of the dreamer hears
  Float down to the dewy sod,
The echoing song of the silver spheres:
  " To the greater glory of God."

O bend thou low unto nature's scorn,
  Self worshipping heart of mine!
O veil thy forehead, thou ingrate, born
  To lead in the hymn divine!
Ay, bend thou low to the ruthless stroke
  Of nature's Nemesis-rod,
Thou mute, when the glorious pæan woke:
  "To the greater glory of God."

Forgive, and the heart of the wayward teach,
  O nature's carolling throng !
And bid its lowlier echoes reach
  The tones of your lofty song.
With the lark's note ringing above the skies,
  And the bee's song on the sod,
O let its carol harmonious rise :
  "To the greater glory of God."

With the sunlight radiance let it shine,
  With the moonbeam brightness glow;
Be its glory won from the source divine,
  And mirrored on earth below.
When night shall wave o'er its day-beams fair
  Her drear and dark'ning rod,
Be still the gleam of its starlight there :
  "To the greater glory of God."

And when the unending day shall fling
  Its light o'er the "crystal sea,"
And the aisles of the endless ages ring
  With the song of the countless free ;
O'er the vast expanse of the kingdom fair,
  By the pure and the ransomed trod,
Its voice in the echoing strain shall share :
  "To the greater glory of God."

THE CROSS AND THE CRESCENT.

THE CROSS AND THE CRESCENT:

A DRAMA OF THE FIRST CRUSADE.

Personages :—

JOSEPH, *an Aged Pilgrim.*
MARY, *his Daughter.*
PETER, *the Hermit.*
SARACEN WARDEN.
SIR HUGH, *a Christian Knight.*
SIMON, *Patriarch of Jerusalem.*
LADY BLANCHE.
LADY AGNES.
MARQUIS DE MERINCOURT.
COUNT DE LILLE.
SOLIMAN, *Sultan of Nice.*
HAMET, *a Messenger.*
GODFREY.
RAYMOND.
TANCRED.
BALDWIN.
Christian Residents of Jerusalem, Soldiers, etc.

PROLOGUE

TO THE DRAMA OF

THE CROSS AND THE CRESCENT.

O PICTURED Past! what privilege to see
Thy golden age of faith and chivalry,
When spell-bound Fancy turns her backward glance
On those proud days of glory and romance!
What wondrous streams, enshrined in rosy light,
What lofty pageants move before her sight!
What visions fair, in swift succession, throng
The brightest scenes of story and of song!
The pomp of tourney, and its knightly train,
The mail-clad hosts that filled the battle-plain;
The hooded falcon and the baying hound,
The fiery steed, whose footstep scorned the ground;
The moated castle, and its massive wall,
The Christmas holly of the banquet hall;
The yule-log's blaze, the wassail's spicy draught,
The courtly train that gayly smiled and quaffed;
The fearless archers of the greenwood free,
The May-day sports beneath the bloom-decked tree.
All these, in "bright confusion," strangely blend—
Framework of visions that can know no end.

But purer scenes, and holier pictures, too,
Circled with halos, rise o'er fancy's view :
Fair scenes that history scorns not to record,
With comment glad and panegyric word.
The gray-robed pilgrim, with his scallop-shell,
His sandal-shoon, and staff that aided well
In wintry blast, and summer's sultry heat,
Still moving on with firm, unfalt'ring feet—
Why roams he thus unceasing, day by day?
To what far region leads his cheerless way?
Seeks he the treasures of some golden mine?
Or would he bend at proud ambition's shrine?
No! no! those faithful feet have longed to stand
Within the limits of the Holy Land.
He seeks the caskets of a priceless gem :
Jerusalem, Nazareth, and Bethlehem!
His infant King he yearneth to adore,
Where sages bowed, and shepherds knelt before.
He greets the cottage of the Holy Child
In lonely Nazareth, obscure and wild ;
And on, beside the Jordan's hallowed stream,
Where once the sacred Dove's mysterious gleam
Shone o'er the baptized Saviour's lifted head,
Still moves the pilgrim's firm, unceasing tread,
Till, from the summit of a rocky height,
Jerusalem shines upon his longing sight.
O ye who cross the mighty deep to tread
Where dim Westminster shrines her noble dead !
Who hail the tombs of kings and warriors brave,
And linger fondly by the poet's grave!
Say, can ye scorn *this* pilgrim's bended knee,
Upon the sacred height of Calvary,

Before the dear Redeemer's rocky tomb,
And 'mid the olive garden's mystic gloom?
Ah! 'twas a holy aim, for love divine
Guided the pilgrim's path to Palestine.
But o'er his way a fearful storm arose:
The dreaded forms of cruel Moslem foes,
Whose bloody spears sustained their erring cause,
And won submission to their Prophet's laws.
The faithful Christians felt their fiendish hate,
And found a dismal doom—a hapless fate.
Insult, oppression, and most grievous wrong—
These woes the zealous Christians suffered long.
And the vast armies of their paynim foe
Still westward swept—a storm of death and woe;
To Christian climes, to Europe's hallowed lands,
Nearer and nearer came the savage bands.
The guarding shepherd of his Saviour's flock
Saw the swift cloud, and heard the tempest-shock;
For the blest Church had shed a holy ray
O'er Europe's pagan night and clouded way;
And long those zealous popes had cherished there
The op'ning bud of learning, bright and fair.
Now must it perish? Must those blighting bands
Destroy the hard-won gems of Christian lands?
The cruel torch that burned fair Egypt's lore,
Must it consume the Christian sage's store?
The thought was anguish! and from favored Rome
Rose many a prayer for bright religion's home.
Heaven sent its answer! With a heart of flame,
And words of might, a holy hermit came.
He saw dread foes pollute the sacred shrine,
He saw the wrongs of fettered Palestine;

And through each realm his tireless steps he bent,
Repeating his sad story as he went,
And urging potent prince and valiant knight
To battle for their safety and the right.
They heard his voice—his sacred call obeyed:
Armed, with their vassals, for the blest Crusade,
And, with the cross upon each noble breast,
Mounted their chargers, laid the lance in rest;
And while the battle-cry, " God wills it," rose
From every heart, went forth to meet their foes;
Resolved, beneath the Christian's holy sign,
To battle well for faith and Palestine;
And bid, through strife and peril, gain and loss,
The cruel Crescent pale before the Cross!

THE CROSS AND THE CRESCENT:

A DRAMA OF THE FIRST CRUSADE.

ACT 1.

SCENE I.—*Before the gates of Jerusalem.*

Enter JOSEPH, *a pilgrim, and his daughter*, MARY.

MARY.—Now, God be praised, my father, thou
    may'st pause!
Lo! here the portal of Jerusalem!
How like a weary dream our journey seems!
But He who led his Israelites of old,
Safe to their promised land, hath guided us,   ·
Through our long, toilsome wand'rings, hither; but
'Tis not the hour of entrance. We must wait
The porter's coming. Meanwhile, seat thyself
Here on this mossy stone. Poor, aged limbs!   '
Sore need have they of rest.

    JOSEPH.—   Nay, nay, my child!
Thus will I take repose. (*Kneels.*) Here, lowly
    bowed
Before the holy city of His love,   ,
The scene of all His matchless sufferings,
Will I adore my Saviour, Sovereign, God!
I thank Thee, Lord, the pilgrim's prayer is heard!
The goal is won! O joy unutterable!

The yearnings of this heart are satisfied :
To look upon Thy loved Jerusalem,
O'er whose proud stubbornness Thy tears have
     flowed ;
To follow where Thy blood-marked footsteps went,
Thou thorn-crowned Monarch ! o'er the royal road
Of pain and anguish to Thy mystic throne—
The cross Thy creatures reared on Calvary.
(Ah, rocky height ! henceforth most fruitful soil,
Bearing bright blossoms of redeeming grace !)
Ay, and to kneel before Thy sepulchre,
Whose narrow limits could not fetter Thee,
When Thy sweet work was done.   This boon, dear
     Lord,
Thou knowest how, through all these weary years,
It was the ceaseless burden of my prayer ;
For I believed that nearer unto Thee
My soul could come—could win a clearer sense,
A deeper knowledge, of the priceless gifts
Thy love hath purchased, if these feet could stand
Upon the soil once watered by Thy blood,
And hallowed by Thy travel-wearied steps ;
If the last glances of these age-dimmed eyes
Might rest upon those consecrated spots,
The scenes of earth's most wondrous tragedy,
Her Maker's death of agony,   And now,
Beyond this gate, the blessed recompense
Of one poor pilgrim's gladly-suffered toils,
The fair reality of his fond dreams—
Jerusalem, with all her peerless wealth
Of hallowed shrines reposes.

Enter PETER *the Hermit.*

PETER.— God be praised!
And when our eyes have feasted on that wealth,
Can we not cry in grateful ecstasy,
E'en as the holy Hebrew cried, of old,
"Lord, let thy servants now depart in peace:"
Our eyes have seen the city of thy love?
JOSEPH.—Ay, holy hermit! for no other scene
On earth is worthy to attract the gaze
Of eyes that have beheld Jerusalem,
And wept on Calvary.
PETER.— Alas! alas!
That earth's most holy treasures e'er should be
In the foul grasp of ruthless infidels!
That Christian pilgrims must await the will
Of their Redeemer's enemies ere they
Can weep in that lone garden where He wept,
Or linger, with His Mother, at the cross,
Or haste, with Magdalen, at early dawn,
To the rent tomb of their triumphant Lord!

Enter SARACEN OFFICER.

SARACEN.—Another troop of crouching Christian
    dogs!
Ha! ha! methinks your pious pilgrimage
Hath been of little profit, for ye seem
A beggar train, in sooth.   But so are all
Your pilgrim tribe.   The staff, the scallop-shell,
The robe of gray, the dusty sandal shoon—
All, all alike.   A Christian pilgrimage!
Bah! what a weary misery must it be!
Away! ye dogs! the Moslem spurns ye thus!

Allah be praised that ye are in our power!
We hold your holy places.   Ay, 'tis well
To make these Christians grovel at our feet.
'Tis thus your brethren crouch within yon walls;
'Tis thus all Christendom shall crouch ere long,
For we have sworn to tear from every tower
In Christian Europe that detested cross,
And rear our flaming crescent in its place.
Away! away! and bid your race prepare
To bend before the Prophet's followers,
The future rulers of the world.   Begone!
Our city hath too many of your kind.

   JOSEPH.—Ah! fatal blow of all my dearest hopes!
Father! Thy will be done!   At least, at least,
I may yield up my worthless life to Thee,
Thus near that mount where Thy own priceless life
Was sacrificed for me. (*Sinks down, exhausted.*)

   MARY (*supporting him*).—   Alas! he dies!
In pity hear my pleading; spurn me not,
But give my father entrance through yon gate—
That hope hath been the day-star of his life.
Fulfil it now, and I will gladly be
A life-long prisoner, a drudging slave.
Nay, more! I'd shed my heart's last crimson drop
To gratify my father's fondest wish,
And think the favor all too cheaply bought.

   PETER.—Refuse them not; as thou would'st find
    sweet aid
And soothing mercy in thine hour of need,
So grant the pilgrim's last petition now,
And let his wearied soul depart in peace,
Within the walls of his Jerusalem.

SARACEN.—-Cease, babblers, cease! Have ye the
   piece of gold,
The tribute-money which your race must pay,
Ere ye can win admission through yon gate?
If so, your prayer is granted.
   MARY.—   Woe is me!
I have no gold.   A cruel robber-band
Of roving Bedouins have taken all,
Save one small coin, and with that, yester-eve,
I bought refreshment for my fainting sire,
For he drooped, worn with hunger, by the way.
Alas! I knew not of this entrance-price.
   SARACEN.—And thou hast dared to talk of
      slavery!
Of willingness to suffer prison-bonds!
Fool! know'st thou not that I could cast thee hence
Into the foulest dungeon yonder, where
Are Christians pining now.   And slavery!
Ay, drudging servitude—a life as hard
As is the toiling over-burdened beast's—·
Is now the fate of hundreds of thy race,
In the fair city of Jerusalem!
Go, then, and think thyself supremely blest
That thou art suffered to depart! And thou,
Most pious pleader! hast thou, then, the sum
To win thy entrance? Nay, I'll warrant me
Thou hast not e'en the smallest coin of brass.
   PETER.—Thy taunt is true.   I have not e'en a coin
Of brass or copper. Nay, for I may bear
Nor purse, nor scrip. It is the Master's law,
To whose blest service I am vowed, and so
I bow me to His holy will. He knows

How I have longed to shed the soothing tear
Of heart-felt penitence upon that shrine—
That rocky altar, where He, Victim-Lamb
And Priest, united, freely offered up
A perfect, priceless sacrifice for man.

    SARACEN.—Go hence, then, to thy cave, and spend
      thy life
In longings for a boon thou shalt not win
Until the tribute-price be paid. Away!
Or must I drive ye hence? (*Advances threateningly.*)

SIR HUGH *rushes in.*

    SIR HUGH.—   Hold! hold! I say,
Thou fiendish savage! Take thy tribute-bribe!
            [*Throws down a purse.*
Here is a goodly heap of that vile trash:
The gold thy soul doth worship. Take it, then,
And straightway ope your gate.
        [SARACEN *stops to count the money.*

    SIR HUGH.—   Nay, linger not!
I am that Christian knight who saved the life
Of thy proud caliph. 'Twill be worse for thee
If thou dost venture to refuse.

    SARACEN.—   Sir knight,
Thy gold hath magic charms, albeit thy words
Are bold, in sooth. Yet, as the Prophet lives,
I like thy proud, outspoken bravery.

    PETER (*extending his hand*).—God's benison upon
      thee, noble knight!

    SIR HUGH (*bowing*).—Nay, holy hermit, if this
      trivial act

Hath won thy prayers, 'tis fuller recompense
And richer meed than I could dare to claim.
                    [*Turns to the other pilgrims.*
Rise, Christian friends! and freely pass yon gate.

MARY.—Alas, sir knight! the rude repulse we met
From yonder Saracen hath proved, I fear,
A death-blow to my feeble, aged sire.
          {SIR HUGH *holds a flask of water to his lips.*
          He opens his eyes.
SIR HUGH.—Nay, courage, maiden! See, thy
    father lives!
Arise, good sir, and enter freely now!

MARY.—Arise, my father, let us thank this knight,
Whose noble act hath won the wished-for boon.

JOSEPH.—Nay, is it so? O, this is life indeed!
I feel my ancient strength return once more. (*Rises.*)

JOSEPH and MARY.—May God reward thee,
    noble cavalier!

SIR HUGH.—Nay, nay, good friends, I merit not
    your thanks!
I were unworthy e'en the name of knight,
Had I refused my aid. But we must haste;
These Saracens are treacherous. Let us, then,
Follow yon warder with all speed. Good sir,
Lean thus on me, and I will lend my strength,
That we may quickly enter. Wilt lead on,
Good father hermit? We shall follow thee.

          [*Exeunt:* JOSEPH, *supported by* MARY, *and*
          SIR HUGH, *preceded by* PETER *the Hermit,*
          closely following the porter.

SCENE II.—PETÉR *the Hermit, soliloquizing at the Holy Sepulchre.*

Ah! this is holy ground! the heart must bow
In silent awe, in rev'rent homage now.
My Saviour's tomb! O words of mystery!
Yet clearest pictures of His love for me.
'Tis good to linger here. 'Tis good to stand
Within the limits of His holy land,
To tread those streets His blessed footsteps trod,
To hail the tomb that hid the martyred God;
To weep in that lone garden, where He wept
O'er sinners' woes, e'en while those sinners slept,
And the pure stars in sympathy looked dim,
As the dread cup was offered unto Him;
To linger where the perfect Victim hung
On that strange shrine, to which He freely clung,
Bidding His sacred blood unceasing flow
A sea of grace, adown the mount of woe.
And this lone, rocky tomb, the wondrous mine
Of love's own treasure, priceless, pure, divine!
Here, here the Conqueror triumphed over death,
And healed the blight of sin's envenomed breath.
How clearly rise upon my spirit's view
Redemption's scenes, in pictures fair and true!
His sepulchre! sweet gate of heaven! here
Can I most fitly shed the soothing tear,
And bid my heart's best tide of love be spent
E'en at this portal, by the Victor rent.
And yet, alas! a foul, polluting race
Invade the limits of this holy place.
Here, 'neath the shadow of His cross they stand,
And rear, with demon might and daring hand,

The false, false symbol of their fiendish hate
For Him whose life hath opened mercy's gate!
E'en, e'en for *them !*   But let me utter, too,
His words: "Forgive! they know not what they
   do!"
Dear Lord of love! give vision to the blind
Who scorn this casket where Thy form was shrined!
Let the dread reign of cruel error cease,
That faithful hearts may seek Thy tomb in peace,
And every nation bless the Crucified,
And love the holy city where He died.

Enter SIMON, *Patriarch of Jerusalem.*

SIMON.—Amen! Good pilgrim, I have murmured
   here
That earnest prayer, through many a weary year;
Yet while mine eyes behold the unchecked wrong,
My saddened heart exclaimeth, "Lord! how long?"
How long, blest Saviour! shall a tyrant hand
Rest on the treasures of Thy holy land?
How long shall those whose love hath led them here,
Above Thy tomb to shed the sacred tear,
Be crushed, insulted, even at that tomb,
And find, in freedom's land, the captive's doom?
When shall Thy faithful children cease to feel
The iron pressure of the despot's heel?
   PETER.—O holy patriarch! to many a scene
Of cruel wrong my shrinking soul hath been
Indignant witness; e'en to-day I saw
Two Christians forced, like drudging beasts, to draw
A laden wain; bound, too, in camel-yoke,
And hailed with scoffs, and urged by cruel stroke!

SIMON.—Alas! dear pilgrim, would such scenes
    were few!
Too oft, too oft, they meet the startled view;
And I, the Christians' patriarch, must see
My children's woes, without the power to free.
O that some valiant host, undaunted, strong,
Would win redress for this most grievous wrong,
And check the progress of this fearful band,
Who swear to conquer every Christian land;
To ride to victory on the boundless flood.   ·
Of Christian tears and hated Christian blood!
To tear the cross from each polluted shrine,
And plant, instead, the Moslem's crescent sign!
    PETER.—List! holy patriarch! full many a knight,
High-souled, strong-armed, and undismayed in fight,
Dwells, even now, in Christian climes afar,
Whose heart would thirst for just, long-needed war
'Gainst the barbarian horde, the savage race,
Whose tyrant hands pollute each holy place,
And whose unconquered sword and unchecked
    hand
Will sweep, like poison blast, o'er every land.
Back to its deserts must that blast be driven—
List to my counsel! 'Tis the will of heaven!
In good Pope Urban thou wilt find a friend;
Unto him, then, thy heart's petitions send,
And to each Christian prince,—for all are brave,
And strong, withal,—the Holy Land to save.
To-morrow morn I take my homeward way,
And thence thy pleading missive will convey.
Throughout each Christian kingdom will I go,
And there recount the tale of matchless woe;

And urge the brave, by every tender claim,
For Faith's dear sake, in Mercy's holy name,
With valiant arm to crush this frightful foe,
And hush their fellow-Christians' wail of woe;
To tear the crescent from this holy wall,
To bid the cruel throne of Islam fall,
And checking error's God-defying reign,
Plant the pure cross upon these towers again.

SIMON.—'Tis heaven's will, and heaven's holy fire
Doth light thy glance, thy earnest tones inspire.
How willingly will I those words obey,
And bid'God speed thee on thy holy way!
My home is near, haste with me hither, then,
And let thy ardent zeal inspire my pen;
And while sweet mercy's charge thou'lt homeward
    bear,
Thy name shall dwell in my unceasing prayer.

[*Exeunt.*

SCENE III.—*A valley of Lorraine. Enter* LADY
BLANCHE.

LADY BLANCHE.—Peace! perfect peace! how,
    like a white-winged dove
It broodeth o'er the landscape! Everywhere
Doth nature own its charm. In soft repose
She rests, as though sweet Eden memories
Were haunting all her heart. An infant's breath
Is not more gentle than this morning breeze,
That scarcely stirs the incense-laden flowers;
And e'en the golden light that softly floods
Each mossy dell, but makes the stillness seem

Deeper and more intense; as beaming smiles
On face of slumb'rer tell of softest dreams.
Alas! alas! that man's discordant strife
Should mar the loveliness of nature's rest!
That he, the lord of all this smiling earth,
Should ever make its sacred quietude
Unwilling witness of his violence.

Enter LADY AGNES.

LADY AGNES.—Ay, ay, sweet friend! thy mourn-
    ful thoughts are mine,
And the same cause, I ween, hath summoned them:
This quiet vale, ere sets yon shining sun,
Must be the scene of fierce, unholy strife.
My brother, and thy kinsman, Guy De Lille,
Have vowed to meet in deadly combat here,
E'en on this tranquil morn. Alas! alas!
This velvet turf shall soon be strangely dyed.
    LADY BLANCHE.—O fiendish feuds! when will
        they cease to fill
Fair Europe's vales with tumult? From yon tower
Of our ancestral wall my glance can rest
On the fair lands and castle of De Lille;
Yet they, whose fields are thus so closely linked,
Are severed by a dark, unchristian feud.
    LADY AGNES.—I fear me much that angered
        heaven will send,
Full soon, dread retribution. Brothers here
Pour out each other's blood, in their blind rage,
Unheeding that a fierce barbarian foe
Speeds now, perchance, like tempest-driven cloud,
On, on o'er Europe's fair, faith-hallowed soil.

LADY BLANCHE.—O gentle friend ! that dark fore-
  boding fills
My daily thoughts and nightly dreams with woe.
My cousin Mary—dost remember her?
Last year she went on holy pilgrimage
With her loved sire, the saintly Sieur De Vaux,
Unto our Saviour's sepulchre. To-day
A holy palmer, on his homeward way
From Palestine, did tell a sad, sad tale
Of my sweet cousin. She is there detained
A captive, pining in a dungeon cell!
My gentle Mary in the Moslem's power!
The thought, the fearful thought, doth chill my
  . heart;
And her poor father, feeble, old, and spent
With the fatigue of his long pilgrimage,
Hath sunk beneath the fiendish cruelty
Of that fierce race who rule the Holy Land.
  LADY AGNES.—'Tis woful tidings! And my
    darkest fears
Wax stronger, darker, by this tale of woe.
But yester-eve, when kneeling at his feet,
In tearful supplication, I did breathe
This fear unto my brother, as I prayed
That, for sweet mercy's sake, he would renounce
This fierce, unnatural strife. He darkly frowned,
And bade me, if I would not share his hate—
His deep, undying hate—to hold my peace,
Nor dare, with childish tears and whining tongue,
To bid a knight forswear his knightly vow.
O that a heart so full of gentleness,
And tender, pitying, bounteous charity,

Should be thus blinded, warped by erring code
Of what the world calls feudal chivalry!
But I have turned my soulful pray'r to heaven;
And now, to yonder consecrated shrine,
The cross-crowned dwelling of a God of peace
And pitying love, I hie me—there to pour
My heart's deep anguish forth in prayer.

    LADY BLANCHE.—   Sweet friend,
I will attend thee thither; we will waft
Our mingled sighs to heaven, and God will hear
Our fond and tearful pleadings.   This sweet day
Shall not be witness of unchristian strife—
Shall not bring death and wailing to our homes.
Pray too, with me, that those now severed hearts
Of Europe's noblest knights may form, ere long,
A sacred league to wrest the Holy Land
From the foul grasp of infidels; to free
Their fellow-Christians from a tyrant's power,
And check the dread simoom, now sweeping on
From Asia's deserts o'er our hallowed clime.

                          [*Exeunt.*

Enter PETER *the Hermit.*

    PETER.—God grant that prayer!   O worse than
        demon strife!
What marvel that the pure, paternal heart
Of our loved pope doth mourn unceasingly
O'er the unchristian feuds of Christian knights,
Who, heedless of his fond remonstrances,
And the pure precepts of a peaceful faith,
Still bid their brethren's blood cry, as of old,
From earth to angered heaven!   And, holy pope,

Well, well, too, may'st thou mourn o'er this fair
    land,
So lately led, from dreary pagan night,
To the clear morning-light of Christian truth,
Now doomed, unless some valiant arm will save,
To feel the with'ring blight of Moslem hand ;
And e'en, while basking in fair learning's morn,
Be plunged again in depths of stygian gloom.
O that my voice could check the coming storm!
Could make these passion-blinded nobles see
The woes that threaten thus, and bid them form
A sacred compact for their own defence,
And the deliverance of the hapless band
Who pine 'neath Moslem, God-defying rule,
By the polluted shrines of Palestine !
Hist! hist! I hear the coming combatants.
Alas ! that hate should darken brows like those!
                    [Conceals himself.

    Enter DE MERINCOURT *and* DE LILLE.

DE LILLE.—This is the place of combat. Nerve
    thine arm,
Marquis De Merincourt, for deadly strife !
    DE MERINCOURT.—Nay, Count De Lille, this arm
    hath strength, I trow,
To cope with thine, as it hath done ere this.

    PETER *the Hermit suddenly appears.*

PETER.—Hold! most unworthy children
       Of a God of love and peace !
      Pause in your demon pastime !
       Your strife unholy cease !

Ye that were linked together
   In faith's fraternal chain,
Can ye thus rudely sever
   That sacred bond in twain?
The pure baptismal water—
   Hath it not laved each brow,
That, stamped with fiercest passion,
   Is madly scowling now?
Those lips that breathed to heaven
   The same sweet words of prayer—
Can they, with tones of discord,
   Pollute the tranquil air?
Ye share one blessed banquet,
   At one pure shrine ye kneel,
Yet, scarce from worship risen,
   Uplift the horrid steel!
And can ye hope for heaven's
   Serene, harmonious life,
Yet pass, O Cain-like brethren,
   Your earthly days in strife?
Men! Christians! pause and listen:
   While ye are warring here,
Your fellow-Christians perish
   Beneath the Moslem spear.
Ye've vowed to aid the injured,
   Ye've sworn to crush the wrong,
Yet Christians pine in dungeons,
   And cry, " O Lord! how long?"
The Saracen hath planted,
   With sacrilegious hand,
His false, triumphant standard
   Within the Holy Land.

Lo! on the walls of Zion,
  And o'er each sacred shrine,
Waves now his blood-stained banner,
  And gleams his crescent sign.
The tomb of your Redeemer,
  The mount whereon He bled,
Have known that haughty presence,
  That foul polluting tread;
And they who fain would linger
  Beside each holy place—
Each scene of man's redemption,
  And heaven's saving grace—
Who've longed to hold, on Calvary,
  Celestial converse sweet,
Like dogs are spurned and trampled
  'Neath unbelieving feet.
And, Christians! pause and listen:
  While ye are warring here,
A just and fearful judgment
  Too surely draweth near.
Within the fairest province
  Of olive-laden Spain,
The Moorish unbeliever
  Holds now his haughty reign.
Would ye see that rule extended,
  And groan beneath his tread?
To the crescent sign of error
  Would ye bow the servile head?
Up! up! renounce your quarrels,
  And form one sacred band,
To guard your own dominions,
  And save the Holy Land!

God wills the holy compact!
  By all ye hold most dear,
By your vow to aid the injured,
  And to break the tyrant's spear;
By your love for faith's pure altars,
  And your zeal for its sweet sign,
Aid the Cross against the Crescent!
  Strive for God and Palestine!

DE MERINCOURT.—Ay, ay, God wills it! These
  are magic words,
They rouse my soul from its unworthy sleep;
The scales of passion leave my sight. Henceforth,
One lance shall ne'er be stained with brother's
  blood.
Give me thy hand fraternal! Let us make
A new, a worthy vow—the vow of peace
And Christian reconciliation; thus
We seal the sacred pledge. Our arms shall be
Linked in the cause of justice, God and truth.
                              [*They clasp hands.*

DE LILLE.—Ay, in this hold, this fond fraternal
  clasp,
Let us crush out our most unchristian hate;
And, linked in unity that maketh strong,
Bid these firm hands begin a nobler strife.
And O what potent voices rouse us now!
Our faith, our homes, the safety of our land;
Our knightly vow to check the tyrant Wrong,
And wrest his victims from his demon grasp;
Our zeal, as children of the thorn-crowned King,
For the protection of each holy place
Whereon our rich inheritance was won—

These voices cry from every sacred mount
And hallowed vale of that fair Eastern land,
The shrine of love's great sacrifice.   At last,
We hear that blest appeal.

DE MERINCOURT.—   Thy magic voice,
O holy hermit! hath awakened us: .
And may all Europe hear those thrilling tones,
And join the sacred compact.   Come, dear Guy,
Henceforth my friend, my comrade! come with me;
A knightly throng within my banquet hall
Are gathered even now.   They, too, shall see
The magic influence of holy words—·
The new, sweet consummation of our strife—
The worthy conquest love hath won to-day.
And thou, too, reverend hermit, haste with me,
And let thy heaven-inspired accents rouse
Yon throng of chieftains to heroic deeds,
In the blessed cause of God and Palestine.

                                    [*Exeunt.*

SCENE IV.—SOLIMAN, *Sultan of Nice.*

SOLIMAN.—Now, out upon that plaguing Persian
    race,
Who, with their wretched schism, so impede
The progress of Moaveah's followers!
In truth, these false Mahometans are worse,
Ay, more vexatious than our Christian foes.
Well, let them strive—the Turkish Mussulmans
Shall never yield to Ali's erring sons.
Ha! ha! we've argued well.   Full many a prize
Hath the scorned Turkman wrested from their
    grasp.

Jerusalem, with all its whining throng
Of Christians, still is ours.   Soon, very soon,
Egypt's proud Caliph may be taught to bow
To the scorned Sultan of the Turkish race ;
And to our heav'n-blest arms, alone, shall be
The deathless glory and the rich reward
Of conquest o'er the longed-for Christian world.
Ay, thanks to Allah and our scymitars,
The crescent still prevails.   Our Prophet's throne
Full soon will crush beneath its conqu'ring weight
The Christian crew, and their rebellious creed.
We triumph by the sword.   No pleading tone,
No fond entreaty, wins *our* convert throng.
The fierce-browed soldier, the relentless spear,
And streaming blood, and death of agony—
These are our priests ! these our baptismal rites !
O Christian dogs ! thus will we win your souls,
Your kingdoms, and your wealth.   Thus have we
      won
Your holy city and your cherished shrines—
Our Emir rules them well.   The hated band
Of meek-faced pilgrims well may testify
How stern, how merciless, how terrible,
Is the dominion of the Mussulman
O'er the opposers of his conqu'ring creed.
" Allah il Allah ! " how that thrilling cry
Will ring, ere long, o'er Europe's haughty realm !
How redly, in the fierce, destroying flame,
Will their proud libraries, their cherished store
Of manuscripts and massive volumes, gleam !
So gleamed they once in Egypt's capital,
When Omar's torches doomed the lettered trash
To ashes and oblivion—hist ! who comes ?

Enter HAMET.

SOLIMAN.—What! Hamet! here? Why comest
    thou from Nice?

Thy looks, thy garments, do betoken haste—

What meaneth this? Speak, fear-struck dotard,
    speak!

What gloomy phantom hath affrighted thee?

HAMET.—Benignant ruler, and most favored son

Of our great Prophet! deign to lend thine ear

Unto thy faithful servant, and forgive

This hasty entrance and unwonted guise.

The weighty message he hath hither borne

Must plead in his defence. The capital

Is in most dismal strait and peril sore.

SOLIMAN.—Ha! ha! thine opium draughts have
    crazed thy brain.

Our Nice in peril? Nice in dismal strait?

How dar'st thou bring thy senseless ravings here?

Off! off! and drive thy phantoms hence by sleep!

HAMET.—Nay! hear me, gracious lord! My
    words are truth.

A Christian army, countless as the leaves

Of a vast forest in the summer's prime,

Are now besieging our great capital—

Thy Vizier bade me hither speed, and say

That, if thou dost not straightway send good aid,

The garrison must yield to Christian arms.

SOLIMAN.—To Christian arms! No! as the
    Prophet lives,

The race of dogs shall not win entrance there.

And I was dreaming of the victory,

The triumph, over hated Christendom,

That seemed so near, so certain! 'Tis most strange!
We had no warning of this host's approach.
Surely they journeyed hither on the wings
Of the swift midnight blast! But they shall die
As dies that blast upon the torrid waste
Of wide Arabian deserts. Dare they hope
To bid the Crescent pale before the Cross?
Presumptuous fools! We'll bid them howl with
    woe
For this, their mad attempt! Away! away!
And summon ev'ry warrior to arms!
Go! bid them straightway sally forth to Nice!
Stay! I'll go with thee, for my presence there
Will be as fuel to their fiery zeal.
Haste! haste! and let our ceaseless summons be:
'Death, unrelenting death, to Christian dogs!

                    [*Exeunt*

———

SCENE V.—*Eve of the conquest of Jerusalem.*
    GODFREY of Lorraine (*solus*).

GODFREY.—O holy city of the Christian's love!
    Why art thou still the cruel Moslem's prey?
Surely our cause is just, is blest above:
    Then why doth needed victory delay?
The paynim crescent gleams, unconquered still,
    Where faith's Crusaders fain would plant the
        cross;
And truth lies crushed beside the sacred hill
    Where Israel's martyred King redeemed our
        loss.

Still, from within those error-guarded walls,
   Forth on the air the captives' shrieks are borne ;
And ceaselessly the lash of torture falls
   On those who, helpless and unaided, mourn.
Our ranks are thinned—each knightly spirit sinks
   Depressed, discouraged by the prospect drear,
While the fierce scymitar in triumph drinks
   Deep draughts of blood—the Christian's life-
      blood dear.
O Lord of Hosts ! how long shall these things be ?
   How long shall thine own land be thus defiled,
And saddest echoes rise, unhushed, to Thee,
   Of wailing servitude and anguish wild ?
In sorrow bowed, O Father ! we repent
   Of every sin against Thy sacred laws.
For much we fear our guilty hearts prevent
   The glorious end of our most holy cause.
A sudden hope dawns on my night of woe—
   We yet may kneel before the holy shrine,
And bid the tear of humble penance flow,
   'Mid grateful hymns for rescued Palestine.
So will I hie me to my warriors brave,
   And bid them win, by penitence and prayer,
The grace to gain the blessed boon we crave,
   Ere night shall hide to-morrow's sunlight fair.
                                             [*Exit.*

Enter RAYMOND, TANCRED, *and* BALDWIN.

RAYMOND.—O brave companions ! 'tis a weary
   strife,
And weary days have passed since yonder walls
First met our longing gaze.   Can we forget

The thrilling scene when, prostrate on the earth,
Our glittering hosts first hailed Jerusalem?
How throbbed each heart with deep and holy joy!
There, there, beyond those walls, the object fair
Of Faith's Crusade, of Faith's sweet visions, lay—
There, in the sunlight, slept Gethsemane;
There rose the rocky altar of the cross,
There knelt the pilgrims at love's sepulchre,
To free those holy shrines from Moslem grasp,
To bid the Christians worship there in peace,
Was our blest aim. "God wills it!" How that cry
Rose in one mighty voice from every heart!

  BALDWIN.—Alas, alas, that aim is not fulfilled,
And bravest souls are sick'ning with despair!
Still, still, yon portal is as firmly closed
As when the Christian army rested first
Outside its massy towers; and little hope
Remaineth of our longed-for entrance there.

  TANCRED.—Yet, courage, knights! success will
   bless our arms,
If we be strong of heart and firm of hand.
"Nil desperandum!" 'Tis a motto fair,
And he who follows it can never fail.
What? Can we faint with Godfrey at our head?
The pure-souled Godfrey, valiant, undismayed,
Saintly in life, adored by all who know
And own him as their leader? Crush the thought!
To-morrow we will strive with trebled zeal:
'Tis our last chance, yet humblest confidence
In heaven's sure aid doth bid me banish fear.

Enter PETER *the Hermit.*

PETER.—Brave Tancred! thy courage will win
thee success—
The hopeful in spirit sweet heaven will bless;
The Christian shall triumph, the cross shall pre
vail—
God wills it! God wills it! His word cannot fail.
He wills the blest triumph of right over wrong,
He wills that the just in the strife shall be strong;
Though the clouds may be dark, yet His light can
shine through—
God wills it! God wills it! His promise is true!
'Tis to chasten, to humble, He sendeth delay—
Though the journey be long, shall we faint by the
way?
No! onward and upward, with hearts strong and
pure!
God wills it! God wills it! His word shall endure!
By virtue, by vigils, by penance and prayer,
Man gaineth the power to do and to dare—
With a purified heart, and an unsullied hand,
We may aim the sure arrow, and lift the true brand;
For He who bade Israel triumph of old—
The just God of armies doth bid ye be bold.
To the helper of Gideon gratefully bow,
God willeth, God willeth, your victory now!
To-morrow—'tis Friday—redemption's bright day,
When the Conqueror passed o'er the death-darkened
way;
To give ye blest ransom, to bid ye be free,
He clung to His throne on the blood-purpled tree.

The garden He wept in, the mount where He bled,
Have felt the pollution of Saracen tread—
Up, up, to their rescue! nor falter, till they
Are won by the Cross, on its festival day.
But O, let sweet mercy with justice be twined—
To the pleading give ear, to the helpless be kind;
And armed thus with virtue, go forth to the fight—
God wills it! God wills it! we strive for the right!

Enter GODFREY.

GODFREY.—O noble war-cry, worthy of our
    cause!
To-morrow it shall ring with thrilling power
From those brave hearts who battle for the right.
Comrades! our task, as leaders in the strife,
Must be, by bright example, to enforce
Precepts of valor, charity, and zeal.
Let us be brave, but gen'rous; let no deed
Of cruelty or passion stain the cross
We wear upon our breasts, and in whose name
We wage our holy warfare.   Let us haste
To our dear chapel, there to win, by prayer
And holy vigil, purest benisons
Upon the Christian arms.   Thy pleadings blest,
O holy hermit! will give strength to ours,
And waft them heav'nward, as an incense-cloud.

                              [*Exeunt.*

SCENE VI.—*The morning after the conquest of Jerusalem.* PETER *the Hermit* (*solus*).

PETER.—The prize is won.   At last, at last,
The Red Sea of our strife is past !
God's chosen ones may safely stand
On thy freed soil, O Promised Land !
And o'er those streets, unfettered, tread
Where Israel's Victim-Lamb was led.
The pilgrim here may freely bow
Before thy holy places now—
May stand upon that summit lone,
The Victim's shrine, the Sov'reign's throne—
Muse 'mid the olive garden's gloom,
And kneel beside his Saviour's tomb.
O loved Jerusalem ! art thou free ?
Hath the dread shadow fled from thee ?
Or am I mocked by cruel gleam
Of glowing fancy's faithless dream ?
No ! no ! the blissful scene is true.
At last, before my longing view,
The Christian symbol gleameth bright
From lofty wall and mountain height ;
No more the crescent's haughty glare
Defies thy sacred sunlight fair ;
No more will sighing captives pine,
Or Moslem hands pollute the shrine.
Fled is the shadow, loosed the chain,
And Faith resumes her peaceful reign.
O Lord of Hosts ! the praise is Thine.
The purchased prize, the ransomed shrine,
By Thy blest aid was won ; Thy ear

Heard the deep wail of woe and fear,
And Thou hast dried the mourner's tear.
My work is done, my prayer is heard :
The heart that trusted in Thy word
Was not deceived. And now I go,
To bid the grateful tear-drop flow
Upon that fair and favored earth
Thy blood redeemed from blight and dearth.
O that my soul might win release
Within this home of love and peace,
And, all her earthly fetters riven,
Rise from Thy sepulchre to heaven !

[Exit.

Enter the Crusaders, in procession, singing the Te
Deum.
All exclaim.—Hail, Holy City ! Hail, Jerusalem !

GODFREY *enters, attended by* RAYMOND, TANCRED,
and BALDWIN.
All shout.--Long live Duke Godfrey, and our
noble chiefs !
GODFREY.—O brave Crusaders ! with o'erflowing
hearts
We here return your greeting. 'Tis a time
For holy joy and blissful gratitude.
Lo ! the rich recompense of all our toils—
Jerusalem, with all her treasures fair,
Her blest associations, her rich store
Of holy memories and hallowed scenes !
'Tis bright reality ; at last, at last,
This glowing prize that mocked our eyes so long,

Like false illusion of the desert waste,
Which showeth crystal streams and waving trees
And blooming Edens, and serene retreats,
Unto the weary pilgrim ; and while he,
Eager and hopeful, quickens his faint steps
To reach his rest, the mocking phantom false
Flies on before, yet ever seemeth near:
But now the true oasis shines at last,
And we have reached its blessed boundary.
Error is checked. Her vile, polluting hand
Removed from fair religion's holy shrines—
From dungeons foul, from weary servitude,
The Christians issue, as the mourning band
Came from the hateful bonds of Babylon.

Enter SIMON *the Patriarch, with a throng of
Christians.*

SIMON.—Ay, noble knight! they come, a grate-
   ful throng,
To thank their brave deliverers—to bid
Heaven's choicest benedictions rest on those
Whose valiant arms have won their blest release.
Long had the Christians' tears of anguish flowed
On the sad spot where once a Saviour wept;
Long had the heart-wrung pray'r and weary sigh
Wafted to heaven their history of woe,
And, with the eloquence of agony
For aid and comfort, and the full redress
That heaven hath promised for the wrongs of earth,
Pleaded unceasingly. Long, long deferred
Was the blest answer, and the needed aid—
But now 'tis won. O blessed be His name

Who, as He armed the Israelites of old
With strength and valor 'gainst their pagan foes,
Hath armed the faithful soldiers of the cross,
And caused their triumph o'er that dreaded race
Who strive, by fearful threat and cruel spear,
To win unwilling homage—to extend
Their erring Prophet's false, ferocious creed.

  GODFREY.—O reverend patriarch! the unworthy
    chief
Of the Crusaders humbly bows to thee,
The shepherd true of Zion's Christian flock,
And faithful minister of that dear Lord
Who won our life on yonder barren height.

  All exclaim.—Hail, holy patriarch of Jerusalem!

  SIMON.—Permit me, noble knights, to utter now
The fond petition of my brethren here:
That from your dauntless band ye would select
A ruler for Jerusalem—a king
O'er the new realm your bravery hath won.
The just enforcement of the laws, the weal
And safety of our city, now demand
A monarch just, beneficent, and wise.

  TANCRED.—Ay, holy patriarch, thy prayer is well.
And, for that dignity, none, none on earth
Is more deserving, or hath firmer hand
To wield the sceptre; or a nobler brow
To wear a sovereign's diadem of power,
Than our loved leader, Godfrey of Lorraine!

  RAYMOND.—Well hast thou spoken, Tancred!
    From my soul
I echo all thy words! Though he would check
The voice that in his presence praiseth him,

Yet will I say, that, if unsullied life,
Valor and justice, tender charity,
And every peerless grace that, as a robe,
Is worn upon a Christian warrior's heart,
Render their owner worthy of a throne,
Then is Duke Godfrey in his fitting place,
Were he the ruler of a world-wide realm !

SIMON.—Most noble duke, I pray thee to accept
The dignity for which, with one accord,
Thy followers do pronounce thee worthy. Ay,
Let not humility bid thee reject
A station which thy duty to the realm
Thine arm hath helped to conquer, and thy zeal,
As faithful Christian, for religion's weal,
Would urge thee now to fill.

GODFREY.—   Revered
And holy patriarch, and too partial friends,
Ill do I merit your so lavish praise ;
And all unworthy am I of that throne
Your friendship would confer. Yet, in the name
Of duty as a Christian and a knight
Whose arm hath lent its weak, yet willing, aid,
In our blest triumph, unto this fair realm—
The casket of so many priceless gems,
Those holy shrines, that must be guarded well—
I do accept, with humble, grateful heart,
The government of loved Jerusalem ;
And, in my urgent need, I now implore
Your potent prayers, that I may win the boon
Of grace to be most faithful to my trust,
And make my reign, as reigns should ever be :
Useful to earth, and blest by well-served heaven.

BALDWIN.—Belovéd leader! let my willing knee
Be first to bend to our new sovereign;
And let my voice salute thee with the words
It shall repeat, when, on thy brow benign,
Our patriarch shall place the jewelled crown:
Hail! hail to Godfrey, our most worthy king!

> *All repeat.*—Hail! hail to Godfrey, our most
> worthy king!

> GODFREY.—Ah! noble comrades! do not bid
> me wear

A sceptre here, or jewelled diadem:
My hand shall never grasp a golden rod
Where my dear Lord's once bore the mocking reed.
Upon this brow no costly crown shall gleam,
Where He hath worn a diadem of thorns.
The name of monarch, even, is too much
Here, in this city of the cross-throned King.
And now, to render fitting thanks to Him
Who gave the victory—who well may claim
The fond Crusaders' heartfelt gratitude—
Let us unto His sacred tomb repair,
As humble penitents; and as He wept
O'er human sins, when that glad multitude
Strewed royal palms in His triumphal way,
So, even in our glad, victorious march,
Let us bemoan the guilt that twined His brow
With cruel thorns, and bade our King repose
Upon a throne of matchless agony.
'Twas by a wondrous chance, upon the day,
E'en at the self-same hour of that strange scene—
The man-God's saving death on Calvary—
That this new triumph of the cross was won:

'Tis meet, then, that another triumph now—
The contrite sorrow of our humble hearts—
Should here be gained by that most blessed cross,
Where first it rose on favored Calvary.
'Tis fitting, too, that thou, O patriarch!
Shouldst guide thy newly-chosen followers
Unto that shrine where oft thy earnest prayer
Hath pleaded for the coming of this day
Of cloudless joy and blest deliverance.
Lead, then, this humble train of penitents
To the dear tomb of their triumphant Lord,
That they, with grateful hearts, may mingle there
The tear for foul offences with their glad
And deep thanksgiving for the victory
That bade the Crescent's false and lurid glare
Pale in the light of Truth's resplendent Cross!

[*Exeunt omnes.*

EPILOGUE

TO THE DRAMA OF

THE CROSS AND THE CRESCENT.

THUS valiant knights a noble conquest made,
And closed triumphantly their First Crusade;
Redressed the wrong, and reared the holy sign
Above the rescued realm of Palestine.
Godfrey, whose virtues hist'ry loves to tell,
Ruled that fair clime, and watched its treasures
 well;
Yet, when his noble life at last was given
Back to its God, to find its crown in heaven,
Again the cloud grew dark above the land,
So long sustained by his victorious hand;
Again the paynim scymitar of dread
Flashed in proud triumph where the Christians
 bled.
From Clairvaux's abbey sainted Bernard came,
And, in Religion's cause and Mercy's name,
Bade the brave heart and strength-invested hand
Battle once more for Faith's beloved land.
Again that sacred summons was obeyed,
Again they gathered for a new Crusade;
And, through alternate victory and loss,
Waged the just warfare of the holy cross.

Long years fled by, and still the strife went on—
Fame tells the deeds of those bright ages gone,
And shows the Lion Heart's victorious name,
That to the Saracen such dread became,
The Moslem mother by it hushed her child,
And horsemen checked the charger foaming wild
Yet, while she smiles o'er many a conquest made,
Fame mourns the losses of the last Crusade ;
But smiles again, as cheeringly she shows
Full many a triumph even in that close.
Error was checked—the Moslem's dreaded lance
No more toward bright Europe dared advance ;
And fair concessions, gladly granted, gave
Freedom to those who sought their Saviour's grave.
For, the proud Saracen no longer chose
To battle 'gainst such hydra-headed foes ;
And, though victorious, had been taught to fear
The Christian sword that so long matched his
    spear.
Fair Science, too, had many a triumph won,
Before the battles of the cross were done :
The pilgrim scholar added to his store
Arabia's tongue, and Syria's starry lore ;
New halls of learning rose and flourished fair,
Watched well by those whose throne was Peter's
    chair.
There pale-browed students found an endless feast,
'Mid the rich treasures gathered in the East.
The needle guide, that seeks the northern star,
First proved its value in the holy war,
And led, at last, the sons of smiling Spain
To the new empire, o'er the Western main.

And commerce, too, could bid her strength expand,
By the new intercourse with Eastern land
Then Venice rose, proud sovereign of the sea
And ruled the world by laden argosy.
Then, in the shining leaf from Syria brought,
Its costly shroud the patient silk-worm wrought;
And, torn from Eastern soil, the slender cane
Transferred its nectar to Italia's plain.
Another triumph Europe's realms had won
Ere the Crusaders' noble work was done:
The savage warfare 'gainst whose guilty reign
Religion's ministers long strove in vain—
The Cain-like strife, when, in unchristian feud,
Fierce knights their hands in brothers' blood
    imbrued;—
This died at last, when, linked in friendship's band,
The Christian army sought the Holy Land,
And Europe saw her direst evil cease,
When feudal lords were clasped in bonds of peace.
So came this good from the dread hand of war—
Well worth renown such noble triumphs are.
Ah! cold contempt should never cast her shade
On those who battled in each just Crusade;
Who, bound by knightly vow to right the wrong,
For Faith and Freedom struggled well and long,.
And, through alternate victory and loss,
Still bade the Crescent bend before the Cross.

THE SIEGE OF GRANADA.

THE SIEGE OF GRANADA,

A DRAMATIC POEM.

PERSONAGES:—

ABEN HASSAN, *the Moorish King.*
BOABDIL, *his Son.*
FERDINAND, *King of Spain.*
DOɪɪ JUAN DE VERA, *Christian Envoy*
ABDALLAH, *Moorish Prime Minister.*
ALI,
MAHMOUD, } *Moorish Courtiers.*
A Santon, or Moorish Prophet.
ISABELLA, *Queen of Spain.*
DONA INEZ,
DONA CATALINA, } *Ladies of Honor to Isabella.*
AYESHA, *Mother of Boabdil.*
MORAYMA, *Wife of Boabdil.*
ZORAYA, *Wife of Aben Hassan.*
MARIA, *a Christian Captive.*
ZARA,
FATIMA, } *Ayesha's Attendants.*

The Siege of Granada:

A DRAMATIC POEM.

ACT I.

SCENE I.—*An apartment in the Alhambra. The Moorish King*, ABEN HASSAN (*solus*).

ABEN HASSAN.—My soul is weary of this listless life,
   And loathes the quiet of its gilded cage;
O for the charger's neigh, the din of strife,
   The trumpet pealing 'mid the battle's rage!
This is the warrior's music, these the strains,
   For which I pine in idle bondage here,—
Ay, bondage base, though formed of silken chains.
   In sculptured halls, than dungeon far more drear,
I pace the broad and tesselated floor,
   And dream of fields bedewed with Christian
      blood;
My flashing scymitar seems red with gore,
   Cleaving its pathway through the fancied flood.
I wake, to curse the idle peace that reigns
   O'er spacious gallery and decked saloon;
To bid the minstrels cease their drowsy strains,
   And chide the tinkling fountain for its tune.
My carpet courtiers, broidered, decked, and bland,
   With snowy fingers pluck the silly flowers,

Or praise the beauty of this goodly land,
   Its verdant fields, its vineyards, and its bowers.
And they are very brave in mimic war—
   In joust and tournament well skilled and bold;
Of peaceful chivalry the boast, the star,
   By ladies praised, and decked with scarfs of gold.
But I will try their bravery ere long—
   Ay, I will lead them to a nobler strife.
Rouse, unscarred heroes, rouse, ye valiant throng!
   I'll bring rare changes o'er your lazy life.

Enter ABDALLAH.

ABEN HASSAN (*starting*).—Ha! who intrudes?
   Abdallah, is it thou?
May not the monarch of this mighty realm
Be left one hour in peace? Hence, hence, retire!
   ABDALLAH.—O gracious sov'reign! Allah's
   favored son,
Benignant ruler o'er earth's fairest clime,
Long may thy royal presence bless this throne!
Long may thine eyes illume these sacred halls!
   ABEN HASSAN.—Enough of adulation! If thou
   hast
Some trifling message, or wouldst beg a boon,
Speak quickly, and withdraw!
   ABDALLAH.—   Thy prostrate slave
Kisses the dust beneath his master's feet,
To thank this condescension, for he has
A weighty message for thy royal ear,
And craves a boon of thy rich clemency—
But 'tis not for himself. The wily king
Who rules the Christian dogs in fair Castile,

Hath hither sent a haughty train of knights,
On special embassy.   An hour since
The throng arrived, in glitt'ring armor dight,
Their steeds caparisoned with cloth of gold.
Sooth, 'twas a goodly sight! and as they pranced
In pompous silence through the quiet town,
The wond'ring citizens stood fixed and mute,
In stupid admiration.   That proud knight,
Don Juan De Vera, envoy of Castile,
And noble leader of this courtly troop,
Now in the royal antechamber waits,
And craves an audience.
    ABEN HASSAN.—   Allah! say you so?
On special embassy?   Nay, this is strange!
Castilian monarchs are not wont to send
Their pompous envoys to our Moslem court.
I read the riddle: 'Tis some cunning scheme
Of that proud plotter, Ferdinand.   In sooth
His insolence shall find as bold retort,
For Aben Hassan is no crouching slave.
Give cordial greeting to Don Juan, and say,
The Caliph grants him audience, and awaits
His coming, here.   But summon, first, two knights,
Two trusty servants, that some show of state
May honor the occasion.   Then attend,
Thyself, the knight unto our presence.   Go!
                       [*Exit* ABDALLAH.
    ABEN HASSAN (*solus*).—Now may our holy
Prophet aid me!   How I long
To fling defiance in the very teeth
Of these proud Christians and their wily king!
Well can I guess their errand.   Ere I pay

The servile tribute wrung from craven hearts,
This thirsty scymitar shall drink deep draughts
Of unbelievers' blood. I dreamed of war:
May Allah and his holy Prophet grant
Its swift and sure fulfilment!

Enter two Moorish knights.

KNIGHTS (*together*).—   Hail to thee,
Commander of the faithful! Death to all
Who dare oppose thy heaven-directed will!

ABEN HASSAN.—Ay, death indeed! stern, unre-
   lenting death!
Behold your places, knights! quick to your posts!
I hear the footsteps of our Christian guest.

Enter ABDALLAH, *with* DON JUAN.

ABDALLAH.—Long live our Caliph! May those
   royal eyes
Look down with favor on the prostrate slave
Who here presents, obedient to thy will,
Don Juan de Vera, envoy of Castile.
         [DON JUAN, *advancing and sinking on
            one knee.*
   DON JUAN.—Permit me, august monarch, in the
      name
Of my most gracious sovereigns, Ferdinand
And royal Isabella, of Castile,
To offer greeting courteous unto thee!
   ABEN HASSAN.—Rise, noble knight! Granada's
      king returns
The royal greeting, with profoundest thanks
For the kind courtesy of Castile's lord,

And his right regal spouse.   Thy presence here,
Most worthy cavalier, is honor more,
Far more, than we could claim.   It well rebukes
Our own neglect of courtly etiquette,
For which we crave our royal neighbor's grace.
Our Vizier hath informed us, noble knight,
That thou art come on special embassy :
Make known thy errand.   Our unworthy ears
Are open to thy words : speak, then, sir knight !

DON JUAN.—Thy will is potent, O most gracious
   king !
And claims a prompt obedience. I have come,
Commissioned by my sov'reigns, to demand
Full liquidation for the long arrears
Of tribute-money which Granada's kings
So justly owe the rulers of Castile.
This is my embassy.

ABEN HASSAN.—   And *this* my reply :
Go, tell thy masters that the craven kings
Who made that compact, and were wont to pay
To the Castilian crown the servile sum,
Are, thanks to Allah, mould'ring in their graves !
Now, the sole coinage of our Moorish mints
Are blades of scymitars and lances' heads !

DON JUAN (*aside*).—Presumptuous infidel ! would
   I might give
The fitting punishment for those bold words !
But slumber yet, good lance ! The time will come.
(*Aloud.*) Thy will is potent, and shall be obeyed
With scrupulous exactness.   May I now
Take courteous leave of fair Granada's court ?

ABEN HASSAN.—Nay, nay, most noble knight!
    Thou art our guest,
And we would show thee how the Moslem king
Can practise hospitality most meet
For our good neighbor's envoy. We implore
That thou wilt honor till the morn, at least,
Our grateful court. Abdallah, in thy charge
We leave our noble visitor; see, then,
That he be honored as befits his rank.
And now receive, most worthy cavalier,
As testimonial of our deep regard,
And true appreciation of thy brave
And knightly seeming, this fair scymitar
Of best Damascus steel.

DON JUAN.—   Most humble thanks,
O gracious monarch! for the regal gift.
He whom thou honorest thus, albeit he is
Most undeserving, ventures yet to hope
That this tried arm may, one day, give good proof
Unto the royal donor of its skill
In wielding this good weapon. Sire, adieu!
I kiss thy gracious hand.

        [Exeunt DON JUAN *and* ABDALLAH, *fol-
        lowed by the two knights.*

ABEN HASSAN (*solus.*)—Now, by the Prophet's
    sword, I like that speech!
It hath the ring of true and trusty steel.
O favored king, who hast within thy reach
    Such matchless souls, so valiant, true, and leal!
I long, brave knight, to cross a lance with thine,
    To meet thee, hand-to-hand, in deadly strife—

And soon the joy I covet may be mine;
  Soon may I know the free campaigner's life,
For my bold words will rouse yon haughty king,
  And call his courtly followers to arms.
Soon to the breeze my banner will I fling,
  And leave this dull Alhambra's drowsy charms;
The battle-cry will greet my longing ear:
  "Allah! il Allah!" 'tis a thrilling strain!
'Twill bid the Christian shrink in very fear,
  And fill his heart with strange, foreboding pain.
But twilight deepens; from yon minaret
  Sounds the muezzin's lazy call to prayer.
Hence, warlike visions, for a season yet—
  Now to the mosque, blithe-hearted, I repair.

———

SCENE II.—*An apartment in the Palace of Cordova.*
  DONA INEZ *and* DONA CATALINA, *two of* QUEEN
  ISABELLA'S *maids of honor, are seated at their em-
  broidery.*

DONA INEZ.—Now, of a certainty, our gracious
    queen
Is ill in mind. Did'st note her altered mood,
So anxious and so absent—pacing now
The echoing floor with quick, uncertain steps;
Then stopping short, as if she fain would chide
Her own strange restlessness, and sinking back
Into her seat with such a weary air,
And sighs so deep they pierced my very soul?
Then taking up yon piece of tapestry,
She feigned to broider, but I saw the tears

Descend like rain upon the glowing tints
Her trembling fingers crushed.   At last she raised
Her drooping head, and met my wond'ring gaze.
A startled flush o'erspread her face, and then
She rose up swiftly, as in sudden haste,
And quitted the apartment.   Verily,
These royal lives are full of cark and care,
And princely diadems too oft, I ween,
Hide cruel thorns beneath their flashing gems
To wound the wearer's brow.   What sayest thou?
   DONA CATALINA.—Thou speakest truly, Inez, but
      the grief
That presses now on our dear lady's soul,
Her subjects should partake, for 'tis their grief
Her mother-heart bewails.
   INEZ.—   Nay, Doña, now
Thy words are riddles.   Prithee, then, explain.
Of all that hath transpiréd at the court,
Or in this goodly kingdom, while my long
And grievous illness lasted, I could have
No knowledge, as thou knowest.   Tell me, then,
What means this trouble? Famine, plague, or war—
Or all, mayhap, combined?
   CATALINA.—   Ay, more than all!
If that may be.   But cease thy jesting tone;
It suits but ill the grave and gloomy theme:
Late yester-night a courier arrived,
A jaded horseman, haggard, wan, and sad,
From far Zahara; and the news he brought
Might well bring sorrow to a sov'reign's heart.
Good angels guard us! 'twas a dismal tale!
Its fearful horrors froze my very soul.

INEZ.—What of Zahara? Say not she hath fall'n
Beneath the cruel swords of infidels?
  CATALINA.—Ay, even so. Her guardians, too
    secure
In the tried firmness of her rock-like wall,
Were wrapped in slumber. E'en the sentinels
Slept on their posts, nor dreamed of lurking harm.
But, in the midnight's fav'ring gloom and hush,
The fierce marauders left their ambuscade,
And scaled, with wary skill and noiseless haste,
E'en the proud summit of the lofty wall.
The drowsy guards awakened, then, to die;
And through the fortress and the fated town
Soon rang that fearful cry, " The Moors! the
    Moors!"
Too late the startled soldiers buckled on
Their armor strong, and seized their shining blades.
Too late! alas, too late! though well and long
They battled for their honor and their homes.
But the fierce foe, within their very hearths,
Had gained strong foothold, nor relaxed his grasp,
Till, o'er the prostrate forms of Christian knights,
He strode to triumph and to victory.
Ah! who can paint the horrors of that scene,
Or know the agony of helpless hearts,
When the broad streets ran red with Christian blood,
And Christian shrieks of anguish blended with
The frightful war-cry of the fiendish Moors?
Now, in fierce triumph, o'er those conquered walls
The hated crescent waves. In dungeons deep
The Christian captives pine, or,—fearful fate!—
Are dragged to proud Granada's capital,
To serve as slaves for their stern conquerors.

INEZ.—O pitying heaven! 'tis a fearful tale,
And bids us cry, " How long, O Lord! how long "
Shall these things be? How long shall Moslem
    taint
Pollute the balmy air of Christian Spain?
    DONA CATALINA.—The end *must* come. Hath
    not our God declared
Vengeance is His, and He will well repay?

Enter QUEEN ISABELLA.

ISABELLA.—Your pardon, noble ladies. 'Tis a day
For earnest thought, and we would be alone.
[*Exeunt maids of honor.*
    ISABELLA (*solus*).—Alas, Zahara! can the care-
    less smile
Live on my lips, and thine be pale with pain?
Can I rejoice in heartless splendor, while
    Thy bravest sons are lying, basely slain?
Ay! shall thy queen be calm, while dungeons deep
    Echo the Christian captive's wail of woe?
No! bleeding hearts, and eyes that wildly weep,
    Your griefs are mine! for you my tears shall flow.
All night I knelt before the holy shrine,
    With hands upraised, in agony of prayer,
That our just God would aid this arm of mine
    From my loved realm its hated pall to tear.
Thou Lord Omnipotent! how long, how long,
    Shall helpless virtue yield to demon might?
Behold, avenging justice! how the wrong,
    Haughty and fierce, hath trampled on the right!
How godless hands destroy the sacred shrine,
    And bind Thy chosen land in error's chain!

O check this outrage by Thy power divine.
Aid Thy unworthy child to save her Spain!
O Thou wilt hear!   My prayer shall granted be!
I *may* retrieve this sad, this fearful, loss:
Soon from her bonds my kingdom I may free:
Soon shall the Crescent bow before the Cross.

Enter FERDINAND.

FERDINAND.—What holy dream, what ecstasy is
    this?
Good faith, my gentle queen, thou art inspired!
There beams such radiance from thy soulful eyes,
There dwells such strength of purpose on thy brow,
Such calm determination on thy lips!
And yet, methinks, thy cheeks are stained with tears,
As if thy soul had battled with the storm,
And bravely conquered
    ISABELLA (*smiling*).—   Even so, my liege.
But, if I read thy troubled mien aright,
That frowning brow, that restless, clouded look,
Tell that the storm still rages in thy heart.
    FERDINAND.—I render homage to thy skill, fair
    queen!
Well hast thou read my chafed and troubled soul.
Twas the war-kindling tale of yester-night
That roused this tempest in my slumb'ring heart;
That bids me grasp my good Castilian blade,
And force yon haughty Moor to rue the day
He made this base, this robber-like assault:
It shall bring ruin on his realm and throne.
I vowed revenge when his bold message came—
His haughty answer to our just demand—

But now the cup o'erfloweth.   By my crown,
Yon fiend shall drain it ; yet my angry mood
Will bid me act too rashly.   Give me, now,
Thy prudent council, thy sagacious plans—
What sayest thou to war ?

    ISABELLA:—   'Tis best, 'tis just :
A heavenly voice hath whispered to my soul,
In answer to my prayer.   It bids us haste
To cleanse this plague-spot from Granada's heart ;
It bids us arm for quick, ay, instant war.
Yet not for love of conquest, or revenge,
But that the Christian captive may be free
From Moorish thraldom ; that the fatal blight
Of vile, unhallowed hands no more pollute
With impious rites the consecrated shrine—
The Crescent fierce no more insult the Cross ;
That demon power be taught to own its God,
And cease its bold defiance of His will.
Ay, we *must* haste to war—God wills it so.

   FERDINAND.—Come, then ; let thy enthusiasm
     rouse
These valiant knights, who, in our audience-hall,
Are waiting thy decision.   Purify,
With these thy holy motives, all base thoughts
Of plunder or of vengeance.   Let us go.

                                 [*Exeunt.*

SCENE III.—AYESHA *and* BOABDIL, *in an apart-
ment of the Moorish palace.*

AYESHA.—Dare I advise rebellion 'gainst thy sire?
Was that thy question, faint heart? Listen, then,
And mark my answer well: I do advise,
Ay, and command it, too. Yon sceptred brute,
Thy fierce, unnatural father, is not worth
A son's esteem, much less submissive love.
His meanest subject loathes the tyrant's name,
And mutters curses on his blood-stained hand.
And shall we bow in vile allegiance here—
I, his insulted spouse, his outraged queen,
And thou? Bethink thee, trembler, who *thou* art:
His lawful heir, Granada's destined king!
Yon throne is thine! From his unworthy brow
Thy power could tear the crown! Then why delay
To claim thy true inheritance? Is't fear
That binds thee here, a helpless looker-on,
While I, who cherished thee, am mocked and
    scorned
For a vile Christian slave? Say, canst thou yield
Thy goodly realm to her usurping brood?

BOABDIL.—Nay, cease these taunts, my mother!
    'Tis not fear
That bids me yield obedience to my sire—
I am no coward, as thou knowest well;
And his stern cruelty hath long since crushed
From my young heart the last faint spark of love
Which nature's hand, in childhood, kindled there.
I long to crush this vile Zoraya's schemes,
And blight the hopes she dares to cherish, yet
My heart assures me 'tis no fitting time

For this bold step.   He hath a mighty host
At his command; and that dark prophecy
That hangeth o'er me like a blighting curse—
O'er all Granada 'tis a household word,
And by the very children I am called
Boabdil the Unlucky.   Ah, my fate!

   AYESHA.—And thou wilt let these superstitious
      fears
Fetter thy hands, and palsy thy young soul?
Now, out upon thee for such cowardice!
Fate! senseless word! I scorn its very sound!
The warrior's sword and dauntless lion-heart
Carve out the only destiny I own.
The stupid prate of vile astrologers
May do for silly peasants: princely hearts
Should laugh at such delusions.   Say'st thou, too,
That 'tis no fitting time to claim thy rights?
Why, Allah never gave a rarer chance—
Success is sure.   Thy father's rash attack
Upon Zahara is rich boon for thee,
But woe for him.   Yon wily Christian king,
Roused by the outrage, hath repaid it well,
As sad Alhama's graves can testify.
War with Castile, ay, long and deadly war,
Is now inevitable.   It must come;
And Hassan's subjects, maddened by the woes
His pride hath heaped upon them, boldly give
Free vent to their deep hate.   Canst thou not hear,
On every side, the fierce and boding sounds
Of execrations, bold, and loud, and deep?
But listen well, Boabdil!   I have caught,
Amid their threats, the glad, the welcome, tones

Of blessings coupled with thy name. Fond eyes
Look pleadingly to thee, and valiant hearts,
Eager and true, are ready, at thy call,
To join thy royal standard. Hasten, then!
Avenge *their* wrongs and *thine!*

BOABDIL.— I will! I will!
My lion-hearted mother, thy brave words
Have roused my soul to new, to nobler life.
I *will* obey thee. This good sword shall cleave
A glorious path to fair Granada's throne,
And, firmly seated there, I will redress
Thy injuries, brave mother. Once again
Unchecked, unrivalled, thou shalt proudly bear
Thy rightful name: Sultana.

AYESHA.— Thanks, my son!
But calm thy youthful joy. E'en walls have ears
And tongues to utter treason. Hark, a step!
It is thy father's heavy, cruel tread.
Thus walks he proudly o'er his subjects' hearts.
Let us away! The tyrant's eye may read
Our secrets on our brows. In sooth, my son,
He fears, each day, the trampled worms may turn
To sting the heel that crushes them. Away!

[*Exeunt.*

Enter ABEN HASSAN.

ABEN HASSAN.—Woe, woe, Alhama! O that
madd'ning cry!
That fierce outpouring of a wild despair!
It rings where'er I turn. In ev'ry eye
Hate, like a savage beast, doth boldly glare—

My people's hate! Their curses, loud and deep,
  Sound in my ear, like mutterings of a storm;
Their anger rouses from its long, forced sleep,
  And boldly rears its fierce, defiant form.
And wherefore? Ah! in characters of blood
  The dread reply is written on my soul.
My rash ambition hath unsealed the flood
  Which o'er my realm, too soon, will madly roll.
O Christian king! thou hast avenged full well
  The wrongs of thy Zahara—woe for woe.
On my Alhama's heart thy lightning fell,
  And crushed her life beneath its fatal blow;
But think not I will tremble. Let it come—
  This dreaded war. It was my daily dream,
And shall I shrink? Shall terror make me dumb
  When the storms burst, the wished-for lightnings
    gleam?
Perish the coward thought! O traitor throng,
  Who dare to curs eyour monarch! Ye shall know
My will is iron, and my sword is strong,
  To crush the rebel, and to quell the foe.
            [*Turning suddenly. A noise without.*
Ha! whence this uproar? Silence, there, without!
Who dares disturb the king?

  Enter the SANTON, *struggling with the guards.*
  SANTON (*to the guards*).—Detain me not! I'll beard
    the lion in his very den!
    ABEN HASSAN (*starting back*).—Demon, avaunt!
      hence, foul and hideous fiend!
Or, stay--Ben Hassan is no trembling loon.
By what vile incantation art thou here?
What sorcerer's art conjured thee? Demon, speak!

SANTON.—I am no slave of sorcery, no restless
    fiend of air—
This frame is worn by holy fasts, and sanctified by
    prayer ;
It is no demon fire that burns within these aged
    eyes—
They caught the light from Allah's throne, while
    gazing on the skies.
> Within the wildest mountain glen,
>   Full forty years, and more,
> I've heard the holy Prophet's voice,
>   And learned his sacred lore ;
> And oft in waking dreams by day,
>   And visions of the night,
> The pageants of the busy world
>   Have passed before my sight.

ABEN HASSAN (*aside*).—A crazed enthusiast,
    whose wildered brain
Hath urged him here, to read his monarch's fate.
(*Aloud.*)—Reveal thy inspirations ; doubtless we
Have played conspicuous part in these strange
    dreams.

SANTON.—Aye! I *will* read my dreams, O king !
>   The Santon knows not fear ;
> He will not quail before thy frown,
>   Nor heed thy haughty sneer ;
> And while I bid my visions rise
>   Before thy royal view,
> Look on the magic picture well,
>   And say if it be true.
> My dream was of a lordly town,
>   I saw its towers rise ;

Each turret rear'd its frowning brow,
    To meet the arching skies.
I looked within the stately walls—
    Ah! rich, I ween, and fair,
Was the proud city of the plain,
    That nestled calmly there.
That city glowed with wealth and life;
    I heard, in every street,
The eager sound of many tongues,
    The tramp of many feet;
And I blessed its stately palaces,
    Its gardens of delight,
Bedecked with sparkling fountains, and
    With blossoms rare and bright.
The picture passed, the night came on;
    A wild, a fearful wail—
A cry it pierced my soul to hear—
    Was borne upon the gale;
Once more I turned my startled eyes
    On that fair town, and lo!
I saw its massive towers rent,
    As by the lightning's blow;
I saw its stately homes despoiled,
    And on the ravaged plain
The bravest of its cavaliers
    Were lying, foully slain.
The Cross was waving where, so late,
    I blessed the Crescent's gleam—
Aye, writhe upon thy throne, O king!
    And read my faithful dream.
ABEN HASSAN.—Thy vision, Santon, is not hard
to read.

Ha! ha! thou art a prophet of the past!
Thy brain is crazed.   What are its dreams to me?
  SANTON.—Within a dungeon's cell I saw
      The Moslem captives pine;
    I heard them curse a tyrant's name! ·
    And list—that name was thine!
    They said the peace was broken by
      Thy fierce and haughty hand;
    Thy pride had brought this flood of war,
      To desolate thy land.
  ABEN HASSAN.—Ha! says't thou so?   Nay, listen
  in thy turn.
I *have* invoked this war!   It was *my* dream—
My dream of glory and of endless fame!
And it *shall* be fulfilled!   Ay, though a host
Of wild fanatics and their trembling dupes
Heaped threats and curses, high as yonder mount,
Upon my careless head.   I laugh to scorn
Thy senseless words, thy prophecies of ill.
  SANTON.—Then hear, thou impious tyrant,
      My dream of future woe.
    E'en as our fair Alhama sunk
      Before the Christian foe,
    So shall this regal city fall,
      In terror and in gloom;
    So shall this Vega rich become
      The patriot's bloody tomb.
    Woe to this fair Alhambra—
      The palace of thy pride—
    For, o'er its tesselated floors,
      A conqu'ring host shall stride.

The Christian king shall rule within
    These gay and gilded halls,
The Christian banner proudly wave
    Above its massive walls.
For Allah's wrath is kindled sore
    Against his traitor son,
And Allah's vengeance shall repay
    The ruin thou hast done.
Woe to thee, cursed by heaven,
    And hated by thy race!
Scarce shall thy body find on earth
    The meanest burial place.
By kinsmen's hands thy death shall come,
    And kinsmen's hands shall cast,
Into a nameless sepulchre,
    Thy haughty form at last.
Ha! ha! thou shrinkest! Do my words
    Disturb thy kingly state?
'Tis well! the madman's curse shall be
    The dread decree of Fate!

ABEN HASSAN.—O gracious Allah! must I bear
    these taunts?
Cease thy insulting words, and quit my sight,
Or this good lance shall still thy rebel tongue!
What! dost thou linger yet? Ho, there, brave
    guards!
Seize this bold maniac, and cast him forth,
And take good care he enter not again.

SANTON.—Thou hast no need to call thy slaves—
    With thee my task is done;
But sadder mission yet is mine—
    Stern duty, scarce begun:

O'er fields and cities I must roam,
   Still uttering, as I go,
This curse against my native land—
   Woe! loved Granada, woe!

                  [Exit.

ABEN HASSAN.—Insolent fanatic! why did I permit
His bold, audacious ravings? Yet, in sooth,
Such wild, weird lustre lurked within his eye,
Such magic power, such fascinating skill,
It bound my kingly soul as by a spell,
And made me helpless as a trembling bird,
Neath the bold serpent's gaze ; and though I burned
With fiercest anger, yet in vain I strove
To break the charm that held me, or to still
His bold, presumptuous threats, which now I heed
As lightly as the wild and wilful blast
Doth heed the mournful wailing of the boughs
Whose leaves it hath despoiled. Hark! yet his voice
Sounds in the outer court. This must not be ;
His demon art will pour into the minds
Of my retainers poison, that may prove
A deadly blight to their weak loyalty.
Now will I burst, like the fierce mountain storm,
On this false prophet, and, despite the looks
Of horror-stricken vot'ries, this good sword
Shall send the Santon's soul to paradise.

                  [Exit.

SCENE IV.—*In the Castle of the Albazoin, after the report of Boabdil's death, at the battle of Lucena.*

AYESHA.—Rouse thee, Morayma! this is vulgar grief!
Hush those wild moans, and check that rain of tears ;
Bind up thy tresses, and compose thyself.
Such childish sorrow ill befits thy rank—
Thou art the daughter of a royal line,
The consort of a prince, and thou should'st leave
Loud lamentation and dishevelled locks,
Fierce, frantic gestures—all excess of grief—
To low-born mourners, who have not yet learned
To curb their stormy passions.   Noble hearts
Must scorn such peasant weakness.   Rouse thee, then ;
Put on the armor of thy queenly pride,
And it will bring thee strength.
    MORAYMA.—   Ah! can it be
That thou, the mother of my murdered lord,
The favored parent of Granada's prince,
Dost thus upbraid my sorrow?   Hast thou not
A mother's love for thy most royal son?
And can thy soul restrain its anguish when,
From ev'ry heart throughout this stricken land,
The bitter wail—a nation's mingled woe—
Is borne upon the gale?   " Alas!" they cry,
" Alas! Boabdil, flower of chivalry,
Our pride, our hope, the day-star of our souls!
Thy light hath set in darkness and in blood,
While yet in its proud zenith!   Woe for thee!"

O royal mother! canst thou yet be calm?
O canst thou steel thy heart, in high-born pride,
'Gainst all its fond affections? Spare me, then;
Mock not my grief with cold and heartless words.
Forgive my weakness; think what bitter cause
I have for tears. My consort and my sire,
Both cold in death on that dread battle-plain!
O fearful, madd'ning grief! All, all I love
Gone from my gaze for ever! Wretched heart,
Bleeding at ev'ry throb! why break'st thou not?

AYESHA.—Thou doubt'st my love, Morayma, for
    my son?
Thou askest if the mother-love is dead
Within my heart—if I can count as naught
The fearful loss that fills thy heart with woe?
Thou art unjust. Have I not shielded him
From yon fierce tyrant's wrath? Did not these
    arms
Cherish and fondly circle his young form,
When dangers threatened helpless infancy?
And as he grew in every manly grace,
Did not my mother-heart beat high with pride?
Oft have I watched, with eager, glist'ning eyes,
His knightly bearing in the brilliant joust;
And as he bore away the well-earned prize
Amid the shouts of thousands, Allah knows '
How my fond heart exulted—how I blessed
All-bounteous heaven for him, its noblest gift.
And when my treacherous rival, yon vile slave,
Had spread her snares around his father's heart,
And fain would win the kingdom for her sons—
Did I not bid him claim his lawful rights,

And tear the brutal tyrant from a throne
He was unworthy of?   Mine were no schemes
Of vain self-exaltation—all my hopes
Of pow'r and fame were for my cherished son.
Ay, when I bade him gather his true band
Of valiant followers, and hold his court—
His rival court—here, 'neath the very gaze
Of his now baffled sire ; and when these hands
Buckled his armor on, and sent him forth
To win new laurels for his kingly brow
In this fierce Christian war, my soul was filled
With glorious visions of his proud success.
I saw his enemies beneath his feet,
Helpless and crushed, and in his native halls
I saw him reign, a monarch undisturbed
By treacherous friends or unbelieving foes.
And thinkst thou, now, my heart is not transfixed
By keenest dart of anguish, when these hopes
Lie withered, blasted, like the dying leaves
The rude blast scatters round us.   O my son!
My loved Boabdil !   'Twas a cruel stroke
That tore thee from me !   Yet, I must restrain
All unavailing grief.   'Tis Allah wills,
And we must meekly bow.

    MORAYMA.—   'Tis vain ! 'tis vain !
I cannot give my loved ones up !   Forgive,
Brave, noble-minded mother, this wild grief!
Bear with me yet a little space—the end
Will shortly come.   This wretched heart will break,
And I shall find, within the peaceful grave,
My welcome rest.   Come, death ! O quickly come!

AYESHA.—Alas, alas, poor, broken, blighted
  flower!
This cruel blast hath crushed its very life.
Summon the minstrel, Zara. She is fond
Of the soft lute and tender madrigal.
Perchance its power may assuage her grief.
                                        [*Exit maid.*

Enter MINSTREL.—(*Lament for Boabdil.*)

O lovely Granada! I see the glad smile
  Flash o'er thy fair mountains and sunlighted
    plains;
Thy fountains laugh softly, yet joyfully, while
  Thy forests reëcho the mirth-freighted strains.
They hail a loved hero, they waft a dear name,
  Afar on the wings of the wandering breeze;
They sing of his valor, they herald his fame,
  And the glad notes resound e'en across the
    broad seas.
That name is Boabdil's—that hero is he
  For whom his Granada looked fondly and long—
Her king, her deliverer! Shall he not be
  The light of her proud eyes, the theme of her
    song?
But, list! ere those echoes have died on the gale,
  The storm-cloud hangs darkly o'er mountain
    and plain;
And a wild cry of anguish—a sorrowful wail—
  Succeeds now the notes of her joy-laden strain.
O lovely Granada! well, well may'st thou weep,
  And shroud thy bright beauty in darkness and
    woe;

Thy hero is fallen, the foul ravens keep
  Their watch o'er the field where thy monarch
    lies low.
Woe, woe, for Boabdil, our glory, our pride!
  Woe, woe, for the hearts that are sad for his sake!
Woe for thee, brave mother, and grief-stricken
    bride!
  In sorrow, in anguish, these fond hearts must
    break.

                           [MORAYMA *faints.*
AYESHA (*to the Minstrel*).—Cease, dotard, cease!
    Did I not bid thee sing
A joyous strain, to soothe this storm of grief?
And thou must needs increase it. Cease this wail,
And quit our sight! (*Exit* MINSTREL.) Poor,
    sorrow-blighted heart!
This is a fearful swoon. Haste, maidens, haste,
Bear her into the garden, near the fount,
That its cool plashing and the fragrant air
May woo her back to life. Go, daughter, go,
And may all-gracious Allah give thee strength!
          [*Exit* MORAYMA, *borne by maids of honor.*

            Enter MOORISH CAVALIER.

CAVALIER.—May't please your Highness, in the
    outer court
A Christian messenger doth wait. He bore
This missive from the sovereigns of Castile
Unto your Highness, and he made me pledge
My knightly word that I would forthwith give
The packet safe into your royal hands.
Its contents are of weighty import: and

He bade me tell your Highness, furthermore,
That he doth crave an answer, and will wait
Until it please your Highness to reply.

AYESHA.—A message from Castile! What mean-
eth this? (*She reads, then speaks aside.*)
O gracious Allah! May thy name be praised!
My son still lives! But, prudence! I forget
Keen eyes are watching me. (*Aloud.*) Well, Hamet, go
Conduct the bearer of this grave dispatch
Into our hall of audience, and say
Her Highness will receive him there, when she
Hath studied well his monarchs' courteous words.
                    [*Exit* HAMET.

AYESHA (*solus*).—A captive in the hands of Christian
dogs!
Nay, Allah Achbar! 'tis a dismal chance,
A grievous insult to our Moslem pride!
I fear this news will chill the loyal faith
Of our too fickle subjects. All was well
When they supposed him dead. He was a god,
A hero, martyred in a holy cause;
The nation sunk beneath its weight of woe,
And raised his name and virtues to the skies.
That tone will change; vile hints of cowardice,
And darkly muttered execrations, will
Salute my ears to-morrow. And his sire,
His fierce, unnatural sire, will exult:
E'en now he thinks his prey within his grasp.
Base wretch! he offers ransom, not to save
His captive son, but to destroy him. Fiend!
He tells the Christian king it matters not
Whether his victim be delivered up

Alive or dead! I thank thee, gentle queen—
Thou hast a mother's heart. Thou did'st refuse
This·cruel offer. But thy terms are hard:
A heavy ransom to be paid at once,
Four hundred Christian slaves to be set free—
But, to this last demand, I render glad
And free consent, to thank thy noble heart.
What more? My son must henceforth hold his
    crown
As vassal to the Christian monarch. Ah,
This is too galling! yet, his safe release
Cannot be compassed else. Then be it so:
If Allah send us victory at last,
The Christian king must humble in his turn!
And what is this? Alas, young stricken heart!
My poor Morayma! thou wilt find it hard
To give thy infant son, as they demand,
In hostage for his father. Yet, thy joy
To know thy dead is risen, and thy lost
So soon to be restored, will give thee strength
For any sacrifice, however great.
Allah be praised! my noble son is safe!
Once more my heart beats high with life and hope.
What, if his people scorn him? That will pass.
His next successful deed will win their hearts.
Courage, my soul! Again indulge thy dreams—
Thy golden dreams of glory and of fame!
But I must meet this messenger, and give
My answer to his sovereign's request.
It shall be prompt assent. Hence, scruples, hence!
All pride must yield to gain my son's return.

                         [*Exit* AYESHA.

ACT II.

SCENE V.—*A garden.*

Enter ZORAYA, *an apostate Christian, and favorite wife of* ABEN HASSAN.

ZORAYA.—Alas, how vain are earth's ambitious
schemes!
For worldly pomp I staked my priceless soul;
To win the phantoms of my fleeting dreams,
I pledged my fairest wealth, and lost the whole:
The bubbles burst, the phantoms fled away.
The spell is broken; o'er my dazzled sight
The sad reality of perfect day
Steals slowly back, and lifts the veil of night.
Alas, alas, the real and the true—
How the false phantoms shrink before its gleam!
And, startled conscience, now thou bring'st to view
My buried years! How sad, how stern, they
seem!
O fierce, accusing spirits, back again
To your sealed sepulchres! In mercy, turn—
I cannot bear your looks! Through soul and brain
Those spectral eyes, like torturing fires, burn.
'Tis vain! 'tis vain! the phantoms haunt me yet—
Those mocking tones will never, never cease.
"List! list!" they cry, "and never more forget
The gloomy retrospect that mars thy peace.
Ay, writhe in anguish, shrink in guilty fear—
Thou can'st not still our clamoring voices now;
Our dark recital thou art doomed to hear,
Till pitying death shall seal thy sin-stained brow.

For the false Crescent thou didst leave the Cross:
　　Thy soul is perjured for a base renown.
Measure thy gain, O traitor! by thy loss:
　　Thy birthright bartered for a worthless crown;
God's friendship lost, that thou might'st be the slave,
　　The toy, the favorite, of a mortal king.
Where is thy master?　In his nameless grave.
　　What is thy diadem?　A worthless thing.
Where is thy regal splendor?　Gone! all gone!
　　Thy palace home is now thy prison cell;
The fierce usurper of thy master's throne,
　　Hath he not paid thy treachery full well?"
Offended God, if I might turn to Thee
　　For aid, for comfort, in this gloomy hour!
Alas, alas, lost soul! this may not be,
　　Thou scorner of thy Maker's love and power!
Mock Him not now in thy unworthy prayer—
　　Endure thy anguish: 'tis a just reward;
But never let thy perjured accents dare
　　To breathe the name of thy insulted Lord!
But, list! a step approaches! well I know
　　That calm, soft tread.　O favored child of grace,
Happy Maria! earthly guilt and woe
　　Never may find in thy pure soul a place.
How tranquil is her eye!　How sweet her smile!
　　O faithful mirrors of the peace within
The quiet heart, unstained by worldly guile,
　　And undisturbed by worldly strife and sin!
It is her hour for holy thought and prayer.
　　Ay, hark! she speaks! now will I list, unseen,
To sacred words which I may never dare
　　Utter with traitor tongue and lips unclean.
　　　　　　　　　　　　　[*Conceals herself.*

MARIA *advances, and seats herself on a grassy mound.*

MARIA.—How calm, how pure, how lovely is
  this scene!
Fair nature, shrouded in the waning light,
With dew-gemmed eyes, yet patient and serene,
  Looks meekly forth, to greet the royal night.
O twilight calm, the lingering embrace
  Of night's sweet stillness with the day's unrest!
The fiery monarch soon will yield his place,
  And slumber softly on her jewelled breast.
O holy twilight, nature's hour of prayer,
  How sacred is the hush thy presence flings!
From the soft stars gleam angel faces fair,
  And fancy hears the rush of angel wings—
So near doth list'ning heaven seem to bend
  Unto the orisons of suppliant earth;
And benisons with evening dews descend,
  Like heralds of a new and perfect birth.
O blissful heaven, so near, and yet so far!
  O bond of earth! O wretched, wretched chain!
My weary soul, beneath the vesper star,
  Pours forth its sigh in sad and longing strain.

  [*She sings to her guitar.*

MARIA'S *Song.—(Air, " Ever of Thee.")*
Still, still for thee, O dear and distant heaven,
  Sadly I pine in hated bondage here!
O that the chains that bind my soul were riven!
  O that her cell, her prison, dark and drear,
Might open now its gloomy, gloomy portal!
  How would my ransomed spirit wing her flight!

Ne'er would she pause, till, on thy shore immortal,
  Calmly she basked in endless peace and light.
    Ever a slave, while here I may be,
    How do I languish, heaven, for thee!

Hush, hush, my soul, thy discontented plaint—
  Bear patiently the cross, to win the crown.
Though on his way the pilgrim oft doth faint,
  Soon shall he lay his weary burden down;
But, God and Father! hear my prayer for her
  Whose need is great.   O pour Thy healing balm
Into her wounds!   O deign to minister
  To those dark woes, which only Thou canst calm!
In mercy save her from the dark despair
  Which broodeth o'er her like a fatal pall.
Thou knowest, Lord, how earnest was my prayer
  That Thou Thy wandering sheep would'st fondly
    call
Back to her place, within the peaceful fold.
  I see Thy hand already stretched to save.
Still in thy grasp the weary wand'rer hold;
  The wolf yet howleth, and the tempests rave.
She pauses, wakened from her sinful dream,
  And backward turns her wild, bewildered gaze;
She sees the wrathful fires of justice gleam,
  And the dark phantoms of her buried days,
Like stern accusers, rise to mock her woe.
  O faithful Shepherd! shield her from despair,
Bid the blest drops of sweet repentance flow,
  Teach the dumb lips to form a trusting prayer.
O tender Mother of her angered Lord!
  Fair pity's home is in thy gentle breast;

Plead for her, then—one mediative word
  From thy blest lips can bring the perfect rest.

ZORAYA *rushes wildly from her hiding-place.*

ZORAYA.—O saintly maiden! dost thou pray for
  me?
For me—a wretch, a rebel? Know'st thou not
That I am stained with crime so base, so black,
That yon pure sun should scorn, methinks, to shed
One ray on such a foul and hideous thing?
I but pollute the earth on which I tread,
And prayers for me would mock insulted heaven;
Then leave the traitor to her fate—despair:
It is her doom, well-merited, well-earned.

MARIA.—My noble mistress, cease these frenzied
  words—
Yield not to dark despair, the demon's last
Convulsive hold upon thy struggling soul;
Shake off his grasp, dear lady, and look up,
Look up to Calvary! Above the cross
That crowns its blessed height, the star of hope
Still sheds its soft and pitying light for thee.

ZORAYA.—Calvary! the cross! those words but
  add new pangs.
The precious blood once offered on that mount
Cries out against me. Every drop doth fall,
Like burning lava, on my perjured soul.
The Cross? I trampled it beneath my feet—
I scorned it for the Crescent's glare; and now
It hath become my judge, and writes my doom!
'Tis changed into a fierce and flaming sword,
To goad me downward to my fitting home.

MARIA.—I do command thee to be calm!   Nay,
    thus
I prison here these restless hands.   List! list!
Thy wild, disordered fancy conjures up
These shapes of gloom and terror.   Nay, look up;
The blessed cross is not a wrathful sword,
It is the symbol of sweet peace, the sign
Of sure salvation.   From its sacred base
A full, unfailing stream of mercy flows;
And, though thy sins were red as scarlet, yet
That saving tide can wash them white as snow.
Behold thy Saviour's dying look of love!
Doth it not bid the prodigal return,
To find glad welcome in her father's house?
From mercy's home, the pure and peaceful cross,
His tender accents softly whisper, "Come,
O weary, burdened, heavy-laden heart!
Come trustingly.   Cast here thy load of grief,
And I will give thee rest."
    ZORAYA.—   Ah blessed words!
Too sweet, too soothing!   Can it, can it be,
That there is hope for me?   No! no! I am
Too vile, too guilty.   Yet, ah gracious thought!
He died to save!   E'en now, around His throne,
Are ransomed souls, once black and foul as mine,
All, in His cleansing blood, washed white as snow,
Ay, in His blood!   O victim lamb!   O love
Ineffable!   Break, break, thou stubborn heart!
                        [*She weeps.*
    MARIA.—I thank Thee, Lord!   Thy servant's
    prayer is heard!
Ay, weep, dear lady!   These are priceless gems.

One tear of true repentance, one sweet drop,
Such as thou sheddest now, the heart's pure dew,
Can blot out ev'ry crime that 'gainst thy soul
Was stamped in blood on the eternal page.
With such pure tears the penitent of old
Bedewed her Saviour's feet.   Now, even now,
Thy precious tears are filling angel hearts
With purest joy, and bidding heaven's court
Ring with their glad rejoicing o'er this soul
Once lost, now found, once dead, now roused to life—
The perfect life of grace!

    ZORAYA.—   O matchless friend!
Sweet comforter!   Thy dear and gentle voice
Recalls my blameless childhood, for its tones
Are like the sainted mother's, at whose knee
I listened to that history of love,
My Saviour's earthly life: a holy peace,
Long, long, a stranger there, steals o'er my heart.
Take up thy lute, Maria, I would hear
The hymn thou sungest yester-night.   How oft,
Ah me! how oft that sweet and soothing strain
Hath floated from her pure and peaceful heart
On the soft twilight air!   O sing it now,
And I will dream of by-gone innocence.

MARIA *sings:* " *The Evening Hymn at the Wayside*
Shrine."

       O'er mount and meadow
         Steals the twilight's dreamy gray ;
       Night's deep'ning shadow
         Hides the ling'ring day.

Pilgrims faint and weary,
  Fondly hail their guiding star,
Through the darkness dreary,
  Shining bright and far.
      Ave Maria!

Beacon gleaming through the wild!
  Star of the wand'rer,
Shine upon thy child!
Soft tones are stealing
  Through the twilight cold and dim,
Earth's children, kneeling,
  Chant their vesper hymn.
Hear their earnest pleading!
  Safety flies with fainting day!
For us, interceding,
  Send the guiding ray!
      Ave Maria, etc.

Lo, the boon is given!
  Dread not now the shades of night!
Stars have bloomed in heaven,
  Earth is crowned with light.
Thus, O Guardian tender,
  May thy starry glance illume,
With its potent splendor,
  Life's last hour of gloom!
      Ave Maria, etc.

ZORAYA.—O blessed souvenirs of by-gone days!
How they come thronging back! O Christian
  home!
Dear, dear Castile! How my heart yearns for thee!

Maria, if I could behold once more
Those loved, familiar scenes: my village home,
My father's ancient hall, the vine-clad cots
That nestled safely 'neath its shelt'ring towers,
And the quaint chapel, with its gilded cross,
Pointing the heavenly road to faithful hearts,—
If I could feast my weary eyes but once
On that sweet picture, I would be content
To spend my life a crouching, toiling slave
In e'en the meanest cottage of that vale.
Oh, I would bless the chains that bound me there
In willing servitude! Alas, vain dream,
Never to be fulfilled!

MARIA.—   Nay, say not so!
Our gracious Isabella hath a heart,
The palace home of every noble thought,
Whose every throb is charity and love;
And, like the Master whom that heart hath served
With faithful zeal, from earliest infancy,
A human soul is precious in her sight,
Its conquest prized above earth's fairest realm.
Toward the Christian slaves who pine, like thee,
In pain and peril, 'neath the Moslem yoke,
She fondly yearns with all her mother-love.
Fly, then, to her. Be sure that thou wilt find
A tender welcome there.

ZORAYA.—   I know, I know
Her generous soul. E'en haughty infidels,
Enraptured, praise its gifts and virtues rare:
And yet I may not fly to her. Alas!
My gilded chains are firmly fastened here,
By hands still reeking with a brother's blood.

The fierce El Zagel, base and cruel wretch,
Detains me, prisoned in these palace walls;
His creatures watch my ev'ry movement—e'en
Would read my very thoughts.   Escape is vain.
How, how can I be freed?

MARIA.—   An easy task.
Only this morn I chanced to overhear
A secret conference betwixt two knights—
Two of his chosen followers.   They said
The fickle populace e'en now had grown
Disgusted with their idol.   Whispered hints
And fierce suspicions of foul fratricide,
Ominous and dark, like boding vulture's wings,
Were floating through the stormy atmosphere;
And all this, while full victory hath blessed
The Christian arms, in ev'ry strife and siege.
And yet, El Zagel crouches in his lair,
And dares not venture forth, lest Boabdil
Should, in his absence, seize his halls and throne.
The Moorish mob are clamorous for war,
As they behold, like maddened beasts at bay,
The cross-crowned banner of the Christians wave
E'en within sight of their proud capital.
Granada must surrender: civil war
Within her gates, and conqu'ring hosts without,
Will bring her speedy fall.   Now hear my plan:
Do thou, most noble mistress, now, this night,
Write to our queen a simple, strong appeal;
State thy whole case—thy sufferings, thy needs,
And signify thy wish to be received
Within the shelter of thy home and faith—
That is thy task, dear lady!   This is mine:

A trusty friend, a watchful Christian spy,
Is lurking now within these very walls—
At my request, this messenger will bear
Thy missive safe unto our gracious queen.

    ZORAYA.—Thanks, gentle friend! O pure un-
    looked-for joy!
I shall be free! Farewell, ye stately walls,
Proud home of guilt, ambition, and unrest!
Far from your charms I seek the longed-for peace
Which royal pomp could never, never, give.
Ayesha, thou mayst reign unrivalled now—
May God forgive my sinful strife for power,
And the deep wrongs I wrought on thee and thine.
My earthly dreams are o'er; I only seek
To win for my young sons a fadeless crown—
Their priceless, true inheritance—in heaven.
But why do I delay? Come, gentle friend,
Sweet angel-counsellor, assist me now
To frame the missive that shall bring me peace.

                  [*Exeunt* MARIA and ZORAYA.

—————

SCENE VI.—*The Surrender of Granada. A Hall of*
           the Alhambra.

    BOABDIL.—O my lost kingdom! O my ruined
    home!
My fair Granada, beauty's favored land!
Ah! must thy king a weary wand'rer roam,
    Far from thy sunny skies and zephyrs bland?
How will the fragrance of thy smiling flowers,
    And the rich verdure of each fruitful plain,

Still haunt my dreams, through all the dreary hours
  Of my lone exile's sad and ceaseless pain !
O wretched fate !   O drear and dismal doom !
  Well might the prophets curse my natal star,
Already shrouded in a night of gloom,
  Soon, soon to sink in rayless death afar !
Mine is a base renown—a fearful fame :
  Cursed by my race, and hated in my time.
All future ages, too, shall scorn my name
  In blighting chronicle and mocking rhyme.
But, Allah Achbar ! God alone is great !
  Alas ! these words of resignation fall
From a reluctant heart, which mourns its fate—
  Torn from its realm, its throne, its ancient hall,
And doomed—O woe ! O anguish, keen and deep !—
  Far from its home to wander and to pine.
My lost Granada !   Let me wildly weep,
  For was there ever grief, O God, like mine?

                                        [*He weeps.*

    Enter AYESHA, MORAYMA, *and Courtiers.*

  AYESHA.—Ay, weep ! these tears become thee !
    Thou art right,
O coward, craven-hearted king ! to mourn,
Like a weak woman, o'er the fallen realm
For which thou couldst not battle like a man.
    MORAYMA.—O royal mother, spare his bleeding
      heart !
Hast thou no mercy ?   Ah ! withhold those shafts
Of thy most piercing scorn.   Thou art unjust :
He is no coward.   Long and well he strove
To save his kingdom and his kingly fame.

All, all in vain. The dread decree of fate
Pronounced his doom, for God alone is great:
. Earth's mightiest monarchs must obey his will.
    BOABDIL.—I do deserve reproaches, though, in
    sooth,
I never failed in bravéry, nor sought
To shield myself when danger hovered near
My cherished people: yet my fate is just.
I have incurred the blighting wrath of heaven
For my rebellion 'gainst my murdered sire.
Forgive, my injured subjects, oh, forgive
The ruin I have wrought on you and yours!
Lay not up wrath against me—'twas my fate:
Well was I nicknamed the Unfortunate.
The seer's prediction, uttered at my birth,
Hath been fulfilled. Alas! I am the last,
The last and luckless Moorish king. My throne
Is vacant now for ever. Yet comply
With those hard offers of the Christians—'tis
Your only means of safety. For your sakes
I did accept the treaty. Now, farewell!
Think kindly of your most unhappy king.
May Allah, who doth hold his royal court
Above our loved Granada, guard and bless
Our once so happy home! May he avert
From my poor subjects his avenging wrath!
Upon my guilty head alone the blow,
Well-merited, should fall. Farewell! farewell!
    All cry.—Long live Boabdil the Unfortunate!
    MORAYMA.—Rouse thee, Boabdil, thou hast one
    true heart:
Though friends forsake, and even hope depart,

In life, in death, one faithful heart shall cling
Fondly to thee, its consort and its king.

   All.—All hearts are his! may Allah guard our
     king!

   AYESHA.—What? do you dally here in maudlin
     grief

And interchange of silly compliments,
When, even now, within the outer court,
I hear their ringing steps, who gaily come
To celebrate their haughty triumph here?
Ay, will ye linger on, till your new lords
Shall drive ye out like dogs? Hence, fly with me,
If ye be Moors, nor stay, like crouching slaves
Or fawning sycophants, to kiss the dust
Beneath the feet of your proud conquerors.

   (*Exeunt all, exclaiming.*)—Farewell, Granada! woe
     for us and thee!

TRIUMPH OF THE CHRISTIANS.

CONCLUDING SCENE.—*The Christian Camp before
Granada. Enter* FERDINAND *and* ISABELLA, *at the
head of a triumphal procession. All sing, in chorus,
the Christians' Song of Triumph.*

Granada is fallen! Granada is ours—
We've conquered her cities, her plains, and her
    towers;
New lustre to add to our kingdom's renown,
New jewels, new jewels, to flash in her crown.

(*Chorus*).—Then down with the Crescent, and up
    with the Cross—
We've crushed the false Prophet, we'll laugh at his
    loss;
And the shouts of our triumph unceasing shall peal:
Granada is ours! Joy, joy for Castile!
    FERDINAND.— Most valiant knights and noble
        cavaliers,
Behold the rich reward, the worthy prize,
Of all your wounds, fatigue and perils! Look
On yonder stately city! It is ours:.
Granada hath surrendered! In the dust
The haughty Moslem bends! Our conqu'ring cross
Shall gleam, this day, on yon proud minaret:
We wait the glorious signal. When ye see
That holy sign on yon Alhambra's towers,
Then proudly enter through its gates, and there,
Within those stately walls, which now belong
To fair Castile, keep joyous gala day.
    All together.—Long live Fernando! Heaven
        bless our king!
    ISABELLA.—But, in our triumph, let us not forget
That gracious hand, without whose mighty aid
Success had never blessed the Christian arms.
When priestly hands have sanctified yon mosque,
And changed the temple of unholy rites
Into a dwelling for the Lord of Hosts,
Then let us there adore and render thanks
Most meet for this blest victory. Nor let
The thrill of earthly pride be blended with
The joyous throbbing of our grateful hearts:
This is the triumph of the cross! The praise

Belongs to Him who vanquished, by that cross,
A proud and stubborn world.   Remember, too,
He conquered by His mildness and His love.
Let us not mar the glory of our deeds
By haughty sneers toward our fallen foes.
For the meek Saviour's sake, O let us be
As noble and as chivalrous, in peace
And triumph, as the conquered Moors do now
Acknowledge we have ever been in war.
   All sing.—Hail, hail, Isabella!   Long life to our
     queen!
Be that heart e'er as tranquil, that smile as serene!
All glory, all grace, hath attended thy reign:
Blest, blest be that heaven that gave thee to Spain.
   (*Chorus*).—Down, down with the crescent, etc.

   Zoraya *advances, and kneels before* Isabella.

   Zoraya.—And now receive, O sweet and saintly
     queen!
This conquered soul within thy shelt'ring love;
Here, at thy feet, I bend the humble knee,
And in the presence of this august court,
I here deplore my base apostasy;
I trample on that crescent, whose false gleam
Betrayed my dazzled soul.   I now renounce
The fiend-led Prophet, with his erring creed,
And promise firm allegiance to the cross.
Forgive my wand'rings from my childhood's faith;
Receive the penitent, who would become
E'en as thy meanest slave, for she deserves
No higher station in her native land.

ISABELLA.—Rise, rise, Zoraya, and again resume
Thy Christian name of Isabella—rise,
Thy prayer is granted. Should His creatures be
Less merciful than God? He hath received
His erring child. Take, then, our kiss of peace,
And all the honors due thy rank. Thou art
Our Princess of Granada, and thy sons
Shall take the title of Infanta. Nay,
No protestations of unworthiness:
Thy penitence atones for every sin.
Ah! here is conquest worthy this proud day:
A soul reclaimed—a precious gem restored
To the bright casket of the King of kings.
Brave knights, our victory is but begun!
How many souls, within this darkened land,
Are groping blindly through forbidden paths!
Be ours the noble task to guide them safe
In the blest road of virtue and of peace;
And now, in humblest homage, let us kneel
Before that God who armed the Christian's hand,
And meekly bge His precious grace, that we
May wear our honors worthily and well. (*All kneel.*)
    ISABELLA'S *Prayer.*—Thou God Omnipotent,
      before whose throne
Earth's proudest places sink, unmarked, unknown!
At whose all-conqu'ring will and kingly rod
Earth's sceptres bend, earth's monarchs own their
      God!
Who biddest worldly kingdoms rise and fall,
Thyself enduring, King and Lord of all!
Accept, O God, our grateful homage now,
Before Thy throne our reverent heads we bow!

And for the joy, the triumph of this day,
To Thee our debt of gratitude we pay.
Great God of armies, Thou hast deigned to bless
The Christian arms, and win their proud success,
That haughty error's dark and dreadful stain
Might thus be wiped from off our lovely Spain;
That rebel hearts might bow their stubborn pride,
And own His power, whom they have long defied.
Thine shall the glory of our conquest be—
This rescued land we consecrate to Thee;
The Moslem mosque, made pure by holy hand,
A Christian temple in Thy sight shall stand.
Low in the dust the cruel Crescent lies,
And in its place the peaceful Cross shall rise;
But shield our hearts from vain ambition's dreams,
From haughty triumph, and all sordid schemes.
To the pure standard of our Lord and King,
Give us Thy grace with faithful hearts to cling.
O blessed Saviour, who beside us stood,
Linked with our race in human brotherhood!
Aid us to hold all earthly things as dross,
And glory only in Thy saving cross; .
And by that sign, more mighty than the sword,
O may we spread the empire of our Lord!
Be this our noblest work, our best renown:
To win new gems to sparkle in His crown.
Then, valiant victors o'er the demon foe,
A fairer prize than earth could e'er bestow,
A fadeless wreath of everlasting fame,
E'en at Thy hands, O Father! we may claim—
The priceless boon to faithful servants given:
An honored name within Thy court of heaven!

All respond.—Amen.

FERDINAND.—Behold the signal! O'er yon
   stately tower

The silver cross is gleaming! Finish, now,

The song of triumph! Then advance, brave
   knights

And noble dames, through yonder portal's arch,

To the new church, the consecrated mosque—

There, with the holy bishop, to intone

Te Deum Laudamus for our victory!

   All sing.—Hail, morning of triumph! Hail,
      glorious day,

And blest be the hearts that exult in its ray!

To the strong arm that aided, success let us sing!

Long life to Fernando! Hail, hail, to our king!

   (*All retire slowly, singing this chorus :*)

Down, down with the Crescent, and up with the
   Cross!

We'll crush all invaders, and laugh at their loss;

And this be our watchword, in danger or weal,

"Santiago! Santiago! Ho! ho! for Castile!"

                                   [*Exeunt omnes.*

THE RANSOMED CAPTIVE;

OR,

THE REGENERATION OF EARTH.

PERSONAGES:

EARTH.	MERCY.
PAGANISM.	EUROPE.
CHILD OF EARTH.	ASIA.
VIOLENCE.	AFRICA.
TRUTH (*or* RELIGION).	AMERICA.
VIRTUE.	SCIENCE.
FAITH.	MUSIC.
HOPE.	POETRY.
CHARITY.	PAINTING.
PEACE.	SCULPTURE.

The Ransomed Captive;

OR,

THE REGENERATION OF EARTH:

AN ALLEGORICAL DRAMA.

———

ACT I.

Scene I.—Paganism *leads* Earth, *fettered.*

Earth.—Yet once more, hear me! Lo, I call
    on thee,
By all thy gods on high Olympus throned,
To free me from these bonds! I faint, I die,
Beneath thy fearful yoke! My smiling vales
Are drenched with blood—the life-blood of my sons,
Poured out upon thy dread, unholy shrines.
Is not the dismal sacrifice complete?
List the fierce echoes, o'er my moaning hills,
Of thy foul orgies. Maddened by thy spells,
The wild Bacchantes fill the quiet air
With strange, demoniac sounds. Lo! ev'ry vice,
Ev'ry dark crime, exalted as a god,
And by my children worshipped, proudly rules,
And fills my once unclouded realm with woe.
Ah, bid this anguish cease! 'Tis time! 'tis time!
Ages ago thy fearful sway began—

Can it not end? Oh, better, better far
E'en formless chaos, than a world like this!
Oh, woe! woe! woe! Thou wilt not hear my
 prayer,
And mockery smiles its triumph on my lips.
  PAGANISM.—Ha! ha! 'Tis joy to see thee writhe!
   Look up,
That I may feast upon thy haggard mien,
And wild, imploring gestures. Clasp thy hands,
O craven trembler! 'Tis a pretty scene!
Proud Earth a captive! Ha! ha! this is well!
This is my triumph. Thou would'st be released?
Fool! Think'st thou Paganism could relent?
Ah! these are galling bonds. I'll tighten them.
            [*She tightens* EARTH'S *fetters*—EARTH
               groans with pain.
That groan was music. Thus I grant thy prayer!
Thus do I bid my gentle reign be o'er!
Why, driveller, weep'st thou for thy children's woes?
The fault is theirs. Have they not called me forth,
From my dark realm, to rule them? In their hearts,
Blinded by pride and passion, lo, the source
Of all their ills! Ay, willing slaves were they—
Slaves to their own proud wills! So let them bear
Their self-forged chains. Ay, let the farce proceed.
Let them bow down, and bring their costly gifts
To Mars and Venus, and the horrid train
Of their own crimes and passions, deified;
Let them pour out their life-blood at my feet,
As foul libation to their demon gods;
Let the Bacchantes in wild frenzy howl,
And keep their fiendish revels. Ay, let all

The ghastly train of woes themselves have wrought,
Now hold high carnival within their hearts.
Let Superstition, from Dodona's oaks,
Utter her lying oracles. Ay, let
Her willing dupes, the *godlike* souls of men,
Seek their own ruin from the demon snares
Which Paganism, whom themselves invoked,
Spreads for her silly prey. Ha! ha! 'tis well!
And they shall have an endless throng of gods—
I'll humor every whim and fantasy,
To lure my victims. Thus, thou craven Earth,
Will I, thy conqu'ror, grant thy prayers. Yet, hold!
Did I not bid thy children worship thee?
Ay, ingrate! Art thou not the turret-crowned
And ancient goddess: Terra, Vesta, Ops,
Rhea, Sylvia, Cybele? Ha! ha! in sooth
Thou shouldst be satisfied, for names enough
Thou hast, great mother; and thy costly fanes
Rear their proud heads from many a classic mount
And smiling vale. What! does that make thee
    writhe?
Methought 'twould ease thy anguish. Even now
The feasts of Cybele commence! Dost hear
The shouts, the pæans, ingrate? All for thee!
'Twill be a goodly sight: the gleaming throng,
In tinselled trappings, shouting, o'er the plain,
To their decked idol, wreathed and garlanded.
I must away, to feast upon the scene,
And thou, anon, shalt follow. Bow thy head,
In homage to thy sovereign. Stay, thy bonds
Will bear a tighter clasp. I'll send, ere long,
To bid thee share my triumph, Mother Earth!
                              [*Exit* PAGANISM, *laughing*

EARTH (*solus*).—O woe unutterable!   O agony,
That findeth no relief!   Ah, happy days
Of blest, primeval innocence and joy,
When, fresh from the Creator's hand, I stood
In blooming loveliness, unstained—in peace
Most pure and perfect.   Seraph eyes looked down,
And smiled upon the incense-breathing flowers;
And angel pinions hovered o'er the paths
Of blissful Eden, where the sinless pair
Walked in their yet unspotted innocence.
Ah, dreary change!   Ah, blighting serpent trail,
That left its slime upon those hapless hearts!
That withered ev'ry flower, and set its seal—
The seal of death—upon my youthful brow!
Sin rests, a frightful incubus, on all,
And Earth must suffer for the fault of man.
And now, to see the great and bounteous God,
The Lord Supreme, by His own creatures scorned;
To see the blooming world His fiat formed,
Polluted by foul demon-worship, chained
In galling fetters by the ruthless hand
Of the dread tyrant, Paganism!   Ah,
'Tis anguish keenest, woe unutt'rable!
O sister-virtues—snowy-pinioned Faith,
Fair, star-crowned Hope, and dove-eyed Charity!
Where are ye flown?   Shall hapless Earth be blest
No more by your sweet presence?   List! that
      moan !
Whence is it?   Ah, my weary-hearted child!
She comes to pour her soul's wild anguish forth
Upon my pitying heart.   Alas! alas!
Pity is all that helpless heart can give!

Enter a maiden, who casts herself wildly on the ground, singing this lament. (Air, "By the Sad Sea Waves.")

O wild night winds! O tempest-breathing gale!
Bear on my song, my soul's despairing wail,
     That some voice, in reply
     To my grief-laden sigh,
May soothe the wild woes that my spirit assail;
     That some spirit of air
     May a soft spell bear
To the maid who haunts the night like a phantom
    pale.

O vain, vain hope! O echo-taunted cry!
O woe-worn face! why meet the mocking sky?
     For its stars point, in scorn,
     At the wanderer forlorn,
And whisper no rest for the soul's agony.
     In vain! All in vain!
     O weary heart and brain,
Why can ye not grow wild? why can ye not die?

(Speaks).—O mother! I come of your pity to crave
A balm for my anguish, a lethean grave.
I am weary of life, I am weary of thought,
I have labored in vain, I have fruitlessly sought;
I dreamed of a bliss that was stainless and pure,
I dreamed of fair joys that for ever endure;
I sought to possess them—in vain, all in vain!
For joy I found sorrow, for freedom a chain;
I sought in the temple, I knelt at the shrine,
Of laurel-crowned idols, of gods deemed divine.

With the white train of vestals,
  By day and by night,
I watched the bright flame,
  And I worshipped its light;
But my fond hopes were mocked,
  And my soul sickened there,
For foulness was hid
  In their raiment so fair.
Other temples I sought, but,
  Alas! 'twas the same:
Corruption concealed in
  Religion's fair name.
I loath'd the proud pomp
  And the idols of Rome—
I left the fair city,
  I fled from my home,
Where the pyramids rear
  Their proud heads o'er the land,
And the dreamy-browed sphinx
  Casts her shade on the sand.
I sought the ideal my soul hoped to win,
And I found but illusion, corruption, and sin.
I turned to that land where the Persian bends low
To the flame-vested sunlight, and worships its
  glow;
Still my longings were mocked, still my dream's
  phantom fled—
To the proud home of science, to Athens, I sped.
To the poets who sung, and the sages who taught,
Still vainly I listened, still vainly I sought,
Though pale-browed Philosophy dimly revealed
The light which Idolatry foully concealed:

Yet, alas! it was wrapped in the shadows of doubt—
'Twas but the fair corpse, with its life blotted out.
For the daylight of truth, I found twilight's pale
    beam,
For waking reality only a dream—
The pure and the sensual, basely combined :
Earth holds not the heaven my soul longs to find.
Like a child in the darkness, I wail for the light,
Like a pilgrim, 'mid tombs I have groped through
    the night—
No balm for my anguish, no star-beam is there,
And I sink to Plutonian depths of despair.
In death and oblivion, oh, let me find rest !
Earth ! Earth ! give me peace in thy pitying breast !
Hear, mother ! I come, of thy mercy to crave
The lethe of death, and the calm of the grave.
Thou mock'st me with silence, thou spurnest thy
    child,
The spent soul is maddened, the weak brain grows
    wild ;
Like the gadfly-stung nymph, over mountain and
    plain,
In my grief and unrest I must wander again :
No cure for my tortures, no balm for my woe,
No light from above, and no solace below.
                    [*Rushes wildly out.*
    EARTH.—Alas ! alas ! I cannot heal thy woe,
My weary child ! My soul reflects the grief,
The wild unrest, the pangs that torture thee ;
Yet, from the hand that drew me from the depths
Of formless chaos, and upon my brow
Placed the bright crown of beauty and of life,

Relief *must* come.　Oh, let me lift my voice,
In wild appeal, in agony of prayer!　(*She kneels.*)
O source of life! Creator, Sovereign Lord!
　　Hear the wild prayer of sorrow-laden Earth.
Fair nature's King, at whose creating word
　　Light rose from shade—a world sprang into
　　birth!
Who bade the mist-wreath'd mountains proudly
　　stand,
Chained the vast sea, and decked the blooming
　　land—
To Thee, great Ruler, lo! I lift my cry—
　　My wild appeal for pity and relief;
Break my loath'd bondage, heal my agony,
　　Comfort my children, calm their stormy grief;
Bid the foul demon-tyrant's reign be o'er,
Bring dove-eyed Peace to weary Earth once more.
Thy promise sweet of perfect sacrifice,
　　Of full atonement, thrilled this blighted heart,
When sin-bowed Adam from lost Paradise
　　Turned, in his lonely anguish, to depart.
'Tis time, O Lord! fulfil Earth's hopeful dream:
Send the Messiah, and Thy world redeem!
Banish the false, and bring Thy truth divine,
　　Let Thine own temples in fair beauty rise;
Let holy hands, upon a holy shrine,
　　Offer the blest, eternal sacrifice;
O'er shrouded earth Thy blessed sunlight shed,
And back to endless life restore the dead.

Enter VIOLENCE.

VIOLENCE.—Rouse thee, pale mother; shrink no
    longer here!
Up from thy craven dream! Thy ruler claims
Thy homage and thy presence. Stare not thus—
Dost know thy ruler? 'Tis my consort meet,
Great Paganism, mistress of the world,
Who gives a god for every fantasy
And passion of her victims. Ha! ha! well
May she thus condescend! Full sure is she
Of her deluded prey. Dost hear their shouts?
Up, dreamer up, and join thy children's cry.
Hail, Error, hail! Live, Crime and Violence, live!
                      [*Drags* EARTH *away*

SCENE II.—*The Regeneration of* EARTH.

TRUTH (*or* RELIGION), *solus.*

TRUTH.—Hail, hail, at last the hour of blest
    release
For sorrow-stricken Earth! The longing cry
Of weary hearts, that in the midnight gloom
Have blindly groped, shall now—O joy!—be heard.
The faint mysterious ray that feebly stole
Through the sin-clouded corridors of time—
O bliss ineffable!—hath burst, at last,
Into the fulness of perfected day.
Each mystic type that blessed the prophet's dream
With a fond, trembling hope, becometh now

Waking reality; and love's sweet song,
That through the echoing ages faintly rolled,
Like the soft melody of distant chimes,
Rings out, in thrilling emphasis, beneath
The starlit sky o'er Bethlehem's favored plain.
O mystery of love! O happy race,
For whom a God hath left His mighty throne,
And in your fallen nature's frail disguise,
Offers Himself a sacrifice for sin!
That trait'rous blow, which, by your daring hands
Aimed vainly 'gainst His regal majesty,
Hath but returned—O rash, O fatal stroke!—.
To wound the impious hearts that sent it forth.
The wound is healed, its pangs for ever o'er,
And Earth from galling fetters shall be freed.

Enter VIRTUE, *with* FAITH, HOPE, *and* CHARITY.

TRUTH.—Welcome, sweet sisters! welcome,
    white-robed train!
What joy to meet in Earth's sad realm once more!
    FAITH, HOPE, *and* CHARITY.—Peace, peace on
    earth! good-will to fallen man!
    FAITH.—Thus let our greeting echo forth the song,
The new, celestial anthem, now begun
On this redemption-morn.
    TRUTH.—   'Tis well! 'tis well!
And now, O shining band, behold your home!
Never again, by sin and darkness driven,
Shall ye be forced to wing your heavenward flight,
And leave poor Earth to ev'ry ill a prey.
The baneful power, the dark despotic rule,
Of **Crime and Error,** hath forever closed;

And now begins the new, eternal reign
Of God-commissioned Truth.

HOPE.— Hail, heavenly Truth!
'Tis joy to greet our sov'reign here once more,
And to resume our holy work on Earth.
Poor fallen captive, from my far-off home
Oft have I heard her anguish-laden cry,
And longed to comfort her, to chase away
The demon of despair.

TRUTH.— The time hath come!
Go, star-crowned herald, on thy swiftest wings,
And bring the joyful answer to her prayer—
The glorious tidings of a Saviour's birth.
E'en now her weary moan, her wail of woe,
Is borne upon the gale. Go, shining Hope,
And soothe her grief with sweetest words of cheer.
[*Exit* HOPE.

FAITH.—O gentle queen, I wait thy blest com-
mand!
My eager steps, impatient of delay,
Would hasten on their sacred pilgrimage.

TRUTH.—O halo-circled Faith, thou shalt depart
On thy sweet mission. Give thine aid to him,
The blest precursor of the coming Lord—
The "Voice that crieth in the wilderness"—
And shed thy radiance o'er the darkened hearts
Of those who, by fair Jordan's blessed shore,
Shall list his holy words. O bid them see
The glory of this new, celestial dawn!
Haste, with thy magic hand, to ope the gates,
The shining portals of that glorious land,
To which, sweet Faith, thy rapt, ecstatic gaze

Is ever lifted.   Heaven speed thy steps,
Fair child of God, bright, gloom-dispelling Faith !

                             [*Exit* FAITH.

    CHARITY.—And I, beloved sovereign—hast thou
    naught
For me to do? Ah, bid me take my place
'Mid those blest laborers in our Master's cause !

    TRUTH.—Queen of the sister train, sweet Charity !
Thine is the noblest work.   Thy golden chain,
Thy magic bonds of balm-distilling flowers,
Must bind the wayward souls of sin-bowed men.
Revenge and Hate, thy darkest, deadliest foes,
Have tinged earth's crystal streams with brothers'
    blood,
And bade the trembling, fear-struck air resound
With tumult wild and wailing agony.
Go! cleanse th' ensanguined tide ! Go, still the
    storm !
Conquer, with gentlest spells, thy demon foes,
And let the joyous air be filled, once more,
With the glad echo of Love's endless song.

                        [*Exit* CHARITY.

    TRUTH.—Sweet sister, we must share our chil-
    dren's work :
Ours is a noble conquest.   Let us haste
To follow, through the olive-shaded plain,
O'er the lone mountain, and beside the shore
Of hallowed streams, that blest, atoning Life,
In Bethlehem, on this fair morn, begun ;
And when it shall be closed on Calvary,
And Love's sweet sacrifice for man complete,
Truth shall receive His blood-empurpled cross

As her fair standard.   By that saving sign
We shall subdue our demon-enemies,
Idolatry and Violence.   Ah, what joy
To free the captive, Earth, and crush her foes!
   VIRTUE.—And, blessed sister, we may claim sweet
     aid:
Mercy shall wait beside the sacred tomb
Of heaven's risen Lord, at early dawn
Of the blest resurrection-morn.   Her, there,
Expectant we shall find.   Her potent hand
Will burst asunder the unhallowed bonds
Of Error-fettered Earth, and—blessed boon!—
The pardon purchased by a Saviour's blood,
To fallen man shall bring.   Ah! let us haste—
In lowly crib our Master cradled lies;
Let us beside the sinless Mother kneel,
And offer homage to our Infant King.
                  [*Exeunt* TRUTH *and* VIRTUE.

SCENE III.—EARTH *enters, still fettered.*

EARTH.—Vainly I plead: no comfort, no release!
   Still, still I writhe, in vilest fetters bound;
I long to hear the soothing song of peace,
   And still dread Moloch's battle-cries resound.
Error and Crime hold fiendish revelry,
   And still my children grovel at their feet;
And bend, at guilty shrines, the willing knee,
   And, day by·day, their sinful rites repeat.
The holy memory of that hallowed time
   When Israel bowed before the living God,

When incense rose, where pealed the chant sublime,
　　And pure libations sanctified the sod,
Like the sweet fragrance of departed flowers—
　　That blest remembrance lingers o'er my heart;
And through the long, long night's slow-pacing
　　hours
The dream-like odor could not all depart.
Oft, too, beneath the star-bespangled sky,
　　With dewy tears upon my brow, I lay,
And watched the kneeling prophet's lifted eye,
　　And caught the glory of a heav'n-sent ray,
Serenely mirrored in his upward gaze.
　　O mystic light, that sent the joyous thrill
Through my lone heart, and bade the flowers raise
　　Their grief-bowed heads, and woke each sleeping
　　rill!
Though ages since the heaven-inspired seer
　　Passed from my lonely solitudes away,
And through the gloomy night, and silence drear,
　　Nor sweet voice woke, nor bright, prophetic ray;
Yet, God of hope! that dream-like memory
　　Hath a strange spell to soothe my wild despair,
And bid the captive kneel again to Thee,
　　And breathe once more her agony of prayer.
Last night a clearer murmur faintly stole,
　　Like the fair seraph's long-hushed song of peace,
And trembling hopes woke in my weary soul—
　　Hopes of the promised comfort and release.
It comes not yet.　Oh, was it mockery?
　　The demon-tauntings of my cruel foe?
Nay! Sov'reign Lord! yet, yet l call on Thee!
　　Fulfil Thy promise, calm Thy children's woe!

(HOPE *sings in the distance.*)
Love hath sent a balm for pain,
   Heaven bids Earth's sorrows cease !
List to the new, celestial strain,
   List to the angels' song of peace:
     Gloria in excelsis Deo !

EARTH. —'Tis last night's song, but ah ! so sweet,
  so clear !
And list ! the rustle of an angel's wing !
'Tis long since those fair pinions stole so near.
  Is it a dream ?   Do mocking demons sing ?

HOPE.—It is no dream, thou hast heard aright ;
Look up, and bask in heav'n's own light.
   Up, up, and echo the seraphs' lay !
The night of sorrows is past and gone.
Look up, look up, and hail the dawn,
   The golden dawn of redemption's day !

In lowly crib thy Saviour lies,
Clad in thy children's frail disguise,
   Hailed by the lowly shepherd throng
Who, watching on the dreary plain,
Caught the first echo of that strain,
   The seraphs' own celestial song.

Lift up, O Earth, thy gladsome voice,
Let hill, and vale, and stream rejoice !
   Pale mourner, in thy joy, be strong !
Behold the realm of fadeless peace,
And hail the boon of sweet release,
   The ransom thou hast waited long.

Through the sin-clouded ages borne,
The echo of thy wail forlorn
   Reached my abiding-place on high;
And fondly have I yearned to bring
Light, joy, and healing on my wing,
   To calm thy cruel agony.

The time is come, the boon is brought,
The light, the solace thou hast sought,
   Are thine, pale mourner, thine at last.
The reign of Tyranny is o'er,
And Truth shall reign for evermore,
   And bid thy anguish all be past.

The light that cheered the patriarch's night,
And beamed upon the prophet's sight,
   With strange, mysterious ray—
Heaven's radiant Sun, its richest gem,
Lies hid in humble Bethlehem,
   Enshrined in lowliest clay.

EARTH.—O joyous tidings! O celestial dawn,
That endeth thus my long, long night of woe!
I know thee, smiling herald, star-crowned Hope.
I saw thee first in that most blissful time,
With thy wings folded o'er fair Paradise;
Again I caught the bright, reflected gleam
Of those blest pinions, when, above the waste
Of surging waters, God's fair covenant—
His radiant bow of blessed promise—hung.
And I have called thee long—with hands out-
   stretched

Have sought to clasp thy robe, to catch its gleam,
And listened vainly for thy blissful song.
O joy at last! to hail thee, brightest one
Of all the heavenly throng, thou sweet-voiced Hope!

FAITH *enters.*

FAITH.—Ransomed captive, welcome me!
    Brightest gift I bring to thee,
    Fairest treasure from on high :
    Sunlight from Love's fadeless sky.
    Incense pure again shall rise,
    And an endless sacrifice
    Offered shall be evermore,
    For the reign of doubt is o'er.
    From the sin-polluted shrine
    Idols falsely deemed divine
    By a demon-fettered world,
    Shall, by angel hands, be hurled.
    I, who led the chosen band
    Safely to the promised land,
    Kindled Israel's altar-fire,
    Woke the psalmist's sacred lyre ;
    And, by mystic starlight, showed
    Their Redeemer's poor abode
    To the treasure-laden band,
    Who, from distant Eastern land,
    Costliest offerings would bring
    To that hidden Lord and King,—
    I will teach thy children now
    At His holy shrine to bow ;
    I will cleanse the sin-stained clay,
    I will wash thy guilt away.

EARTH.—Hail, hail to thee, upon whose seraph
  brow
Heav'n's glory hovers, as a gleaming crown,
The purest ray from Love's eternal throne—
O glorious Faith ! Earth gladly welcomes thee;
And may my sin-duped children hear thy voice,
With willing ears and rev'rent hearts. Ah, then,
Joy shall awake within those care-worn souls,
And every longing wish be satisfied.

    CHARITY.—I come, I come, with glowing heart,
      And ever open hand,
    I bring a chain of fragrant flow'rs—
      Tis Love's own magic band.
    I come a guiltless conqueror,
      In bloodless strife I win ;
    Thy children's souls my subjects are,
      My well-fought foe is sin.
    By gentle words and soothing smiles,
      By kindly deed and thought—
    Thus is my glorious conquest won,
      My glorious labor wrought.
    I still the storm of vengeful hate,
      I break the sword of war,
    And free the hapless victims whom
      He fastens to his car.
    I turn the heart from gods of clay
      To the true God of love,
    And fill the world-worn spirit with
      Sweet dreams of bliss above.
    I come to still thy wild unrest,
      To charm from demon-snare,
    To bind upon thy woe-worn breast
      The potent shield of prayer.

I come to fill thy children's hearts
　　With love's celestial fire,
And I will.bid that holy flame
　　Burn clearer yet, and higher.
It glows in perfect purity
　　Within her sinless breast,
Upon whose fond, maternal arm
　　The Lord of love doth rest.
It beams upon her radiant brow,
　　It lights her perfect face,
For 'tis her regal ornament—
　　Her richest, brightest grace.
The hearts that love her blessed Son
　　This royal gift shall share,
And I will guard the sacred flame
　　That burns, unfading, there.
And I will bid that blessed light
　　Shine out with steadfast ray,
To form a pure, celestial path,
　　A heavenward-guiding way.

EARTH.—Welcome, sovereign of the shining
　　three,
Thou of the burning heart and beaming smile!
Thou, in whose radiant eyes the ready tear
Of pity shineth, like the crystal dew
Upon the bosom of a sunlit flower!
All hail! all hail! fair, dove-eyed Charity,
Thrice blessed be thy gentle reign on earth!
In thy sweet fetters may my children's hearts,
O peaceful conqueror! be firmly bound.
Fair sister-graces, heav'n's own brightest band,
Once more the Eden-happiness returns,

And decks my realm as with a festal robe,
To hail your blessed coming. And yet, hark!
The dreaded step! Ah, shield me! lo, they come!
My tyrant foes, my demon enemies!

Enter PAGANISM *and* VIOLENCE. *The Virtues gather
round* EARTH.

PAGANISM (*aside to* VIOLENCE).—Our fears were
faithful messengers! Behold
Yon soft-voiced three, our hated, heaven-sent foes,
Descended here, in answer to the prayer
Of Earth! Bewailing driveller! Ours will be
Hard task, indeed, to break the magic spell,
The potent influence of those silver tongues.
Yet we must battle on; it will not do
To yield our long-enjoyed dominion thus.
Stay! I will speak in honeyed syllables—
Will win, by flattery, yon deserter back,
And conquer her new champions, even here,
By their own magic weapons. (*She advances.*) Hail
to thee,
O sovereign Terra, mother of the gods!
We come to lead thee forth in triumph now;
We bring thy oaken wreath and turret crown,
And, in thy car, by royal lions drawn,
We, thy retainers, thy most willing slaves,
Will lead thee to Olympus—to thy throne
Amid the nectar-nourished deities.
Forgive the wanton game we played with thee—
We hasten now to loose those chafing bonds:
'Twas but a trick to try thy fortitude.

EARTH.—Away, base flatterer, thy reign is o'er,
The spell dissolved, the weary burden raised
From my crushed heart! Earth shall no longer
    bow
In vile allegiance to thy fiendish rule.
The song of Hope hath soothed my wailing woe,
The lifted hand of halo-circled Faith
Hath raised my glances heavenward at last;
And from the glowing heart of Charity
Warmth, light, and life, shall animate once more
The dying heart of Error-fettered Earth.

    VIOLENCE (*to* PAGANISM).—Your arts are vain—
    all vain. One struggle more
To grasp again the prey we must not lose—
I'll make the effort. By my darkest frown
And direst threats the conquest shall be won.
(*She approaches* EARTH.)—Think not, O coward, to
    escape us thus!
Thou art our prey. Was not the compact sealed
Ages ago, when Israel bowed down,
And offered costly sacrifice to Baal?
You shining train can not release thee now—
Thy fetters are too firmly riveted.
Our temples rear their heads from every land;
Before our shrines thy children prostrate lie,
In servile homage to our gods of clay.
Haste thee to join us. What? Dost thou refuse?
Nay, then, I'll force thee, and thy craven heart
Shall tremble to its centre! False one! Come!
                    [*Rushes forward.*

Enter RELIGION (*or* TRUTH), *bearing the cross, and
      followed by* MERCY *and* VIRTUE.

   TRUTH.—Demons, avaunt! Fly, vile deluders,
     fly !
See ye this cross?   It is the sword of Truth,
The weapon of the world's new Conqueror!
To-day, on Calvary, a Victim hung,
And, by His death on this empurpled cross,
Won the blest triumph o'er thee, Violence,
And thee, O impious Idolatry!
The Paschal Lamb, by mystic words foretold,
By mystic types prefigured, was, this day,
On this new altar, this most precious cross,
Offered in blest, atoning sacrifice.
The world's redemption, by His royal blood,
Is fully, freely gained.   Your reign is o'er,
O demon tyrants!   Back, then, to your home,
In darkest Hades!   Hide for ever there,
(*Advances*) Or bow before the Saviour's conqu'ring
     cross,
The standard pure of all-subduing Truth!
        [PAGANISM *and* VIOLENCE *hastily retreat.*
   TRUTH.—Rejoice, O ransomed captive! let thy
     tears.
For ever cease!   Thy starless night is past,
Behold the glory of thine endless day!
By death, thy wayward children are redeemed;
By death, eternal life is freely won!
To gain the souls so precious in His sight,
The Son of God hath offered up His life;
And now the Father's wrath, appeased, hath changed

To an unfading smile of tenderness
And reconciliation, most complete.
Mercy, His gentle messenger, hath come
To bring thy ransom, and to loose thy bonds.

(EARTH *throwing herself at the feet of* MERCY.)

EARTH.—Pardon, most blessed minister of grace,
The insults offered by the daring hands
Of my deluded children to the King,
The sole and Sovereign Lord of once-bright Earth.
I have been forced to bear upon my brow
The weary weight of sin-polluted shrines—
Of temples reared to gods of vilest clay.
I have been forced to see the revels foul,
And pageants proud, of base Idolatry ;
To feel the tramp of war's destroying hoof,
The blighting steps of rampant vice and crime,
Crushing upon my heart—to echo back,
O'er all my shrinking hills, and through the depths
Of sighing forests, the most direful sounds
Of fiendish orgies—shrieks and wails of woe,
Sent from my children's overburdened hearts.
Now, at thy feet, sweet Mercy, lo! I kneel,
Weighed still by sense of foul unworthiness.
  MERCY (*raising her*).—Pardon in full for crimes of
      deepest dye
Is freely promised to repentant hearts—
Thy children shall receive the blessed boon.
And now lift up thy drooping brow again,
And let the beaming Eden-smile return,
In radiance o'er thy realm, now purified
From every blot and foul, sin-blighting stain.

Poor, fettered hands, how have they borne the
    clasp
Of these vile cords?   My strength shall rend them
    now.
Away, ye signs of basest servitude!
        [*Breaks the cords, and throws them from her.*
Rejoice, poor Earth!   Thou art for ever free!
    TRUTH.—I greet thee, favored one, regenerate
        Earth,
And I will be thy gentle sovereign!
My potent arm shall hurl the idol down
From its proud place, and plant my standard there;
And each unhallowed fane shall be transformed
Into a temple of the living God.
The bloodless sacrifice of Calv'ry's Lamb
For ever offered on the sin-cleansed shrine
Shall henceforth be; and smiling heaven will bless
With every grace and Eden-loveliness
The ransomed realm, where now begins the reign
Of heav'n-sent Virtue and eternal Truth!
    EARTH.—All hail, all hail, O clear-eyed, heav-
        enly Truth!
I bow in fond allegiance unto thee.
What rapture thrills my heart, what joy illumes
My blooming plains, and lends a brighter glow,
Like smiles of heaven, to the rich brilliancy
Of its fair sunlight!   Dewy tears of bliss   .
Rest in the radiant eyes of gentle flowers,
That send their fragrance, like sweet incense, up—
Their new, fond tribute to the conqu'ring Lord.
The wildwood choir have learned Redemption's
    song,

And dancing rills bear on the joyous strain,
In gentle murmurs, to the waiting sea,
That swells in louder cadence, endlessly,
The glorious anthem.   Hasten, blessed Truth,
With thy fair band of sister virtues, now,
Through every nation of my ransomed realm,
And bear the precious tidings to those hearts
That sigh in darkness for the hoped-for dawn !
May all my children, 'neath thy gentle yoke,
In glad allegiance bow !
    TRUTH.—   Ay, we will go,
Armed with the cross, salvation's blessed sign,
And thou shalt follow in our train, fair Earth.
Error is not yet conquered utterly—
It will return, and use its deadliest arts
To stay our triumph-progress.   Blood must flow—
The blood of martyrs—which shall nourish thus
Faith's newly-planted seed.   By that blest tide,
So freely laved, it shall become, at last,
A stately tree.   Amid its spreading boughs
The captive birds, the weary human souls, .
Flying from Error's snares, shall freedom find,
And safest shelter.   They who thus shall wash
Their garments white in their own cleansing blood,
Shall bear the palm of victory on high ;
And chant a new, eternal song of " praise
And benediction to the Lamb once slain,
Whose death has won our new, undying life."
    EARTH.—Once more, O star-eyed Hope, ere we
        depart
On this blest mission, sing thy soothing strain,

And in its sweet refrain let all unite:
" Glory to God on high, and peace to Earth!"
  HOPE.—Blend your sweet notes with mine, O
    sisters fair,
And let all hearts the chorus blest prolong!

FAITH, HOPE *and* CHARITY, *sing together.* (*Air*—"*Les
    Anges dans les Montagnes.*")
    Angels sung our glorious song
      When our Lord in Bethlehem lay:
    Still the bright, seraphic throng
      Chant it on this blessed day:
(*Chorus.*) Gloria in excelsis Deo.

    Clear o'er Calvary's mystic height
      Still the glorious strains resound;
    E'en through dark and dreadful night,
      E'en through direst gloom profound:
(*Chorus.*) Gloria in excelsis Deo.

    .In the radiant Easter dawn,
      From His tomb the notes arise,
    For the night is past and gone,
      Sunlight dawns in fadeless skies:
(*Chorus.*) Gloria in excelsis Deo.
             [*Exeunt omnes, singing chorus.*

SCENE IV.—*Enter* CHILD OF EARTH. *She sings.*
(*Air*—" *Je suis la Bergère Fidèle.*")
O blissful and radiant heaven,
    Fair dwelling of freedom and light!
Soon, soon shall these fetters be riven,
    Soon, soon shalt thou dawn on my sight.
        The night of pain is o'er—
        Nevermore
    'Shall its shadows chill my heart,
        The restless night is o'er,
    The sunlight can never depart.

PEACE *enters, unobserved, and joins the refrain.*
        O hasten, Lord, the day
          Of martyr victory,
       When, freed from bonds of clay,
       My soul shall speed to Thee!

CHILD OF EARTH *greets* PEACE.
CHILD OF EARTH.—O olive-crowned Peace, I
    have found thee at last,
And the storm of my anguish for ever is past!
Thy spell hath been laid on the world-fevered brow,
And sweet is the calm that encircles me now;
I have conquered at last, I've successfully wrought,
I have found the blest treasure so ceaselessly sought;
Thy wings have enfolded my pain-tortured breast,
And gladness succeedeth its wailing unrest.
Thou changest the passionate cry of despair
To the music of praise, and the murmur of prayer;
There is balm e'en on Earth for its suff'ring and woe,
For Truth hath reflected her heaven below.

Ah! blest be the day when the wanderer heard,
In Faith's holy temple, the soul-soothing word;
When the tear of repentance suffused the proud
    eye,
And the haughty heart heaved with contrition's
    soft sigh,
And, humbled and grateful, she bowed and adored
The God of the Christian, her Master and Lord.
Thrice-blessed the dawn of that glorious day,
When the baptismal tide washed her guilt-stains
    away,
And, robed in her white festal garment, she shared
The banquet of love, for His children prepared.
How perfect, how full, is the answer returned
To the prayer of the heart that so restlessly yearned!
One longing remains: 'tis to wing my glad flight
To the kingdom eternal, the dwelling of light.
Soon, soon 'twill be granted, and with the glad
    throng
This martyr shall sing the victorious song;
In garments washed white in the blood of the
    Lamb,
This victor shall rise with the conquering palm.
O hasten, bright dawn of that glorious day,
When my spirit, released from the thraldom of
    clay,
Through the portals of death triumphant shall
    spring,
Heaven's song on her lips, and its light on her wing!
    PEACE.—O daughter of Earth, lo! thy ransom is
    near;
Stern trial awaits thee, but solace is here!

I bless thee, I charm thee, from feàr and from snare,
With the armor of strength, and the bright shield
    of prayer.
Faint not, till the tumult of battle is done—
Soon, soon 'twill be ended, the victory won;
The crown of the martyr shall gleam on thy brow,
Heaven's glory, eternal, awaiteth thee now.
The rack and the torture, death's anguish and pain,
Shall win life unfading, and break the loath'd chain.
On, conqueror, on! With thy strength-giving blood
Enrich the new Church—let it lave in its flood.
    CHILD OF EARTH.—I am ready, fair guide, I am
      armed for the strife—
On the altar of Faith let me offer my life.
Let me pour the libation; the hour grows late,
The victim is crowned: must the sacrifice wait?
Joy, joy! they are coming! Ah, blissful release!
It is mine! mine, at last! let us meet them, fair
    Peace.
They thirst for my blood! Ah, did they but know
How willing the sacrifice—quick! let us go!
                  [*Exeunt.*

SCENE V.—*Enter* TRUTH *and* VIRTUE, *and seat
    themselves on thrones.* MERCY *and* PEACE *stand
    on each side.*

TRUTH.—Let us rejoice, sweet sister.   Earth is
    ours—
Her children hail the sacred sign of Truth,
And bow in humblest homage to its God.
Ah! this is blissful triumph, this is joy,
That wakes in angel hearts a deeper thrill,
And fills the echoing courts of joyous heaven
With new, enraptured harmonies.   Once more,
As in that happy time of Eden-bliss,
Our peaceful empire is established here,
Blest by the promise of our Lord and King:
That ne'er again shall demon foes prevail
O'er His fair Church, that on her radiant brow
Bears, firmly stamped, her Founder's seal of Truth.
    VIRTUE.—Ay, and her shining robes—how bright
        their gleam!
They gained that lustre from the blessed tide
Which, with its royal dye, hath stained thy sign,—
The peaceful sword, the all-subduing cross.
And on her radiant breastplate, lo! I read
The priestly motto, "Holiness to the Lord!"
How fresh, how fadeless, is her loveliness!
Ages have passed since that strange tragedy
Of pain-fraught Calv'ry, yet she standeth now
As fair, as youthful, as when then she sprung
Into bright being from the sacred stream
That flowed adown the mystic mount of woe.

MERCY.—How many a sad, sin-burdened human
  soul
Hath laved in that all-cleansing sea of grace !
Yet full, exhaustless, lo ! it gusheth still
From its pure source in Love's o'erflowing heart.
  PEACE.—And O how fondly do my shelt'ring
    wings
Rest o'er each sin-washed soul, as o'er that pair
Who walked in fair, primeval guiltlessness
In heaven-reflecting paradise. How great,
How precious, in our Master's sight must be
The souls His fiat drew from nothingness,
And stamped with his own image, and for whom
He stooped to their weak nature's frail disguise ;
And when the time of sacrifice was come,
And He would then put off that mystic robe,
His creatures' cruel hands performed the deed.
Ay, He, their hidden God, permitted them
To give him death, that He might bring them life !
And even now, the priceless legacy
Of His own sacred flesh, still deeply hid
In the strange mask of mortals' daily food,
He gave these favored souls ; and they shall feast
Upon this Bread of Life until the end
Of Time's mysterious reign. O privilege
Ne'er given to the sinless angel-band,
Yet freely lavished on ungrateful clay !
O mystery of Love ! O mighty power
Of the pure God of Virtue and of Peace,
Of tender Mercy and all-conqu'ring Truth !

Enter FAITH.

FAITH.—Sweet sovereigns, your grateful subject,
    Earth,
And her bright children, whom ye have subdued,
Crave gracious audience from their rulers fair.
She of the dusky brow and gleaming zone—
Weird, mystic Africa—hath led the train;
Asia, the dreamy-eyed and rose-wreathed, next;
Majestic Europe, with her queenly tread,
And cross-crowned brow, succeedeth; then the last,
The youngest of the treasure-laden band,
And best-loved daughter of our ransomed Earth,
The newly-won America.   They come
To pay their willing meed of gratitude
To heav'n-sent Virtue and eternal Truth.

                             [*Exit* FAITH.

Enter EARTH, *attended by* FAITH, HOPE *and* CHARITY,
   and followed by AFRICA, ASIA, EUROPE, *and*
   AMERICA.

EARTH.—Most welcome rulers, gentlest sover-
    eigns,
Receive the tribute of your subjects' love !
Approving heaven hath blest your earthly reign—
Your golden reign of happiness and peace.
Ages of bliss have sweetly, gently rolled
Since Earth's Redeemer won the priceless boon
Of blest regeneration, yet no cloud
E'er dims the brightness of the Father's smile,
Which sheds soft benisons o'er ransomed souls,
And brings sweet sense of pardon and of peace
To my long-burdened heart.   Before your throne,

O Virtue fair, and ever-blessed Truth,
I bow in fondest, deepest thankfulness! (*She kneels.*)
My children blend their gratitude with mine,
And give the tribute of their willing love
Unto their bright celestial sovereigns, (*They kneel.*)
To whose sweet influence and guidance blest
They owe their progress o'er the path of right—
The path that leads to never-ending bliss. (*They rise.*)
  ASIA.—I was the first to learn thy teachings
    pure,
O clear-eyed Faith! The first to hear his voice
Who, in the wilderness, prepared the way
For the Messiah's coming. In my realm
Is many a hallowed spot, where Israel bowed
Before the living God, when, dimly seen
In mystic types, the wondrous Sacrifice
Was offered on Jehovah's holy shrine:
The mount about whose lofty summit played
The lightnings of His pow'r, when awe-struck man
Received the heav'n-sent law: the lonely wild
Where lay the sacred prophet of the Lord,
Weary and travel-worn, yet won new strength
From mystic nourishment, by ravens brought.
Ay, many a spot revered by that blest race
Who erst enjoyed the benisons of heaven,
I keep within my fair domain. Ay, more
And purer treasures are yet hidden there:
The lonely cave, the favored dwelling-place
Of Israel's unknown God. The humble home
Of His pure childhood, bleakest Nazareth,
Where, docile to His blessed Mother's word,
He dwelt concealed until His time should come.

The hallowed stream, whose bright baptismal wave
" Mirrored the sacred dove" with snowy wings,
Descending softly o'er the Saviour's brow.
The woods, the deserts lone, the busy towns,
Where He, the meek and lowly Teacher, went,
And in His soul-entrancing tones subdued
The rebel hearts of error-burdened men.
The crested waves of depthless Galilee,
Upon whose shore He rested, faint and lone,
Yet wearied not in His sweet task of love ;
Upon whose azure breast the majesty
Of nature's God revealed itself, when He
Walked safely o'er the tranquil, spell-bound wave,
Or calmed its fury with His " Peace ! be still ! "
The haughty city, on whose turrets fair,
And stately palaces, His yearning gaze,
Tear-dimmed, yet loving, lingered, when the
　　thought
Thrilled with keen agony His tender soul,
How she, the cherished, whom He came to save,
And would have folded in the sheltering wings
Of His redeeming love, yet turned away,
Scorning the off'ring of her God and King,
And walked,with haughty tread, to death and woe.
Sad, sad Gethsemane, which through the night—
That drearest night of sorrow—saw the pangs,
The anguish, of her God ; whose barren soil
Was moistened with the mystic dew of blood ;
Whose air, in the lone midnight, pitying rang
His wailing cry : " Let the dread chalice pass,
If it be possible ; yet Thy will be done,
My Father ! " And the last, the closing scene

Of that dark drama—lonely Calvary,
Where rose the throne of Israel's thorn-crowned
　King,
The blood-empurpled cross, close to whose foot
The sinless mother, in her anguish, clung,
And gazed upon her Son's pain-tortured face,
Until the mystic words, " 'Tis finished," burst
From those death-pallid lips.　The rocky tomb
Whose bonds the victor broke, and thus from
　death
Won endless life for lost and erring man.
The olive-shaded mount, from whose bright brow
The glory of a God revealed itself,
When He, before the kneeling, awe-struck throng,
Ascended brightly to His fadeless realm,
Blessing, with outstretched hands, His faithful band.
These are the gems, the consecrated spots,
Which favored Asia shrineth in her heart ;
For these she giveth all her grateful love
To thee, O heavenly Truth ! whose God bestowed
Such grace and blessing on her favored clime.
　AFRICA.—And I, within my deserts vast and
　drear,
And lotus-freighted river, treasure, too,
Bright places hallowed by His blest abode :
The weary paths His faithful guardians trod
To my lone Egypt, from the cruel king
Who sought his fancied rival's hated life ;
Where, as the sacred legend verifies
The mystic words of holy prophecy,
The idols foul of demon-worshippers—
Osiris, Isis, all the horrid train—

Down from their pedestals, in terror, fell,
Soon as those way-worn pilgrims rested on
The very borders of that realm of sin:
For e'en the demon rebels dared not raise
Their hideous standard 'neath the kingly glance
Of Earth's Child-Conqueror, their dreaded God
Ay, and when all that history of love,
His life's atonement, was fulfilled, again
Those desert solitudes were sanctified
By hermit-lives of penance and of prayer.
There dwelt the desert-saints, alone with God,
There rose the incense of their soulful praise,
There rang the echoes of their holy hymns.
The youthful Church put on her fairest strength
Won from the pleadings of an Anthony,
And his blest train of world-forsaking souls,—
Fair flowers of that sand-strewn solitude,
Making the desert " blossom like the rose,"
With graces from the garden of their God.
In Afric's glowing realm the cross-armed band
Of Truth's bright warriors won the mystic strife
O'er dark-robed Error and her demon gods,
And poured their life-blood out, a precious tide,
In glorious martyrdom for Christ's dear sake.
Lo! from that blest baptism I arose
Cleansed and transfigured by the light of Faith.
For this I thank ye, gentle sovereigns;
And may your noble conquest never cease,
Till not a trace of vile idolatry
Be left in Africa's redeemed domain.

    EUROPE.—The boon of Faith, by His apostles
      brought—

Those chosen fishers of deluded men—
Still blesses Europe's smiling, sunlit plains
And rocky-fortressed isles. Lo, queenly Rome!
Crumbled to dust her gods of sculptured clay!
A moss-grown ruin, that once haughty pile,
Whose arches rang with fierce, exulting shouts,
When savage beasts, athirst for human blood,
Revelled upon their life's pure tide who stood,
Firm and serene, with upward-gazing eyes,
And met their death with songs upon their lips,
And triumph written on their tranquil brows.
Ah! martyr-blood hath cleansed the guilty stain
Of Earth's imperial mistress, cross-crowned Rome!
Fair Christian temples shrine the Victim pure,
The endless sacrifice of Love. She is
The sepulchre of purest, saintliest dead—
'Tis fairer wealth than all the gleaming pomp
Of foul Idolatry. Behold the seal
Of Christian Truth, stamped fair on ev'ry land:
Majestic Spain, and smiling, sunny France,
The vine-clad empire of the castled Rhine;
Fair Britain, rock-throned mistress of the sea,
Where once the cruel Druid offered up
To demon-gods the human sacrifice.
Now, in the green and smiling English vales,
O'er Scotland's fragrant heaths and lofty heights,
The sweet-toned bell rings out its joyous peal
On the calm Sabbath air. Still fondly shrined
In Erin's bleeding heart, still firmly stamped
Upon her cross-sealed brow, Faith safely dwelt
Through the long night of suffering centuries;
Still, pallid mourner, on her rocky shore,

She holds her Master's priceless legacy
Clasped firmly, fondly, in those fettered hands,
To her grief-laden heart.   Ay, e'en the North,
Where once the savage Viking ruled supreme,
And fiercely drank, in Odin's hideous name,
His foeman's blood from ghastly human skulls,
Now bends the humbled knee at holy shrines,
And owns the Christian's God, the God of Truth,
And olive-sceptred Virtue.   This ye've won,
Sweet messengers of Love's eternal King.

    AMERICA.—What rapture thrills the gladsome,
       youthful heart
Of newly-won America!   Thy hand,
O heavenly Truth! hath wrought this magic work.
Scarce three bright centuries have rolled away
Since spell-bound silence slept in solitude
Within the pathless wilderness, where roamed
The forest's dusky son, in blindness clad—
The thoughtful-browed explorer broke the spell
Where once the Aztec's bloody shrines arose
In the fair, fragrance-laden South ; and where
The mighty rivers of the North speed on
Their march of triumph to the boundless sea,
Loyola's saintly sons have nobly wrought— .
The saving stream upon the swarthy brow
Hath sweetly flowed, and savage hearts have bowed
To the Great Spirit's heaven-descended Son ;
And stately forms have gladly, freely knelt,
To thank the efforts of the " black-robed chiefs."
Now, o'er thy new, bright empire, gentle Truth,
The peaceful fanes of pure Religion rise ;
And every smiling vale and verdant hill,

And fair, majestic river, beareth on,
In joyous echo, the harmonious strains
Of Christian hymns, of Christian pray'r and praise.

Enter SCIENCE *and the Sister Arts.*

SCIENCE.—Fair, bright-browed Virtue, sweet,
  celestial Truth,
Let Science greet ye, with her daughters fair,
The radiant Sister Arts! We offer here
Our aid in the most holy cause of Truth.
The light that faintly gleamed above the path
Of pale Philosophy shall fadeless shine,
In noon-day lustre, o'er the sacred way
Of Truth's pure sages. Long we toiled in vain
To guide the erring steps of man aright.
Fair Earth is ransomed now : our dearest wish
At last is granted. Since the blessed reign
Of Truth began, success has crowned our task ;
And many a pure-souled scholar, bending low,
In lonely cell, above the sacred page,
Hath felt my strong, inspiring power, when thoughts
Depthless and pure, have gleamed upon his brain,
And flowed beneath his consecrated pen.
The Sacred Word, the wisdom-breathing page,
Which wrought such magic in the cause of Truth,
When wily Error spread her sophist snares
And specious reasonings o'er the path of man :
These potent weapons which, with holy skill,
Have parried oft the demon's fiercest thrusts,
I offer here, and may they be preserved
Long in the sacred armory of Truth !
      [SCIENCE *offers volumes and manuscripts.*

Music.—I rule the sweet, harmonious strain; I
    bring
The gentle offering of lute and lay.
My thrilling cadences rang firm and clear
From martyr-lips, and through the caverned depths
Of dark, sepulchral catacombs arose,
And woke a strange, mysterious thrill of fear
Within the startled heart of pagan Rome.
And when the night of persecution passed,
My clear, triumphant anthems proudly swelled
Through vast cathedral aisles, that echoing rang;
Or through the small, secluded chapel stole
In the soft murmur of the vesper hymn,
Soothing with sweet, seraphic melody
The burdened hearts of sorrow and of care—
Calming the storm of wrath, with magic spell,
And conquering the demon of despair.
                    [*Offers lyre and music.*
  Poetry.—I light, I sway, the bard's inspiréd
    dream,
I bid him wake his purest, noblest lays;
Full·many an ode to Virtue and to Truth
Hath thrilled the listening and enraptured world,
And wrought blest service in Religion's cause.
  Eloquence.—I rule the silver tongues of those
    who sway
The spellbound throng with magic eloquence;
Whose bright, anointed brows and glowing eyes
Are lit, transfigured, with the holy flame,
When, in their burning words, the sacred truths
Of pure Religion are as fiery darts
To pierce the captive, awe-struck souls of men.

PAINTING.—1 guide the gifted hand which brightly
   blends
The rainbow tints, the hues of gorgeous flowers,
The starry radiance of bright-winged birds,
The sunset glory, all earth's loveliness,
Upon the glowing canvas.   In that land
Whose artist sons have wrought their glowing
   dreams
To deck the massive walls of stately fanes,
I joy to dwell.   There, there, I reign supreme.
Raphael, Correggio, Titian!—shining names!
The sons of genius leave their distant homes,
And o'er the sounding sea enraptured throng,
To gaze transfixed, in silent ecstasy,
Upon the blest Madonna's pictured face—
The sinless Mother and the Child Divine.
Ah, holy visions of the artist-soul,
What aid ye lend to great, eternal Truth!
   SCULPTURE.—In that same realm of art and
   loveliness
Another heart is blest with magic dream,
And in the deathless marble bids it live,
In almost breathing beauty—perfect fair,
Wanting alone the fiat of a god
To make the finished type of lovely life
A being real and animate.   And all,
All these bedeck the temples of the Lord:
And thus I aid ye, gentle sovereigns.
Ay, more: I bid those stately temples rise,
The vast cathedrals, with their vaulted domes,
And pillared aisles, and sculptured turrets, rich
With tracery rare, and carvings delicate;

And now we bring, as offerings of love,
The pictured beauty of a holy dream,
     [PAINTING *offers a picture.*
And Israel's Lily, wrought in marble pure.
   [SCULPTURE *gives a statue of the Madonna.*
 VIRTUE.—Fair, gifted band, I thank ye in the
  name
Of my most royal sister, heavenly Truth,
For your sweet aid and welcome offerings.
Continue, gentle ones, your blessed work.
Let Science with her wealth of depthless thought,
Let Music's thrilling strains and harmonies,
Fair Poesy's sweet fancies, Eloquence
With silver voice and magic syllables,
Art's radiant dreams, and Sculpture's perfect works,
With Architecture's stately temples blend,
In union blest, to give the reign of Truth
A brighter charm, a fit embellishment.
 TRUTH.—And now 'tis meet, O heaven-favored
  Earth !
Who, with thy blooming daughters, offer here,
Before our throne, the tribute of your love,
And the fair meed of fervent gratitude,
That we, your monarchs, render full return
By words of fond, approving sympathy.
O may the freed, regenerate race that dwell
Within your favored realm press nobly on,
With firm, unfalt'ring footsteps, in the path
Of Virtue and of Truth ! it is the path
That leads to heaven and to happiness—
Look upward, dear ones, with the eye of faith !
Behold how brightly gleameth, far, yet near,

The fadeless city, with its gates of gold,
And walls of flashing gems! The sons of men
Are the true heirs of all its loveliness,
If they but follow whither Truth doth lead,
And list, with docile hearts, to Virtue's voice.
And now, O dove-eyed Peace, extend thy hands,
So fraught with benisons, above the heads
Of the freed mother and her daughters fair,
And bid them win thy wealth of golden gifts.

[EARTH *and the nations kneel.* PEACE
raises her hands over them.

PEACE.—Receive the gifts of white-robed Peace,
The benisons that ne'er shall cease;
And take the wealth I gladly bring,
The gifts that ever closely cling.
The sons of Earth, on heart and brow,
With spells of Peace are bound, e'en now:
The soul serene, and the heart of Truth,
That winneth the fadeless bloom of youth;
The stainless hand and the noble will,
The lip that is free from a word of ill;
The gentle voice, and the tranquil eye,
Serenely turned to the home on high:—
These, these are the gifts of the angel Peace,
These are the blessings that ne'er shall cease.
Rise, daughters fair, to ye are given
The richest boons of bounteous heaven.

TRUTH.—Fair subjects, let us humbly bow before
The shining throne of Truth's eternal King;
There let us give Him soulful gratitude
For this most glorious conquest. Let us win
New benisons, the priceless gifts of prayer. (*All kneel.*)

Great God of Truth! Thy servants prostrate fall
Before thy throne, and hail Thee Lord of all.
Thou who hast checked proud Paganism's sway,
And crushed her idols false, her gods of clay;
Thou who hast blessed Thy Truth's eternal reign,
And freed the captive, Earth, from Error's chain,
And sent the bright, the world-subduing band
Of sister virtues to each darkened land,—
To Thee, O Lord! our rev'rent hearts we raise
In grateful prayer, and loftiest notes of praise.
May every nation bend the willing knee,
And offer fond allegiance unto Thee!
May every soul be cleansed from earthly dross,·
And bow, submissive, to the conqu'ring cross!
So shalt Thou bless Thy Truth's victorious way,
And change Earth's night to heaven's endless day;
So shall the stream of saving mercy flow
From Thy fair throne o'er ev'ry heart below,
And Peace, with folded wings, like nestling dove,
Rest, as in Eden, o'er the home of love,—
Her new, regenerated home on earth,
The home made holy by a Saviour's birth.
Deign still to shed Thy fair, benignant smile
O'er ransomed Earth, washed pure from Error's
       guile;
O'er all her children let that radiant beam
Of heaven-sent light in new effulgence gleam,
Till, in bright course, fair Nature moves no more,
And Thou shalt bid the reign of Time be o'er.
Then, from reflected radiance, may they rise
To Light's fair home, beyond the sunlit skies;

And robed in righteousness, all fetters riven,
Bask 'neath the gleam of Glory's source, in heaven.

> [*All rise.*

Ere on our ceaseless mission we depart,
Let Music wake the lofty hymn of praise
And holy triumph. In its glorious strains
Our voices and our hearts shall all unite ;
.And, as we journey o'er our conqu'ring way,
The joyous notes shall sweetly, firmly swell,
Until the future's distant ages bear
Their lofty echo, through the realms of Time,
To the dim shores of vast Eternity.

> [*Exeunt omnes, singing the psalm,* "*Laudate Dominum, omnes gentes,*" *etc.*

THE NATIVITY.

PERSONAGES:

First Sage, *or* King.
Second " "
Third, " "
First, Second, *and* Third Shepherds.
Angel.
Herod.
Rabbi Simon.
Barah, *a Page to Herod.*
Angels, *etc.*

THE·NATIVITY.

ACT I.

SCENE I.—*A plain near Bethlehem.*

FIRST SHEPHERD.—How full of solemn mystery
   is night!
In the weird glimmer of her starry light,
In the low moaning of the wintry gale,
In the still stream, enrobed in icy veil,
In leafless boughs, that point like ghostly fingers,—
In all things hid, night's solemn secret lingers!
O thou mysterious and unseen God,
Whose seal is stamped upon earth's velvet sod!
Whose secrets slumber in each trembling star,
Whose voice is borne upon the blast afar!
We worship Thee with humbly offered hearts,
With souls untaught, yet free from worldly arts.
We dare not lift the proud, presumptuous eye,
To read the mysteries of the Deity;
We ask not how Thy all-creating hand
Formed the vast sea, and spread the blooming land;
We know Thou'rt God—we seek to learn no more:
Our simple minds, unskilled in sage's lore,
Shall own Thy might, and tremblingly adore.

SECOND SHEPHERD.—This night hath holy gifts.
    A perfect calm
Descends on earth, like sweet celestial balm.
Fair, white-robed Peace, that erst did softly rest
On Eden's soil, a loved and constant guest,—
She comes again, and o'er my spirit flings
The soothing influence of her magic wings,
While, like long-dimmed, yet sweetest mem'ries, rise
Bright, blissful visions of lost paradise.
    THIRD SHEPHERD.—Brother, that nameless peace
        my soul doth share;
I feel its spell upon the tranquil air.
The mystic light that from the sacred shrine
Gleams with a starry radiance divine,
Shines o'er me now, while on my ravished ear
Steals angel-melody, remote, yet clear.
My thoughts have found a new, continual theme;
The holy prophet's blest, inspiréd dream,
The strains that thrilled Isaias' sacred lyre,
When on his lips was laid the living fire,—
The promise of a Saviour, who shall dwell
A welcome monarch in lost Israel,—
These musings o'er my spell-bound spirit throng,
Like the sweet tones of some seraphic song.
I draw strange pictures of the matchless grace,
The tender sweetness, of that Saviour's face—
For, ah! that countenance I cannot see
Mid the dread lightning-flame of majesty!
No, no, He seems a fair and lovely child,
With smiling brow, and eye serene and mild,
Yet with that glance of tender, mournful love
That fills the soft eyes of the brooding dove;

Or, as ye've marked the look, resigned and calm,
Upon the face of a young victim-lamb,
Blended with gentle pleading, as the knife
Aims the dread blow against its guileless life:
So tender, lamblike, innocent, doth seem
Messiah's face, that haunts my constant dream.
But lo! what glory fills the midnight sky?
What bright, celestial legions throng on high?

      [*All prostrating themselves.*

Lord, veil Thy glory, or Thy creatures die!

      An ANGEL *appears.*

 ANGEL.—Fear not; we come on love's exultant
  wing,
And blissful tidings unto earth we bring.
The night is o'er, and lo, the fadeless morn!
Messiah reigns, the Saviour Christ is born!
Heaven lends to earth its fairest, brightest gem—
The man-God lies in lowly Bethlehem!

   [*The Shepherds remain kneeling and gazing
    upward, while a throng of Angels sing.*

Angels' Hymn.—(Air, "Les Anges dans les campagnes.")

  Love hath sent a balm for pain,
   Heaven bids earth's sorrows cease;
  List to the new, celestial strain,
   List to the angels' song of peace!
Chorus.—Gloria in excelsis Deo!

  Mortals, join the strain we sing,
   Welcome your Redeemer's birth.

Glory to the Lord, our King!
Peace to faithful men on earth!
Chorus.—Gloria, etc.
        [*In which the Shepherds, rising, join.*

ANGEL.—Come, favored ones! Concealed in
    lowly guise,
Poorer than ye, your God and Saviour lies;
The low estate, the simple heart, is dear
To Him who comes the woes of earth to cheer;
And simple shepherds first shall bow the knee
Before the crib of hidden Deity!
Haste, then, O faithful watchers on the plain,
Whose favored ears first heard the seraphs' strain!
Away, away, your Sovereign to adore,
Whose reign shall last till time shall be no more!
        [*Exeunt, singing the chorus of "Adeste
        Fideles, Venite Adoremus."*

SCENE II.

FIRST KING.—O guiding star! when shall our
    journey cease?
When shall we hail the longed-for Prince of Peace?
Thy faithful beams have cheered our weary night,
When will they show the source of fadeless light?
How strange, O friends, our pilgrimage doth seem!
Like the swift journey through a blissful dream,
Still safely led, from Eastern climes afar,
By the sure guidance of yon shining star!

SECOND KING.—Ay, and what joy and rev'rent
    awe were mine,
When first I saw that fair, celestial sign!
'Twas at the solemn midnight's mystic hour,
When visions rise of strange prophetic power,
When, as I bent above the treasured store
Of pages rich with Syria's starry lore,
And prayed to find that pure, yet hidden truth,
So vainly sought e'en from my earliest youth—
Yet, baffled still, upon the sable sky
Turned my wild gaze, and with imploring cry,
I called upon creation's Lord and King
Upon my gloom one shining ray to bring:
Quick came the answer to my eager prayer.
A silv'ry brightness filled the midnight air,
And, as a jewel on night's sable crest,
Yon shining herald sparkled in the west;
With heav'nly radiance it smiled, it shone,
Like a blest ray from the eternal throne,
While thrilling, clear, yet soft as zephyr's sigh,
These words seemed wafted from the realms on
    high:
"Go forth, O searcher! thou shalt find the truth,
And win the visions of thine earnest youth;
For Israel's King begins His blessed reign—
The golden age revisits earth again.
Behold thy guide! Yon gleaming, heav'n-sent star
Shall lead thee safely to His home afar.
Bring richest treasures from thy royal store,
And at His feet in faith and love adore."
What bliss, what rapture, thrilled my favored soul!
What magic bound me in its blest control!

Lowly I bowed upon the dewy sod,
And paid fond tribute to my new-found God!
Then gathered all my gifts of royal worth,
The rarest treasures of our native earth,
And hied me forth upon my Western way,
Led by my starry guide's mysterious ray.
Scarce had I issued from my city's gate,
When there I met, urged by the same blest fate,
Ye, O my brethren! following, too, the beam
That sent me on, as through a holy dream.

  THIRD KING.—For we were searchers for the
    pure and true,
And thy inspired dream was ours, too.
We knew Chaldea's weird and ancient lore,
And read the stars, e'en as a volume, o'er;
We saw thy herald at the midnight hour,
We heard the voice with words of wondrous power;
We rose, obedient to that summons blest,
And turned our willing steps toward the West.
O'er many a land those eager feet have passed,
And we have gained Judea's realm at last.
Within its limits He we seek must dwell—
The hope of earth, the heir of Israel!
Quick, to the summit of yon rocky hill—
The star of faith moves on before us still!
'Tis gained at last, and, framed in silver light,
Lo! a proud city rises on our sight,
With massive walls, and darkly frowning towers,
Fair, terraced courts, and olive-shaded bowers.
Still floats our guide toward that city fair—
It points our way! Our Prize is hidden there!

The Jewish capital His home must be—
There, there at last, our Saviour shall we see!
O let us haste where He, our King, is known,
Where eager worshippers surround His throne.
Quick, past the gate, amid that joyous throng,
To join their shouts, to swell their gladsome song!
                                        [*Exeunt.*

SCENE III.—HEROD, *and his attendant*, BARAH.

HEROD.—Most strange, most wondrous story
    dost thou bring!
Three princes, sent from Eastern climes afar,
Seeking the home of Israel's Infant King,
    And guided thither only by a star!
And they are sages, skilled in starry lore,
    And in the tongue of ev'ry clime can speak;
And gold and spices from their royal store,
    They bring, as tribute, to the Lord they seek!
So runs thy tale, good Barah, that doth seem
    The fevered vision of some star-crazed brain;
Yet would I read this strange, bewild'ring dream,
    And make its truth or baseless folly plain.
Go, summon Rabbi Simon—he is wise
    In mystic lore, and learned in the law:
Can tell of dreams that blessed inspiréd eyes,
    And future scenes those holy seers foresaw.
                                    [*Exit* BARAH.
HEROD (*solus*).—Fool, to be tortured by a dotard's
    tale!
And yet a nameless terror fills my soul—

A spell that bids my inmost spirit quail,
  And holds each thought within its dark control.
A rival king! A monarch of the Jews!
  And I, who deemed my earthly bliss complete,
Must see my fair hopes blighted by this news,
  And throne and kingdom crumble 'neath my feet.
It shall not be; for, if this tale be true,
  And one hath dared my rightful crown to claim,
With ceaseless hate will I my foe pursue,
  And with his life blot out his kingly name.

Enter RABBI SIMON.

SIMON.—Hail, mighty Herod! hail, our lord and
    king!
  Thy faithful servant hath thy call obeyed,
And at thy feet, in humblest offering,
  Lays his poor counsel, and most willing aid.
HEROD.—Thanks, thanks, good Rabbi. Thou
    art welcome here.
  Hast heard the tale these Eastern sages bring?
It seems a fancy of some brain-sick seer,
  This story of a new-born Hebrew king.
SIMON.—Ay, royal Herod, 'tis most strange, in
    sooth;
  And yet the words of holy prophecy
Are now fulfilled, and stamp the seal of truth
  Upon these tidings, wondrous though they be.
HEROD.—Ha! say'st thou so? It is enough! yet
    hold!
  I would know more of this bewild'ring news.
Good Rabbi, have our holy seers foretold
  The birthplace of this ruler of the Jews?

RABBI SIMON.—Ay, royal Herod; rock-girt
  Bethlehem,
The city ruled by Judah's kingly band,
Is the blest shrine of Israel's promised gem,
  The longed-for Saviour of our fettered land.

HEROD.—Go, then, wise Rabbi, bid the strangers
  wait
Until the king shall hear their tidings blest—
Until the strange adventures they relate
  Of their star-guided journey to the West.

                                    [*Exit* SIMON.

HEROD (*solus*).—My plan is woven as a cunning
  net,
  Hypocrisy shall bind it well and fast;
By artful wile my hate shall conquer yet,
  And my unconscious prey be caught at last.
I'll feign a pious eagerness to know
  The hiding-place of Israel's promised king,
That I unto that favored spot may go,
  My homage fond and royal gifts to bring;
Then will I bid them hither haste again,
  With the glad news we yearningly await,
They, unsuspecting, will obey, and then
  I'll win the triumph over adverse fate.
When this usurper's hiding-place I know,
  I'll hither send a true and trusty band,
To give the death-stroke to my hated foe,
  And wrest the Hebrew sceptre from his hand.
O happiest plan that ere hath blessed my brain!
  Hence! blighting dreams of dark, corroding care!
Now, with the zeal I can so truly feign,
  Unto these dreamy sages I'll repair,

                                    [*Exit* HEROD.

SCENE IV.

FIRST KING.—Our star of hope still cheers our
  sight,
And earth is blest by heav'n's own light.
Yon rocky summit, lone and bare,
Transfigured, gleams serenely fair,
And shows, upon its radiant side,
A sleeping city, glorified,
Until it seems, to mortal eyes,
The pearly gate of Paradise.
  SECOND KING.—Lo! how the day-star gleameth
    now
Above yon tower's lofty brow!
Brighter and brighter grows its ray;
Dark seems the fairest summer's day,
When matched with thy celestial beams,
Thou beacon of our brightest dreams!
  THIRD KING.—O joy! O joy! it moves no more,
And our long pilgrimage is o'er;
Look, brethren, o'er yon rocky hill
Our guide doth rest, serene and still.
O let us wing our footsteps there,
The home of Israel's chosen heir!
His palace blest, His earthly throne
Amid the mountains, bleak and lone.
And yet no turret gleaming fair,
No royal dwelling, rises there—
A lonely cave, a stable poor,
Like that wherein the cowherd boor

Shelters his charge from tempests chill,
Is hewn beneath that rocky hill:
Surely He doth not slumber there,
For whom yon heaven is not too fair.

An ANGEL *appears.*

ANGEL.—Ay, 'tis His home—this humble shed
Shelters the man-God's royal head;
Beneath yon stable roof doth dwell
The Hope of captive Israel.
He chose earth's meanest, humblest lot—
The proud, the worldly, know Him not;
A helpless babe, He rests alone,
Poor, weak, unhonored, and unknown.
His Virgin Mother, Mary mild,
There kneels beside her Holy Child;
His foster-father well doth keep
Adoring vigils o'er His sleep;
Poor shepherds, led from yonder plain,
There bend, His earthly courtier-train!
And cattle, thronging where He lies,
Still own their Lord in mortal guise.
These are the honors earth doth bring,
To hail her Saviour and her King;
This, all the homage man can give
To Him who dies that man may live!
Yet heaven is ringing with His name,
His glory, power, endless fame;
And seraphs leave their native skies,
To guard the hovel where He lies!
Yet He hath loved this mean estate,
And shuns the proud, the worldly great;

And He hath chosen first to wear
The form of childhood, pure and fair:
For childlike innocence must be
Loved by the Lord of purity.
The poor, the mourners, too, are dear
To Him who cometh grief to cheer;
And ye who haste with earthly store,
Great princes, rich in pomp and lore,
Must kneel where shepherds knelt before!

FIRST KING.—'Tis well! 'tis well!   We own our
        King,
We bring our hearts' free offering;
And we will bow the willing knee,
In love's most fond humility.

ANGEL.—The humble heart, the guileless soul,
Shall ever claim love's sweet control.
When wealth, and rank, and lore are given,
To aid the search for truth and heaven,
That heaven the sacrifice will bless,
And crown the effort with success.
Thus have ye done: each act, each thought,
Was given to the God ye sought;
On lofty thrones each heart bowed low,
And God alone ye longed to know.
Your holy search is not in vain—
Your toil shall reap its endless gain.
Haste, then, to bend the humble brow
Before your loved Redeemer now.
I am the angel of the Lord—
The herald of His Sacred Word!
                    [*They are about to kneel, but the
                        angel prevents them.*

ANGEL.—Nay, rise, and kneel alone to Him
Before whose face yon sun is dim,
Whose glory veils the Cherubim !
But follow me, O favored band,
To yonder cave, your promised land ;
And look on heaven's fairest gem
Shrined in the crib of Bethlehem !

THE BRIDE THAT NEVER GROWETH OLD.

.

THE BRIDE THAT NEVER GROWETH OLD.

NOT hers the life that waxeth old
In face and form of earthly mould ;
Not hers the beauty carved from clay,
That bears the brand of dark decay.
She dwells in youth's immortal prime,
Nor dreads the ruthless hand of time ;
For never can its touch erase
The radiance of her royal face,
Nor spot nor wrinkle e'er may blight
Her cheek of bloom and brow of light.
Her life-spring flows from source divine,
Her form is truth's eternal shrine ;
No clinging trace of earthly clod
May mar the beauteous bride of God !
E'en when the primal curse began
To work its woe on fallen man,
She came, in types yet veiled and dim,
To trace the heavenward way for him.
She dwelt in Israel's lonely tent,
In long Egyptian banishment ;
On Crimson Sea, o'er desert drear,
She cheered his path of gloom and fear.
His altar, with its emblem-light,
Its victim-types and mystic rite,

She made her blest abiding-place,
And thence bestowed her gifts of grace.
She spoke, in prophet's potent voice,
The words that bade his heart rejoice :
Sweet promise of a glad release
In advent of the Prince of Peace,
When He, whose reign should e'er abide,
Would show, unveiled, His spotless bride,—
His bride, that never groweth old,
By sacred canticle foretold.
It came at last, that blissful reign—
Day dawned upon the night of pain ;
And she, that holy spouse, was there,
Though hidden yet her brightness fair.
She blessed the cave of Bethlehem,
When bloomed the bud on Juda's stem ;
She shed her "aromatic breath"
O'er heaven-favored Nazareth,
She followed where His footsteps led,
"Who had not where to lay His head."
She saw His loving labors wrought,
She heard the priceless truths He taught ;
She learned to keep, with Mary's art,
"His sayings treasured in her heart."
And when He sought, beside the sea,
His fishermen of Galilee,
She smiled upon that chosen band,
So docile to their Lord's command ;
And in their train she followed still,
While Love fulfilled His Father's will.
And when, as neared His mystic hour,
He gave the blest commission-power

Unto His twelve, assigning each
His sacred task, "to preach and teach;"
Ay, when He bade His deathless "Rock"
Give shelter to the world-wide flock,
Then, then she rent her mystic veil,
And from the shadowy twilight pale
She rose, in royal grace bedight,
Upon that Living Rock to plight
Her willing troth's undying vows
With Love Divine—her kingly spouse.
Still brighter grew her beauty's bloom,
When first, within that "upper room,"
With loving care her Bridegroom spread
Her nuptial feast of "Living Bread,"
And bade her evermore repeat
His banquet's consecration sweet,
Thus saying: "Till the end shall be,
This do in memory of Me."
Ah! never shall that faithful bride,
Whate'er of weal or wo betide,
Neglect her sweet and sacred task,
Her Lord's commemoration-pasch.
For ever, by anointed hand,
In ev'ry age, in ev'ry land,
It hath been, as it shall be, done
From rising dawn to setting sun.
She lingered where His watch He kept,
E'en while His loved disciples slept,
And from His heart, by anguish riven,
New vigor to her life was given;
And, moistened with its bloody dew,
Her bridal robe yet fairer grew.

And brighter still its beauty glowed
When love's sweet stream more swiftly flowed
Through all the morrow's dismal morn,
By scourges wrung, and cruel thorn.
Upon her poured, in fuller flood,
His boon of life-bestowing blood,
Adown the mystic mountain sent,
From hands and feet by mortals rent!
But when love's " Consummatus est "
Proclaimed salvation's tidings blest—
Ay, when from out His opened side
Was poured her full baptismal tide,
What radiance of perfected grace
Enshrined her form, entwined her face!
She made His cross her royal throne,
Upon her brow His thorn-wreath shone,
And o'er her queenly form she threw
His " seamless robe " of regal hue.
But not on ransomed earth alone
Is reared her bright, immortal throne,
For love to her dominion gave
The penance-realm beyond the grave.
With Him, that drear abode she sought,
With Him, from weary exile brought
The elder saints, the Hebrew band,
Triumphant, to their promised land ;
And with Him, robed in brightest bloom,
She burst the portals of the tomb,
And showed His risen form to her
Who greeted first the Conqueror.
Not long on earth its Saviour stayed,
For now the mighty debt was paid,

Yet depthless is the heart of love ;
So, ere He sought His throne above,
He bade His pure, immortal bride
Within His earthly realm abide,
To give, upon his Living Rock,
Safe shelter to His helpless flock.
New gifts she won, new strength and light,
To keep her sacred charge aright.
The Spirit of eternal truth
Confirmed love's boon of fadeless youth,
When, once again, in " upper room,"
Still brighter grew her beauty's bloom,
As on her pure apostles came
The Pentecostal tongues of flame ;
And they who fled but yesternight
Went forth, undaunted, to the fight,—
Went forth to crush the demon foe,
And lay his pagan standard low.
But long and deadly was the strife
Against the monster's hydra-life ;
A mighty nation owned his sway,
Fast fettered to the gods of clay.
She vowed beneath her haughty hand
To crush the Christian's hated band,
And in a depthless gulf of shame
To fling, ere long, His very name.
Then gushed the glorious martyr-blood
O'er all her realm—a boundless flood.
By crisping flame, and cleaving steel,
By rending rack, and riving wheel,
By wildest beasts of desert lands,
Upon the dread arena-sands—

By every death, with anguish rife,
She sought to crush the Christian life.
Yet all in vain; though ne'er was heard
From Christian lips one vengeful word:
They passed to death, serene and calm,
As is the helpless victim-lamb.
Yet waxed they stronger, day by day,
While weaker grew her tyrant sway,
Until at last the saving sign
Bright promise bore to Constantine.
Ah! then the fiend bewailed his loss,
While shone that bright, redeeming cross,
And from their thrones the Christian hurled
The idols of a conquered world!
Then brightly gleamed, by furnace tried,
The beauty of the deathless bride!
From rock-built throne, beneath the dome
Reared o'er the heart of pagan Rome,
Through ages, bright with cloudless ray,
Spread o'er the world her sacred sway.
She raised the stricken from the dust,
Redeemed the lost, sustained the just,
While Science wrought her labors grand,
And Art grew fair beneath her hand;
The savage owned her voice of might,
That showed his steps the path of right—
That turned aside his vengeful blow,
And bade him bless his hated foe.
Anon the clouds grow dark above,
And storms assail the spouse of love.
The crescent rose, with baleful light,
And fain would crush her standard bright;

And rebel subjects oft disown
The sway of truth's eternal throne.
And still they strive, with cruel art,
To rend her seamless robe apart;
Yet paled the Moslem Crescent's dross,
Before the glory of the Cross.
And rebel hands shall strive in vain
To rend the robe of truth in twain—
Her Spouse shall check the demon-pride
That seeks to harm His chosen bride,
While Mary keeps her vigil blest
O'er her, as o'er His infant rest,
And Joseph guards—O, fond his care
As when he watched the childhood fair!
O holy Church, O shrine of truth,
O beauty bright with endless youth!
I bow before thy rock-built throne,
My loyal heart thy sway shall own;
And till its tones are stilled in death,
My voice shall praise, with ev'ry breath,
The spouse by sacred bard foretold:
The bride that never groweth old!

SURSUM CORDA.

LIFT thy heart, O sordid schemer!
Lift thy heart, thou idle dreamer!
Turn from worldly plans perplexing,
Turn from visions vain and vexing;
Leave the fast-corroding treasures,
Leave the false and fleeting pleasures.
From the world's delusive glitter,
And its Dead Sea fruitage bitter;
From its pageant-phantoms gliding,
From its glories ne'er abiding,
Shifting scene and baseless vision,
False mirage of joys Elysian:
  Sursum corda.

From its wild, discordant voices,
Grief that wails, while mirth rejoices;
Festal songs with dirges blending,
Glees in mournful cadence ending;
Jarring notes, that, born in sweetness,
Die in harshest incompleteness;
From the silv'ry tones that call thee,
From the strains that would enthrall thee.
Trumpet-blast of fame and glory,
Vain ambition's mocking story;
Syren song that sweetly urgeth
Where destruction's torrent surgeth:
  Sursum corda.

Upward to the stores that fail not,
Upward to the dreams that pale not ;
Sacred schemes, sweet rest bestowing,
Dreams with heaven's own brightness glowing ;
Earnest toil for fadeless treasures,
Blissful search for purest pleasures ;
Thought sublime, and aim supernal,
Hero-strife for fame eternal :—
Turn to these thy life's endeavor,
Look not downward, linger never—
E'en beyond the shining portal,
Upward to the joys immortal :
      Sursum corda.

List the echo, softly ringing,
Of the far-off seraph singing !
Bid those wondrous tones be clearer,
Up ! that thou may'st listen nearer,
For no minor wail of sadness
Mars that choral strain of gladness ;
In its notes no discord blending,
Checks the tale of bliss unending.
To that song of deathless sweetness,
Rife with full and glad completeness ;
To that pæan tone of glory—
Fame's eternal triumph-story :
      Sursum corda.

THE MIST.

I WATCHED the folding of a soft white wing
  Above the city's heart ;
I saw the mist its silent shadows fling
  O'er thronged and busy mart.
Softly it glided through the Golden Gate,
  And up the shining bay ;
Calmly it lingered on the hills, to wait
  The dying of the day.
Like the white ashes of the sunset fire,
  It lay within the West,
Then onward crept above the lofty spire,
  In nimbus-wreaths to rest.
It spread anon—its fleecy clouds unrolled,
  And floated gently down :
And thus I saw that silent wing enfold
  The babel-throated town.
A spell was laid on restless strife and din,
  That bade its tumult cease ;
A veil was flung o'er squalor, woe, and sin,
  Of purity and peace.
And dreaming hearts, so hallowed by the mist,
  So freed from grosser leaven—
In the soft chime of vesper bells could list
  Sweet, echoed tones of heaven ;
Could see, enraptured, when the starlight came,
  With lustre soft and pale,
A sacred city crowned with " ring of flame,"
  Beneath her misty veil.

THE TEAR-CLEANSED SCROLL.

[Having heard this legend related by one of the Paulist Fathers, during their recent missions in this city, and being much struck with the beautiful lesson therein contained, I have attempted, rudely enough, to render into rhyme this sweet and tender story of the Ages of Faith.]

AH! list, I pray ye, to a legend olden,
A quaint, sweet story of the ages golden,
   Rehearsed in rudest rhyme;
Yet hides the tale a teaching pure and tender,
That bids each heart the tearful tribute render,
   E'en in our colder time.

The awesome midnight, silent, dark, and solemn,
Hung over stately street, and arch, and column,
   In the proud city's heart;
Save where the "olive star," serenely shining,
Showed the new Bethlehem of love's enshrining,
   Lone, hidden, and apart.

There softest murmurs broke the silence holy,
For gary-robed monks were bowed in worship lowly
   Within that radiance dim;
While calmly slept the worldly throng, unheeding,
Thro' the lone midnight rose their blended pleading,
   And sweetly chanted hymn.

The strain was hushed in sudden fear and wonder,
Wide flew the door, its fast'ning wrenched asunder
  By fierce and frenzied blow ;
A giant man stood framed within the portal,
Soul-rent he seemed with anguish more than mortal,
  With wild, supernal woe.

" Haste, father abbot, ere I sink unshriven,
In vision dread my soul hath well-nigh riven
  Its prison-walls of clay."
The abbot rose : " I come, my son, to hear thee—
Be patient, brethren, 'tis a case, I fear me,
  That will not brook delay."

"Nay, father, *here* let all my sins be spoken,
Be thus with shame the haughty spirit broken,
  And crushed the stubborn will.
Bold were my crimes, and loud be their revealing,
The cancer-wound must needs have sharpest healing,
  To save from deadlier ill."

The sinner knelt, in self-abasement lowly,
And told his woes before those watchers holy—
  Sooth, 'twas a fearful tale ;
So foul, so dark, that picture, penance-painted,
Well might those simple hearts, by guilt untainted,
  With shudd'ring horror quail.

That horror changed to reverence, deep and tender,
That kneeling form seemed garlanded with splendor,
  And by its side they saw
A figure fair, so robed in dazzling whiteness,
That scarce their gaze could bear the Tabor-bright-
 ness
  That filled their souls with awe.

The crimson wreath, like ruby-jewels gleaming,
Showed where that forehead, so divinely beaming,
    A thorny garland wore;
One wounded hand bestowed its tender blessing,
And one unto His Sacred Heart seemed pressing
    The open scroll it bore.

And on that scroll the list of foul transgression,
At each clear word of penitent confession,
    Waxed ever faint and dim,
Till ev'ry line of that so dismal tracing,
By love's command, and sorrow's skill effacing,
    Fled from the record grim.

And when, at last, the woful tale was spoken,
And died the voice, in sobbing murmurs broken,
    The gemmed brow bent above;
The nail-rent hand received the tear-drop shining,
With fondest care each priceless pearl enshrining
    Within its clasp of love.

O'er the dark list it poured the rain of brightness
Till all one gleam of fair, resplendent whiteness
    Was now that dismal scroll.
And then they knew, those joyful watchers holy,
How contrite tears and self-abasement lowly
    Had cleansed that guilty soul.

Said I not rightly of this legend olden—
This quaint, sweet story of the ages golden,
    Though told in rudest rhyme—
Reveals it not a lesson pure and tender,
That bids each heart the tearful tribute render,
    E'en in our colder time?

O grant me, Lord, such gift of true contrition,
And be Thou near, my soul's benign Physician,
    To soothe its sickly fears!
With Thy dear hand blot out my dismal story
Flooding its record with the cleansing glory
    Of my repentant tears.

AN UNKNOWN SISTER OF CHARITY.

[Among the list of victims to the frightful yellow fever, which, a
few years since, so devastated the South, was registered "An unknown
Sister of Charity." Unknown by the worldlings, indeed, but known
and honored in heaven, are those angels of earth, the heroic Sisters of
Charity.]

UNKNOWN to fashion's tinsel throng,
    The soulless and the vain;
Unknown where ringeth folly's song,
    And pleasure's syren strain.
Unknown where fickle fame bestows
    Her evanescent crown,
While, for a fleeting instant, glows
    The light of earth's renown.
Unknown in life, unknown in death,
    Thus would she live and die—
She needed not the trumpet-breath
    To waft her deeds on high;
But where the plague, at noon-day, trod
    O'er earth his fatal way,

And where, beneath his blighting rod,
  The stricken thousands lay;
Where fiercely burned the fever-flame,
  And rung the dying groan,
Full well the Sister's holy name
  And gentle face were known.
And while life's latest murmur breath'd
  On her its blessings fond,
Her fadeless coronal was wreath'd
  The "jasper walls" beyond.
She saw, in every tortured one,
  Her anguish-laden Lord;
For Him her holy work was done,
  From Him it claimed reward.
What! though no flaunting banners wave,
  Where mercy's martyr sleeps;
What! though above her nameless grave
  No earthly mourner weeps;
When soared her soul, on eager wing,
  Beyond the gates of pain,
The white-robed legions of the King
  Were her triumphal train.
And where Love wrote her blessed name
  Above His radiant throne,
In heaven's light of fadeless fame
  She lives, forever known.

THE GOLDEN SEA.

A Song for the golden sea!
A song for the wide and wondrous main!
For the wind-swept waves of the golden grain
    That sway on the sunlit lea!

Over the mighty deep,
Over the waste of the waters vast,
The stormy rack and the roaring blast
    In Nemesis-fury sweep.

Woe for the ships that gave
Their priceless freight to the trait'rous tide,
And dared, in their boasted strength, to glide
    Over the slumb'ring wave!

Woe for the storm-rent sails,
For the riven masts, and the parted ropes.
And the human power that vainly copes
    With the strength of ocean gales!

O terrible unto me,
In peaceful mask, or in warlike crest,
With storm or zephyr to stir its breast,
    Is ever the watery sea.

But sing for the wave of gold—
For the shining billows that whisper low
To the summer breezes, that come and go,
    Of their magical wealth untold.

Sweet store of the sunlit lea!
Ah, richest treasures of golden grain!
Ah, priceless freight of the creaking wain,
    Of the land's proud argosy!

From heaven, that smiles above,
From the golden touch of the royal sun
The shining sea of the vale hath won
    The rarest gift of his love.

For he came in regal pride
To bathe in the dewy and verdant sea,
And lo! on the breast of the fragrant lea,
    A bright Pactolus-tide!

Gone was the emerald hue,
But over the wind-swept meadows rolled
The wondrous billows of shining gold,
    With diamond crests of dew.

While ships to death go down,
The golden waves of the plain are rife
With glorious dower of wealth and life,
    Their glad explorer's crown.

This is the priceless boon
Of the golden sea, that the sickle cleaves—
The billowy heaps of the banded sheaves,
    Upreared in the summer's noon.

Then swell the harvest glee!
Of gleaner's carol and reaper's strain
Be this the ringing and glad refrain:
    "All hail to the golden sea!"

ROSSINI'S FUNERAL WREATH.

[Suggested by an incident connected with the funeral obsequies of Rossini. Upon his coffin was placed a wreath, formed of two branches of laurel—one taken from the tomb of Virgil, the other from the grave of Tasso. These had been planted by Mèry, in the garden of the composer, some years before.]

Ay, weave for him a matchless crown,
    Bright daughter of the sun!
Meet tribute to the proud renown
    Thy gifted child hath won.
Each charm amid thy bloom entwined
    His magic chords have caught--
There is thy voice of music shrined,
    Thy loveliness enwrought.
Well may he claim the minstrel's bays,
    Well may he bid thee bring
The classic laurel of thy praise—
    Thy fairest offering.
O worthy garland, proudly placed
    Upon the master's bier!
A twofold crown hath interlaced
    Its shining leaflets here.
Ay, from this fair Italian land
    Comes matchless meed of praise—
The king of earth's poetic band
    Hath brought his classic bays.

O favored minstrel! thou hast gained
  Proud summit of renown,
For Mantua's royal bard hath deigned
  To grace thy funeral crown.
The sunny land of light and song
  Another treasure keeps:
There, shrined amid her gifted throng,
  Her princely Tasso sleeps.
Within the cloister's holy shade,
  'Mid wealth of balm and bloom,
The reverent hand of fame hath made
  The poet's peaceful tomb.
That tomb its priceless off'ring sends,
  And love the chaplet weaves;
Lo! Tasso's laurel brightly blends
  With Virgil's classic leaves!
A prouder wreath than ever graced
  The mightiest victor's brow,
Rossini! on thy tomb hath traced
  Its twofold glory now.
He of the " verse men deemed divine"
  In Rome's imperial noon,
And he who sung of "Salem's shrine,"
  Have brought their blended boon.
For Poesy his meed should give,
  To him her homage pay,
Who bade her verse in music live,
  Who wedded lute and lay.
Rest, master of the magic tone,
  Beneath thy wondrous crown;
Yet shrined not 'mid the pomp alone
  Of earth's too frail renown.

The radiance of a purer light,
　　A fadeless beam is shed,
By potent prayer and holy rite,
　　Above the Christian dead.
Rest, while thy voice, undying, clear,
　　A world with rapture fills ;
Rest, while above thy sable bier
　　Thy matchless *Stabat* thrills.
Rest where the seraph-chorus swells,
　　Whose echoes sweetly stole,
And wrought their pure, celestial spells
　　Within thy earth-bound soul.
Rest in His blissful calm, who "gives
　　To His belovéd sleep,"
And where eternal glory lives,
　　A fadeless chaplet keep.

THE CONSECRATED MONTHS.

THE CONSECRATED MONTHS.

THE HOLY CHILDHOOD.

O FAVORED cave of Bethlehem!
　Within thy rock-built shrine
Heaven hid its angel-guarded gem,
　Its light and life divine.
O bleak, yet blessed, desert sands!
　Rare beauty graced the wild,
When, clasped in Mary's sinless hands,
　It saw the Holy Child.

Land of the lotus-freighted Nile,
　Long held in demon thrall!
Love sent an Infant's magic smile,
　To bid thine idols fall.
O rock-encircled Nazareth!
　His presence made thee fair;
His seraph court, with incense-breath,
　Filled all thy favored air.

O cottage walls, enriched with beam
   Of heaven's wondrous glow!
O new and lasting Eden-dream!
   O Paradise below!
The scions of a royal race
   Lived here, unknown, obscure—
The "just man," rich in ev'ry grace,
   A toiler 'mid the poor.

The lily-bloom of Israel,
   Blest Sharon's queenly flower,
Fair Cades' palm, content to dwell
   Within her lowly bower.
The Child that " grew in age and grace"—
   Their treasure—who is He?
That Child, with sweet and smiling face,
   And brow of majesty,

Is God! at whose supreme command
   The radiant sunlight shone;
Whose glory bids the cherub-band
   Bow, veiled, before His throne.
Messiah! theme of psalmist's song,
   And hope of holy seer—
The King of Judah, promised long,
   Earth's Saviour, hideth here.

Through haughty-browed Jerusalem
   A " child of twelve years " trod—
Emmanuel, with the diadem
   And sceptre of a God!

O self-willed teachers of the law,
  That youthful sage ye heard!
O error-blinded ones, who saw,
  But would not own, "the Word"!

Child-Saviour! Thou from human eyes
  Hast rent the veil of pride:
We own Thee, 'neath Thy human guise,
  Our model and our guide.
Thy mystic childhood's graces fair
  Our heritage must be,
That so our white-robed souls may share
  Thy crowning legacy.

Obedience, bloom of heavenly soil,
  A spirit simple, pure,
And patient diligence to toil,
  E'en nameless and obscure:
And so each heart, by sin defiled,
  Freed thus from evil leaven,
Becoming "even as a child,"
  Shall win its mirrored heaven.

Second Month,
February.

THE PASSION.

His hour is come.   Love's mystic labor endeth,
   His wondrous life anears its cruel close,
And on the willing Victim-Lamb descendeth
   A world's vast weight of woes.
O lonely garden, strangest Eden-bower,
   Where the new, guiltless Adam waits His doom,
And bears the torture of His trial-hour,
   Within thy midnight gloom !
Thy favored soil receives the priceless treasure,
   The boundless wealth of love's own crimson sea ;
The anguish-tide that knew nor check nor measure
   Is thine, Gethsemane.

Each sighing leaf that o'er thee sadly waveth,
   With that strange dew of agony is wet ;
Redemption's first baptismal torrent laveth
   The brow of Olivet.
When dawns at last the drear and dreadful morrow,
   Thy thronged and busy thoroughfares are dyed,
O haughty city, theme of heaven's sorrow !
   With love's resistless tide.
Behold your King ! What treasures have ye given,
   Children of clay—what tributes rare and meet,
To grace His triumph, while the hosts of heaven
   Bow, trembling, at His feet ?

Insult, and mockery, and mad derision,
  A ragged robe, a reed for kingly rod:
These are your off'rings; this,—O fearful vision!—
  Your homage to a God.
From glowing mines, or fair, sunlighted bowers,
  From shining caverns of thy southern sea,
Dost bring, O earth, thy gifts of gems and flowers,
  His diadem to be?
Alas! no jewelled chaplet's starry gleaming,
  No floral wreath, His royal brow adorns;
Gemmed with the blood-drops o'er His forehead
    streaming,
  Earth gives—a crown of thorns!

O'er His drear pathway bloom no fragrant roses,
  No regal damask decks His lofty throne;
On a rough cross the Sovereign reposes,
  Pain-tortured and alone,
Save for His faithful few, and His dear Mother,
  In voiceless woe, beside His wounded feet:
Thus the death torments of our God and Brother
  Redemption's boon complete.
Thus is the ordeal of His passion ended,
  Thus love's strange history hath reached its close;
And earth was saved, when on His brow descended
  Her weary weight of woes.

O ransomed ones, give homage, earnest, tender,
  To Him whose life redeemed your woful loss!
Fondly remove the thorny crown, and render,
  As tribute for the cross,
A throne unshared, within each heart immortal,
  A fitting home, a "swept and garnished shrine."

Sealed from the world be e'er the sacred portal
 That guardeth grace divine,
That so, with heaven's royal wreaths entwining,
 In fadeless bloom, o'er brows of changeless calm,
Ye may put on the " garments washed" and shining
 With life-blood of the Lamb.

———

Third Month,
 March.

ST. JOSEPH.

EARTH'S lot of lowliness was thine,
Son of her proudest princely line !
As regal gems lie darkly hid
The cavern's gloomy depths amid ;
So, by patrician pride forgot,
Concealed in labor's humble lot,
The royal gifts that shone in thee
Lay shrined in dark obscurity.
The glory of thy kingly birth,
Thy graces rare, thy matchless worth,
Thy fair soul-jewel's wondrous glow,
The worldly vision might not know—
Its scornful glances could but see
The artisan of low degree ;
Yet heaven watched, with tend'rest smile,
Thy hidden royalty the while,
And sent its white-winged angels down,
To guard the glory of thy crown.

And well the seraph-courtiers knew
Thy regal vesture's peerless hue;
In firmest clasp they saw thee bear
Thy lily-sceptre pure and fair,
And keep, unstained by earthly dust,
The bright escutcheon of the just.
'Twas meet that such transcendent grace
Should seek thy soul's fair dwelling-place,
And make thy heart its matchless shrine—
For, ah, what privilege was thine,
Fit guardian of the queenly flower
That bloomed in Israel's favored bower!
Keeper of heaven's royal gem,
The hidden boon of Bethlehem—
Protector of thine Infant God,
O'er desert paths thy footsteps trod,
Obedient to the blest command
That bade thee seek a kinder land,
Where, safe from earthly harm, might be
The mystic Babe of Galilee,
Thy patient labor, fondly given,
Sustained the Lord of earth and heaven,
And all His holy childhood fair
Received thy fond paternal care.
Ay, heaven to thee its homage paid,
The King of kings thy voice obeyed,
Led by thy kind, protecting hand,
Submissive to thy loved command.
Close following where thy footsteps trod,
Behold thy Saviour and thy God!
Sweet spouse of Mary, Christ's dear guide,
By light celestial glorified—

Ruler of saints, thy wondrous life
With love's unmeasured wealth was rife!
Thy Jesus lent His presence blest,
When sweetly dawned the day of rest;
The music of His tender voice
Bade thy departing soul rejoice.
Thou gav'st unto His hand again,
Undimmed by shade of worldly stain,
The gift He gave, thy soul's fair gem,
To deck the Father's diadem.
O blessed Joseph! be our guide
O'er weary wastes and deserts wide;
Give us thy kind paternal care,
The treasure of thy potent prayer;
Aid us to keep, through sin and strife,
The lily of a blameless life.
And when earth's day of pain shall close,
And death's calm angel brings repose,
With Jesus and with Mary, lend
Sweet presence at life's welcome end;
Then from its broken casket bear
The spirit-jewel, pure and fair,
To gleam where shining seraphs bow
Before th' Eternal's kingly brow.

ST. JOSEPH, PATRON OF THE UNIVER-
SAL CHURCH.

HAIL, patron of the Church of God, receive thy
    fitting trust!
O thou on love's evangel-page forever named "the
    Just!"
Well didst thou guard the Word made flesh, well
    didst thou watch beside
The manger-crib, the shrine of straw, where love
    had deigned to hide;
And safely bloomed, in lowly home, beneath thy
    tender care,
The rosebud of a royal root, and Israel's lily fair.
These were thy treasures, favored one—this was the
    charge conferred
On thee, O foster father blest! O guardian of the
    Word!
And now the mystic spouse of Christ thy pure pro-
    tection craves,
While round her rock-built home of love the win-
    try tempest raves;
While searching for her Hidden Gem, the Herod
    minions flood
Her desecrated Bethlehems with streams of martyr-
    blood.
Accept the trust, and guard again the treasures of
    thy God,
And safely guide the spouse of Christ, with lily-
    blooming rod;

Support her steps till, at her glance, Egyptian idols
　　fall,
And bid her blossoms safely shine by Nazareth's
　　cottage wall.
Direct the wondrous work of love, O builder wise
　　and strong!
Till, 'neath his finished temple fair, the gathered
　　nations throng;
And to his eucharistic shrine the star-led monarchs
　　bring
The penance-myrrh, the golden vow, the prayerful
　　offering.
Then shall the grand prophetic dream in fair fulfil-
　　ment shine,
And mighty on the earth shall be Jehovah's name
　　divine;
For Joseph, patron of the Church, accepts his fitting
　　trust—
Rest, faithful hearts, your gems are safe, protected
　　by "the Just."
Safe is the shepherd, high-enthroned on truth's
　　Eternal Rock,
And safe, in Joseph's potent care, the universal
　　flock;
Safe are the sacramental founts that soothe the
　　noontide wrath,
Safe holy shrine and sacred rite, that deck the
　　desert path;
And through the weary waste, behold! the lily-
　　blooming rod
Of Joseph leads the pilgrim-band, as once it led
　　their God.

ITE AD JOSEPH.

"Go to Joseph! Lo, he keepeth
  All the treasures of the king!
Unto him your homage render,
  And your supplications bring.

"I have made him lord of Egypt,
  Placed my ring upon his hand,
Bade him keep the robe of purple,
  And the sceptre of command."

Thus the proud Egyptian monarch
  To his thronging people said,
When, to share his mighty kingdom,
  Forth the captive youth he led.

And unto that Hebrew stranger,
  From his lowly prison freed,
Came the suppliant throng, unceasing,
  In the time of direst need.

When the golden grain was withered
  On the parched and arid plain,
And the harvest treasures filled not
  Gleaners' arms and creaking wain;

When the fearful famine hovered
  Darkly o'er the desert land,
Then the royal stores were opened
  By the Hebrew's tender hand.

"Go to Joseph!" Blessed summons!
　Well that eager throng obeyed—
Egypt's sons, and Syrian strangers,
　Sharing all the willing aid.

"Go to Joseph!" Blessed summons!
　Lo, 'tis uttered once again!
'Tis the universal Monarch
　Speaks it to His subject-train.

Go to Joseph, tender guardian
　Of the world's anointed King;
Bearer of the lily sceptre,
　Wearer of the signet-ring.

Go to Joseph! for he keepeth
　Richer treasures, fairer store,
Than the saintly Hebrew guarded
　In that mighty land of yore.

Israel's lily bloomed securely
　Where he kept his vigil blest,
And a God in safety slumbered
　On that pure and faithful breast.

When the golden store of graces
　Withers in the desert soul,
And a dread and dreary famine
　Holdeth there its dark control,

Go to Joseph! Richest harvests,
　Ripened on the fadeless land,
In an infinite abundance
　Guarded are by Joseph's hand.

Go to Joseph! Never, never
  Can that tender hand refuse
Whosesoe'er the glance uplifted,
  Whosesoe'er the voice that sues.

Go to Joseph! When life's pathway
  Stretcheth through the desert land,
Think that once unto his guidance
  Jesus gave His infant hand.

He will save from tyrant Herods,
  Who thy priceless soul would seek;
He will guard from ev'ry peril,
  In thy journey long and bleak.

He will lead through dread Saharas,
  Guide thee o'er the crimson sea,
Till, beneath the peaceful palm trees,
  Evermore thy rest shall be.

LILIES OF SAINT JOSEPH.

O, OF all the lovely flowers
That bedeck the garden bowers,
Or illume, with rainbow light, the woodland and
    the lea,
One is fair, amid the fairest,
Richer, rarer, than the rarest—
Ay, the sweet and stainless lily is the queen of
    bloom for me!

When I see its snowy chalice,
Like a white and shining palace,
From its stalk uprising grandly, I bethink me of the
    rod,
With its mystic lilies laden,
That to Israel's royal maiden
Showed the fitting spouse, selected by the miracle
    of God.

Other blooms of earthly bowers
Sisters are to starry flowers,
That within the " fields above us" have their bright
    celestial birth ;
But thy sheen, O royal lily !
Is the moonlight, calm and stilly,
Shedding streams of silv'ry splendor o'er the
    " firmament of earth."

Lily leaves of balm and brightness!
Ye have shrined the fragrant whiteness
From the angel wings, reflected downward through
    the desert gloom;
And ye blossom sweetly, solely,
For the lighted altars holy—
Emblems of the blessed Joseph, types of Mary's
    virgin bloom!

———

Fourth Month,
  April.

THE RESURRECTION.

ALL hail to the glory and gladness of day,
Transfiguring earth in its magical ray!
Exult, O ye nations! the shadow hath fled,
And life waxeth fair in the realms of the dead.
The sunlight dispels, with its roseate glow,
The phantoms that filled the long night-time with
    woe;
And the tempest that blighted a world in its wrath,
The anguish that wailed o'er its conquering path,—
Their discord is hushed, for a radiant form
Flung the bright bow of peace o'er the way of the
    storm;
And the spell of its brightness hath silenced the
    might
Of the demons that rode on the blasts of the night.

O fair dawn of Easter! O beauty benign,
Whose glory celestial for ever shall shine!
Thy life-spring hath gushed from the gloom of the
    grave—
From the tomb of the Victor who suffered to save.
Love kindled thy splendor, and gilded thy gleam,
Fulfilling the promise that brightened earth's dream;
The long-brooding darkness for ever is past,
The light, long awaited, for ever shall last.
O'er the realms of a world, lo! its magic is shed,
Bringing strength to the stricken, and life to the
    dead.
O'er the hamlet's low roofs and the city's proud
    walls,
O'er Scythian tents and Athenian halls;
O'er desolate deserts, o'er valleys that smile,
Where the lotus flings beauty and bloom o'er the
    Nile;
Where the " white cliffs " of Britain rise, girded with
    foam,
Where, throned by her Tiber, sits glorious Rome;
Where the far Southern Sea slumbers, shining and
    calm,
Enchained by the spell of its islands of balm;
Where, safe in his Alp home, the vulture looks forth,
Where the ice-seal is laid on the lids of the North;
Where silence hath built,'mid the cedars, her nest,
And majesty reigns in the forest-walled West,—
O'er all the vast home of the children of clay
Redemption hath lavished the wealth of its ray.
Exult then, O nations! sweet Easter-bells, ring,
Let gladness her anthems triumphantly sing;

Let the altar be decked for the jubilant rite,
Let the tapers shed o'er it their halo of light;
Let the odor of incense, the bright blossom's breath,
Waft praise to the Risen, the Conqu'ror of death—
To Him who hath loosened the bonds of the slave,
Illumed the dark valley, and gladdened the grave:
For no terrors can lurk in the pathway once trod
By the Master of heaven, earth's Saviour and God!

———

Fifth Month, May:
THE MOTHER OF GOD.

THE MONTH OF MARY.

FAIR queen of months, bright moon of flowers,
  O rainbow-vestured May!
When earth, through all thy smiling hours,
  Keeps ceaseless gala-day.

The morning air is sweetly stirred
  By hum of golden bees,
And joyous trills of woodland bird
  Float on the fragrant breeze.

Pure incense riseth gently up
  From nature's floral shrine:
From rose's heart, and lily's cup,
  And jasmine's clinging vine;

While sunlight crowns the purple hills,
    And dances o'er the lea,
While light, with joy and music, fills
    All earth, and sky, and sea.

Thus gentle May her bounty brings
    To nature's banquet-hall,
And peace doth sit with folded wings,
    Serenely ruling all.

Sweet month, thou hast a blessed name:
    Thy light and bloom are given
To her who well the boon may claim,
    The gentle Queen of heaven!

Mary, each floral gift we bring
    That decks the dewy sward;
And bid each voice thy praises sing,
    Dear Mother of our Lord.

The triumph thou didst prophesy
    Is thine: all time shall bless
Thy matchless truth and purity,
    Thy spirit's loveliness.

" Hail to thee, Mary! full of grace!"
    Thus fondly we repeat,
While gazing on thy pictured face—
    The angel's homage meet.

O Sharon's Rose! shall we refuse
    To bow before thy shrine,
When He who readeth hearts would choose
    No mother-love but thine?

" Behold thy mother !" Thus He gave
 Thy love our hope to be :
Can we, then, scorn that love to crave,
 Our Saviour's legacy ?

Grace, then, our feast ! Alas ! "no wine,"
 No wealth, no worth, have we—
O Mother, beg thy Son divine
 To aid our poverty !

In vessels frail, a draught defiled
 Before Him now we place—
O bid Him change it, Mother mild,
 To His pure wine of grace !

And while the sweet May blossoms shine,
 And light gilds earth and sea,
These floral gems we fondly twine,
 A coronet for thee.

And so a worthier banquet shall
 Enrich our gala-day,
And thou wilt rule our festival,
 And reign our Queen of May.

A FAREWELL RHYME TO MAY.

Too swiftly fades the " moon of flowers,"
Too swiftly fly its smiling hours,
Till but the last sweet days remain
Of May's benign and blooming reign.
'Tis not alone thy wealth of bloom,
Thy golden rays and rich perfume,
That makes thy ev'ry moment dear,
Thou sweetest month of all the year.
It is because each charm of thine
Is offered at our Lady's shrine;
Because the Maiden-Mother stands,
At thy fair dawn, with open hands:
Rich gifts she bringeth for the day,
Rich gifts she claims, O happy May!

It is because thy dewy eves,
That crown with gems the golden leaves,
Are freighted, too, with manna-balm,
To shed o'er hearts a holy calm—
Are bright with beams of starry grace,
Reflected from her shining face.
Sweet gifts she brings for night and day,
Sweet gifts she claims, O favored May!
The holy rite, the matin prayer,
To rise upon thy morning air;

The tender strain of vesper hymn,
Clear ringing through thy twilight dim ;
The wreath of balm and bloom to twine,
In garlands, round her gleaming shrine,—
This tender tribute must thou pay,
Thou dear and dainty-footed May !
And these the charms that make thee dear,
O queenly month of all the year !

This prompts the sad, regretful sigh :
" Too swift the sacred moments fly ! "
But she who reigns, belovéd Queen,
O'er thy sweet days and nights serene,
Still at thy closing portal stands,
With tender smile and outstretched hands,
And bids us hail, as priceless boon, .
The Sacred Heart's resplendent June.
And on the fair and final day
A blended tribute must thou pay,
And by her last sweet " Festa " show
That, in His triumph and His woe,
The sinless Mother bore her part—
Dear " Lady of the Sacred Heart ! " *

---

* The 31st of May is the Feast of Our Lady of the Sacred Heart,
and the Month of June is, as all know, specially consecrated to the
Sacred Heart of Jesus.

HOUSEHOLD SHRINES OF OUR LADY.

In the sacred month of flowers,
While o'er bright, enchanted bowers
Dance the fairy-footed hours,
Mary's handmaids, fond and tender,
Haste, in household shrines, to render
Tributes of the vernal splendor.
Then the frescoed oratory,
Garlanded with rainbow glory,
Tells its glad and grateful story.
In the stately mansion shining,
Lo! the radiant wreath entwining,
Fair Madonnas sweetly shrining.
Home of beauty! tributes fairest,
Gleaming gold, and gifts the rarest,
Like the kings of old, thou bearest;
Yet no dearer is thy splendor
To the Sovereign, sweet and tender,
Than the simple gifts they render
Who, in humblest scenes, have sought her,
And, in pause of toil, have wrought her
Simple boons, and fondly brought her
Lowly blooms of waysides, knowing
No rich breath and gorgeous glowing,
Only freshest charms bestowing.
Moss-clad cot in verdant valley,
Narrow room in crowded alley,
Where love's poorest, dearest, rally;

Altar rude, and lowly bower,
Shrine whereon the single flower,
Withering, lies, its only dower,—
Thou art fair as is the fairest,
Thou art rich as richest, rarest,
For our Lady's love thou sharest.
Household shrines, by love-beams lighted,
Earthly Edens, e'er unblighted ;
Bowers of peace, in wastes benighted ;
Stately shrines, and altars lowly,
Rich or rude, alike the holy ;
Loved by her who looketh solely
On the souls that in your shining
Mirrored are, where graces, twining,
Wreathe the hearts, her love enshrining.

OUR QUEEN OF MAY.

RIGHT royal is our Queen of May,
And regal in her rich array
    Of queenly grace ;
Her vesture gleams with glory rare,
For priceless gems for ever there
    Hold willing place.

Not from the deep and gloomy mine,
Nor from the hidden caves that shine
    Beneath the sea,
Hath toiler's hand the jewels brought,
That, in her robe's bright texture wrought,
    Glow fadelessly.

But where the wondrous glory falls
From "gates of pearl" and "jasper walls"
    On streets of gold;
Where shines the mystic "glassy sea,"
Where bloometh life's unfading tree,
    Heaven's caskets hold

Each jewel rare, each shining gem,
That decks her royal diadem
    With living light;
A hand divine hath wove their sheen
In the fair mantle of our Queen,
    Our Lady bright.

Would'st know how, in her kingdom rare,
Are named the jewels glowing there,
    Her treasures meet?
Humility, serenely set
First in her radiant coronet,
    Sheds lustre sweet.

And purity, with silver light,
Illumines all her robe of white,
    Her starry crown;
And, throned her shining brow above,
Her richest gem, celestial love,
    Casts ever down

On earthly night its cheering ray,
To light the drear and darksome way
    Of pilgrims faint—
Of weary ones that feebly toil
'Mid thorny paths, and wild turmoil,
    And venom-taint.

The sinless Maid, the Lily-flower,
That dwelt in Nazareth's lowly bower,
  And Bethlehem's cave;
That drooping, wan, yet faithful, clung,
Beside the cross, whereon He hung,
  Who died to save.

His Mother, chosen ours to be—
A dying Saviour's legacy
  To mortals given;
Sweet Sovereign of the shining band
Of dwellers in the better land—
  The Queen of heaven.

She is *our* Queen, our ruler fair,
And wondrous is her glory rare,
  Her queenly state:
To her, the star of earth and sea,
This month of bloom and birdling-glee
  We consecrate.

Time's favored daughter, fair and sweet,
Bright moon of blossoms, tribute meet
  For heaven's flower!
Thine, Mary, be its song and bloom,
Its tinted skies, its soft perfume,
  Its beauty's dower.

We bow before thy pictured face;
The angel-greeting, " Full of grace, "
  We fondly breathe;
Round altars decked for holy rite,
Thy fragrant types, the lilies white,
  Our love shall wreathe.

And while from earnest hearts arise
The tones of tender litanies,
    To hail thy name;
Thy mother-love, thy ceaseless care,
The power of thy pleading prayer,
    Thy children claim.

O be our hearts thy kingdom bright,
Bedecked with lily-graces white,
    In pure array;
And so, within its fragrant shrine,
Each heart shall keep its feast divine—
    Its endless May.

Sixth Month,
  June.

THE SACRED HEART.

It throbbed with an infinite, yearning love,
    When shepherds on earth adored,
And the wandering seraphim watched above,
    The manger that hid their Lord.

Each pulse of His mystical childhood stirred
    With the strength of that love divine;
And a mother treasured each priceless word
    That welled from its sacred shrine.

And O, when the labor of love began,
    And the tempests of wrath were stilled
By the gentle voice of the God made man,
    By the magical tones that thrilled

The awe-struck throng of the busy street,
  The fisherman by the sea;
And the crowd that followed His tireless feet,
  By the margin of Galilee:

In the lonely wild, and the noisy mart,
  Wherever His journey lay,
How the mighty throbs of that longing heart
  Held ever their ceaseless sway!

In the woful watch of that dreary night,
  When He bowed as the storm-swept flower,
And earth was dumb at the dismal sight
  Of her Maker's anguish-hour;

How that heart with its whelming sorrow heaved,
  Till its shrine was wellnigh rent;
And the pale, yet willing, lips received
  The cup by the Father sent!

And it quivered and glowed with its matchless love
  When its life-blood drenched the sod;
And the trembling angels watched above
  The cross of their suff'ring God.

The Sacred Heart! how it burneth yet,
  With the flame of its love divine,
When the hidden gem of heaven is set
  In an humble and earthly shrine!

Where the altar-lights unfading glow,
  And the altar flowers gleam,
And silent mortals are bending low,
  As rapt in a holy dream;

Where the incense bears on its fragrant breath
  The priceless burden of prayer,
And the " tantum ergo " of star-eyed Faith
  Floats up through the charméd air;

There the Sacred Heart of the man-God lives,
  There broodeth the silent Dove,
And unto the lofty and lowly gives
  Rich store of its boundless love.

Shall we, the children of worthless clay,
  Yet washed in that Heart's pure tide,—
Shall we from its tenderness turn away
  In coldness, and doubt, and pride?

Ah no! While the bowers of earth are thrilled
  With the wild bird's gleeful tune,
And forest, and meadow, and vale, are filled
  With the wealth of glowing June,

With praise and prayer the golden hours
  Of this bright month we twine:
A chaplet of gratitude's fragrant flowers
  To place at Thy holy shrine.

O make our spirits Thy worthy throne,
  And bid each heart-throb be
An ever-clear echo of Thine own,
  In holiest harmony;

That so, in the bowers of bliss above,
  Our spirits may form a part,
Entwined with the flowers of fadeless love,
  Of Thine own sweet Sacred Heart.

THE PRECIOUS BLOOD.

STREAM of salvation,
  River of life,
With strength and sweetness
  And benisons rife!
Ceaseless thy flowing,
  Since the dread hour
When a lone garden
  Gathered thy dower.
Laving the olive-roots,
  Moist'ning the sod,—
This thy beginning,
  Ocean of God!
Through the proud city
  Onward thy flow,
Treasured by angels,
  Trampled below.
From the pierced forehead
  Streaming adown,
Purpling His royal robe,
  Gemming His crown,
Till the thorn-garland
  Radiant grew
With thy pure splendor,
  With thy rich hue.

Wrung by the scourges,
  Drenching the clay
Where the meek victim
  Trod His lone way;
Down the bleak mountain,
  World-wide thy course,
Eager its torrents,
  Wondrous its force.
Nail-shattered hands and feet,
  Spear-wounded side—
These are thy fountains,
  Life-giving tide!
Earth, " It is finished ! "
  Loosed is thy chain,
Fled is the nightshade
  Of sin and of pain.
Strong Rock of Ages,
  Scorning the sea!
Lo, on thy firm breast
  Springs a blest tree!
Lost birdlings roaming
  Through the chill air,
Rest in those branches
  Fadelessly fair.
Rich is each bright bough
  With balm and with bloom,
Scenting earth's desert,
  Lighting its gloom;
Lavish its treasure
  Of life-giving fruit,
Boundless its shadow,
  Depthless its root.

Whence its bright beauty?
  Whence its fair dower?
How won it fragrance,
  Freshness, and power?
At its foot flowing,
  Lo, the rich stream!
Fountain of Calvary,
  Ceaseless thy gleam!
Fresh from His Sacred Heart,
  Fadeless and free,
This thy pure life-spring,
  Wonderful tree!
Drink, weary pilgrims,
  Gratefully lave
Sin-fevered foreheads
  In its bright wave.
Sing with the angels:
  Hail, precious blood!
Life-stream of heaven,
  World-saving flood!

HYMN TO THE PRECIOUS BLOOD.

RIVEN hands, in love extended,
  Wounded feet, and sword-rent side!
Forth ye pour, in torrents blended,
  Mercy's bright, baptismal tide.
Hail, sweet stream, for ever flowing!
  Hail, O blest and boundless flood!
Fount with life eternal glowing,
  Love's own pure and precious blood!

In the olive garden, lonely,
  When He drained the cup of woe,
Tender eyes of angels only
  Saw the saving life-blood flow.
Softly sighed the branches o'er Him,
  Bending o'er that mystic flood,
And the long grass bowed before Him,
  Purpled with His precious blood.

Scornful eyes that knew not pity,
  Saw it, on the dreary morn,
Flowing o'er the sinful city,
  Fiercely wrung by scourge and thorn.
Marking all His pathway weary,
  Onward flowed the ceaseless flood;
Via Dolorosa dreary,
  Cleansing earth with precious blood!

Downward, from the mystic mountain,
  Feet, and hands, and opened side
Poured their bright, baptismal fountain,
  Poured their clear and cleansing tide.
Crimsoned cross, so brightly glowing
  With that blest, redeeming flood,
Still we hail, with hearts o'erflowing,
  Thy sweet stains of precious blood.

Ransomed saints, in garments whitened
  By the life-blood of the Lamb;
Pilgrims, with your burdens lightened,
  Martyrs, crowned with purpled palm!
Let us join your songs of gladness,
  Let us hail redemption's flood;
Christians, cleansed from sin and sadness,
  Praise, O praise, the precious blood!

THE IMMACULATE HEART OF MARY.

GONE was the sinless Eden-time,
  Dark shadows dimmed its glow,
And earth was foul with reeking crime,
  And wild with pain and woe.
No sunbeam pierced the weary gloom
  With bright, celestial dart;
No virtue-blossom brought its bloom
  To man's polluted heart.

Long ages fled, and lo! a light
  Broke on the darkness drear;
A garden shone, unstained with blight,
  To angels fair and dear.
Bright virtue's chosen dwelling-place,
  Adorned with heav'nly art,
A temple, rich in ev'ry grace,
  Rose in one sinless heart.

Thy spirit shed that blessed ray,
  O Virgin pure and bright!
Thy radiance brought the beams of day
  O'er earth's unholy night;
The lily-garden's bloom divine,
  Where blemish had no part,
The temple fair, the gleaming shrine,
  Was thy unsullied heart.

Thy truth, a rare and radiant gem,
  Thy love, with incense-breath,
Illumined lonely Bethlehem,
  And perfumed Nazareth.
And thou did'st break the spell of wrong,
  And calm the storm of hate,
With magic of thy seraph song,
  O Heart Immaculate!

Clear mirror of the Heart divine,
  Its image pure and fair!
Its matchless loveliness was thine,
  Its glory thou didst share.
Thine, too, was ev'ry thrill of pain,
  Thine every anguish-dart:
Its sorrow flung a mystic chain
  Around thee, sinless heart.

Its agony was all thy own—
  Its griefs renewed in thee.
The suff'rings of the garden lone,
  The pangs of Calvary:
In all that history of woe
  Thy love hath borne its part;
Its keenest tortures thou did'st know,
  O faithful, sinless heart!

And in thy realm of fadeless bliss,
  In joy's own world above,
Thou keep'st the charge He gave in this:
  The legacy of love.

Thy children know thy constant care,
  They feel the holy art
That leads them to His kingdom fair,
  And to His Sacred Heart.

O mother-heart! deign thou to bless
  My journey through the wild,
And in thy shelt'ring tenderness
  Still keep thy wayward child,
Until, within its sunset glow,
  Life's shades are rent apart,
And heaven's own brightness I shall know,
  With thee, unsullied heart!

———

Ninth Month, September:
THE CROSS AND THE RELIGIOUS ORDERS.

CLING TO THE CROSS.

CLING to the cross, for the wild tempest rages,
Fasten thy hold on the firm Rock of Ages;
Vain, then, the wrath of the wreck-freighted ocean—
Safe shalt thou rest from its angry commotion:
     Cling to the cross!

Cling to the cross, for the darkness increases,
Gaze on the star-beam that fades not, nor ceases;
Pillar of light o'er the Red Sea of danger,
Beacon of hope to the wave-beaten ranger:
     Cling to the cross!

Cling to the cross, for the syren is singing,
Heed not the strain o'er the wild waters ringing;
Lend not thine ear to the echoes that haunt thee,
Ruin lies hid in the tones that enchant thee:
        Cling to the cross!

Cling! 'tis thy shield from the snares that would
    hold thee,
Let its strong arms in their shelter enfold thee;
Safe shalt thou be from the storm-clouds that lower,
Safe, ever safe, from the tempest's wild power:
        Cling to the cross!

Shun thou the perils thy beacon shall show thee—
See the rich argosies ruined below thee;
Tremble and turn from the treacherous ocean,
From its dread calm and its angry commotion:
        Cling to the cross!

Cling with a strength that no art shall dissever,
Till the wild waves shall be silenced for ever;
Till o'er the Red Sea of ruin and danger,
Path shall be made for the storm-beaten ranger:
        Cling to the cross!

THE RELIGIOUS ORDERS.

HAIL to the warriors, leal and strong!
  Hail to the dauntless band!
For a goodly sight is that noble throng,
  A goodly sight and grand.
From forest glen and from mountain side,
  From the desert's trackless waste,
From the narrow lane and the prairie wide,
  The gathering legions haste.
And on with silent and ceaseless tread,
  On in their joyous way,
While the years decayed, and the ages fled,
  They have known nor check nor stay;
For they are strong with immortal life,
  And glad with a mystic wine;
And each hath brought to the field of strife
  A lance and a shield divine.
Yet not in trappings of pride bedight,
  Not in its glittering dross,
Come the stalwart chiefs of a noble fight—
  The warriors of the cross.
The humble monk, in his robe of gray,
  The nun in her sable dress,
From shrines by the busy and broad highway,
  And the lonely wilderness:

These are the conquerors in the fight,
  This is the peerless throng,
With the swords of truth, and shields of light,
  And hearts sincere and strong.
Boldly they battle, from age to age,
  With the hydra-hosts of sin ;
Oh, a fierce and lengthened war they wage,
  And a glorious prize they win !
Ye who have passed in the cloister's shade
  Sweet childhood's hours of joy,
Have felt its pleasures that cannot fade,
  Its bliss without alloy ;
Have drunk from its fountain of crystal truth,
  Have tasted its feast of love,
And won the spirit's immortal youth,
  And shared in the joys above,—
Ye know how the daughter of virtue strives
  To conquer the fresh young soul ;
Ye know how the glory of noble lives
  Is traced to her blest control.
In the alley foul, and the noisome lane,
  'Tis a glorious sight to see
The angel-work at the couch of pain,
  The conquest of charity.
A simple nun is the victor now,
  But the grateful orphan's prayer
And the penitent's tears are worth, I trow,
  An army's trumpet-blare.
In the dreary depths of the pathless wild,
  Where the mournful breezes moan,
And the stealthy step of the forest child
  Scarce wakes an echo-tone ;

There the " black-robe chief" hath boldly borne
  Redemption's blessed sign,
And the savage weeps o'er the crown of thorn,
  And the cross of love divine.
Then hail to the warriors, leal and true!
  Hail to the foes of sin!
For a grand and glorious work they do,
  And a worthy strife they win.
The sacred Orders that ceaseless guard
  The rock-built home of faith,—
With her tireless sentinels' watch and ward,
  Can she yield to the hosts of death?
Hail to the founders, the leaders brave!
  Honor to each bright name!
While the shining standard of truth shall wave,
  Theirs be a deathless fame.
On, on, glad host! to the raging fight,
  Each with his gleaming sword,
And his glowing breastplate stamped in light
  With " Holiness to the Lord!"
" By this sign, win!" see, traced on high!
  Oh, the fiend shall wail his loss,
While Faith reveals to her warrior's eye
  Her motto, beneath the cross!

THE HOLY ANGELS.

FROM out the sheen of star-lit skies,
　From out the morning's glow,
The tender smile of angel-eyes
　Illumes the world below.

How shone that smile o'er Eden's vale,
　Ere guilt had brought the gloom,
And evil left the serpent-trail,
　Upon its light and bloom !

Yet when its blighted human flowers,
　Cast forth by sword of flame,
Turned from their lost and ruined bowers
　In agony and shame;

Then from their fadeless homes of light
　The white-winged angels sped,
And o'er the way of woe and night
　Their tender love-light shed;

And Israel, rapt in holy dream,
　Beheld its brightness fair,
And saw their starry pinions gleam
　Adown the shining stair,

As o'er that golden path they bring
  Earth's weary prayers and sighs,
And waft, in ceaseless journeying,
  The boons of paradise.

Beneath the lattice-shading vine
  Kneels childhood pure and fair,
And messengers of love divine
  Receive the priceless prayer.

And o'er its soft and tranquil sleep,
  Illumed with holy dream,
Sweet angel-eyes their vigils keep,
  And snowy pinions gleam.

And when the sinner, worn with woe,
  Bends low the humble knee,
And tears of sorrow softly flow,
  In mystic brilliancy ;

His angel bears the peerless gem,
  As tribute pure and bright,
A pearl to deck love's diadem
  With hues of holy light.

O shining band ! O seraph throng¹
  Through heaven's eternal calm
For ever rings your triumph-song
  Of " Glory to the Lamb."

Your legions stand as erst they stood,
  Ere bright creation shone,
Where fadeless light's transcendent flood
  Gleams from the " great white throne."

And joyous carols once ye sang
  To hail a Saviour's birth :
" Glory to God ! " the echoes rang,
  "And peace to men on earth."

O bright-winged messengers of grace,
  Through whose pure hands are given
The boons that cheer the human race
  With benisons of heaven !

Earth brings the meed of grateful love,
  And solaced hearts shall bless
Those angel-eyes, that gleam above
  With tender watchfulness.

O pure attendant, guardian bright,
  Beneath whose shelt'ring wings,
From tempest blasts and snares of night,
  My shrinking spirit clings !

Still guide my weak and wayward feet
  O'er life's uncertain way,
Where dangers lurk, and wiles entreat,
  O shed thy heavenly ray,

Till, on my freed, enraptured ear,
  To earthly tumult dim,
Shall fall, in cadence soft and clear,
  The song of seraphim !

COMMEMORATION OF ALL-SOULS.

O FAITHFUL Church! O tender mother-heart,
That, 'neath the shelter of thy deathless love,
Shieldest the blood-bought charge thy Master gave;
Laving the calm, unfurrowed infant brow
With the pure wealth of heaven's cleansing stream;
Breathing above the sinner's grief-bowed head
The mystic words that loose the demon-spell,
And bid the leprous soul be clean again;
Decking the "upper chamber" of the heart
For the blest banquet of the Lord of love;
Binding upon the youthful warrior's breast
The buckler bright, the sacred shield of strength,
The fair, celestial gifts of Pentecost,
Borne on the pinions of the holy Dove!
And when, at last, life's sunset hour is near,
And the worn pilgrim-feet stand trembling on
The shadowy borders of the death-dark vale,
At thy command the priestly hand bestows
The potent unction in the saving Name,
And gives unto the parched and pallid lip
The blest Viaticum, the Bread of Life,
As staff and stay for that drear pilgrimage!
Thy prayers ascend, with magic incense-breath,
From the lone couch, where, fainting by the way,
The frail companion of the deathless soul
Parteth in pain from its immortal guest.

And when, at last, the golden chain is loosed,
And through the shadows of that mystic vale
The ransomed captive floateth swiftly forth,
In solemn tones thy *De Profundis* rings
O'er all the realms of vast eternity ;
Thy tender litanies call gently down
The angel-guides, the white-robed band of saints,
To lead the wand'rer to the "great white throne,"
To plead, with heaven's own pitying tenderness,
For life and mercy at the judgment-seat.
The account is given, the saving sentence breathed,
Yet He who said that naught by sin defiled
Can take at once its blessed place amid
The spotless legion of His shining saints,
Will find, upon the white baptismal robe,
Full many a blemish: stains too lightly held,
Half-cleansed by an imperfect sorrow's flood.
" The Christian shall be saved, yet as by fire :"
So, to the pain-fraught, purifying flame
The robe is given, till every blighting spot
Hath faded from its primal purity ;
Still, faithful Church, thy blest communion binds
Each suffering child unto thy mother-heart.
Full well thou know'st the wond'rous power of
    prayer—
That 'tis a holy and a wholesome thought
To plead for those who in the drear abode
Of penance linger, that " they may be loosed
From all their sins ;" that on each spotless brow
Love's shining hand may place the starry crown.
And so the holy sacrifice ascends,   .
A sweet oblation for that wailing band.
Thy regal form in mourning hues is draped,

Thy pleading *Miserere* ceaseth not
Till, at its blest entreaty, Love descends,
As erst from His rent tomb to Limbo's realm,
And leads again the freed, exultant throng,
Within the gleaming gates of gold and pearl
To bask in fadeless splendor, where the flow
Of the "still waters" by the "pastures green"
Faints not, nor slackens, through the endless years
O Christians, brethren by that holy tie
That links the living with the ransomed dead!
Children of one fond mother are ye all,
White-robed in heaven, militant on earth,
And sufferers 'mid the purifying flame.
O ye who tread the highway of our world,
Join now your voices with that mother's sigh!
And while the mournful Autumn wind laments,
And sad November's ceaseless tear-drops fall
Upon "the silent city's" marble roofs,
O'er lonely graves, amid the pathless wild,
Or where the wayworn pilgrim sunk to rest
In some lone cavern of the crested sea,—
List to the pleading wail that e'er ascends
From the dark land of suffering and woe:
"Our footsteps trod your fair, sun-lighted paths,
Our voices mingled in your joyous songs,
Our tears were blended in one common grief;
Perchance our erring hearts' excess of love
For ye, the worshipped idols of our lives,
Hath been the blemish on our bridal robes.
Plead for us, then, and let your potent prayer
Unlock the golden gates, that we who beat
Our eager wings against these prison bars,
May wing our flight to endless liberty."

REQUIESCANT IN PACE.

O FATHER, give them rest—
Thy faithful ones, whose day of toil is o'er,
Whose weary feet shall wander nevermore
    O'er earth's unquiet breast!

    The battle-strife was long;
Yet, girt with grace, and guided by Thy light,
They faltered not till triumph closed the fight,
    Till pealed the victor's song.

    Though drear the desert path,
With cruel thorns and flinty fragments strewn,
Where fiercely swept, amid the glare of noon,
    The plague-wind's blighting wrath,

    Still onward pressed their feet;
For patience soothed with sweet, celestial balm,
And, from the rocks, hope called her founts to calm
    The simoom's venom-heat.

    Their march hath reached its close,
Its toils are o'er, its Red Sea safely passed;
And pilgrim-feet have cast aside at last
    Earth's sandal shoon of woes.

    Thou blissful promised land!
One rapturous glimpse of matchless glory caught,
One priceless vision, with thy beauty fraught,
    Hath blessed that way-worn band.

And to thy smiling shore
Their ceaseless messengers of longing went,
   And blooms of bliss and fruitage of content,
   Returning, gladly bore.

   Yet sadly still they wait;
For, past idolatries to gods of clay,
And past rebellions 'gainst the Master's sway,
   Have barred the golden gate.

   The magic voice of prayer,
The saving rite, the sacrifice of love,
The human tear, the sigh of saints above,
   Blent in one off'ring fair,—

   These, these alone, can win
The boon they crave: glad entrance into rest,
The fadeless crown, the garment of the blest,
   Washed pure from stain of sin.

   Hear, then, our eager cry.
O God of mercy! bid their anguish cease;
To prisoned souls, ah! bring the glad release,
   And hush the mourner's sigh.

   Mother of pitying love!
On sorrow's flood thy tender glances bend,
And o'er its dark and dreadful torrent send
   The olive-bearing dove.

   Thy potent prayer shall be
An arch of peace, a radiant promise-bow,
To span the gulf, and shed its cheering glow
   O'er the dread penance-sea.

And on its pathway blest
The ransomed throng, in garments washed and
white,
May safely pass to love's fair realm of light,
To heaven's perfect rest.

THE DE PROFUNDIS BELL.*

THE day was dead; from purple summits faded
Its last resplendent ray,
And softly slept the wearied earth, o'ershaded
By twilight's dreamy gray.
Then flowed deep sound-waves o'er the silence holy
Of nature's calm repose,
As from its lofty dome, outpealing slowly
Through the still gloaming, rose
The deep and dirge-like swell
Of De Profundis bell.

---

* Among the many beautiful and pious customs of Catholic countries,
none appeals with more tender earnestness to the pitying heart than
that of the *De Profundis* bell. While the shades of night are gathering
over the earth, a solemn, dirge like tolling resounds from the lofty
church towers. Instantly every knee is bent, and countless voices, in
city and hamlet, from castle and cottage, repeat, with heartfelt earnest-
ness, the beautiful psalm, "*De Profundis*," or, "Out of the depths," etc.,
for the souls of the faithful departed. Thus is illustrated, in a most
touching manner, the blessed doctrine of the Communion of Saints.
Thus does the Church Militant clasp, each day anew, the holy tie which
binds her to the suffering Church of Purgation.

The compassionate heart of the Christian is stirred to its inmost
depths by the plaintive call of that warning bell; and as, in the holy
hush of nightfall, he obeys its tender appeal, how fully does he realize
that "it is a holy and wholesome thought to pray for the dead."

To heedful hearts each solemn cadence falling
    Through twilight's misty veil,
An echo seemed of spirit-voices calling
    With sad, beseeching wail;
And thus outspake the mournful intonation:
    " Plead for us, brethren, plead !
From the drear depths of woe and desolation
    Our cry of bitter need
        Floats upward in the swell
        Of De Profundis bell."

Then bowed each knee, that plaintive summons
    heeding,
    And rose the blended sigh,
As incense-breath of fond, united pleading
    E'en to the throne on high:
" Hear, Lord, the cry of fervent supplication
    Earth's children lift to Thee;
And from the depths of long and dread purgation
    Thy faithful captives free,
        Ere dies on earth the swell
        Of De Profundis bell.

" If, in Thy sight, scarce e'en the perfect whiteness
    Of seraph-robe is pure,
Shall mortals brave Thine eye's eternal brightness?
    Shall man its search endure?
Ah! trusting hope may meet the dazzling splendor
    Of those celestial rays,
For with Thee, Lord, is pardon sweet and tender,
    When contrite sorrow prays.

Ay, Thou wilt lead, from desert waste of sadness,
  Thine Israel's chosen band ;
And Miriam's song of pure, triumphant gladness
  Shall, in Thy promised land,
     Succeed the dirge-like swell
     Of De Profundis bell."

Twelfth Month, December:
THE IMMACULATE CONCEPTION.

MATER IMMACULATA.

O WONDROUS vision of the winter night!
O picture fair, impressed on sable cloud,
Yet flooding all that sad, perspective shade
With the soft splendor of a summer's dawn,
The glad reflection of thy matchless glow:
' A woman, crowned with twelve unfading stars!"
The crescent-moon, a subject at her feet ;
A countless throng of cherub faces twined
In dazzling wreaths around that royal form ;
And crouching, crushed beneath her potent tread,
The serpent-fiend, whose " trail is over all "
The bloom of earth, save one unblighted flower.

Lo, this the fair apocalyptic dream!
The brightest revelation erst vouchsafed
To the pure eyes of loved evangelist.
Hail, radiant vision! hail, thou peerless queen!

O lily sweet, whose petals hid no stain
To mar their white and fragrant loveliness!
O royal rose, at whose earth-fostered feet
No canker-worm in secret silence gnawed!
Pure fountain from thy life-spring! Jewel fair,
Unflecked, unmarred, by flaw of primal sin!
Immaculate! the bending seraphs sing;
Immaculate! lo, earth has caught the strain,
And all a glad, sin-ransomed universe
Rings with the echo of that blest refrain,
And eager lips, through earth and heav'n, repeat:
" All fair art thou, beloved one, all fair!
The spot original is not in thee."

THE TREASURES OF DECEMBER.

O FAVORED month of all the year,
  What privilege is thine!
Upon thy clouds, reflected clear,
  What magic splendors shine!
Through all thy wintry atmosphere,
  What radiance divine!

The Christmas-light that dowers earth
  With heaven's richest rays;
The dawn that filled the midnight dearth
  With flood of seraph-praise;
The beam that hails a Saviour's birth,—
  The wondrous day of days.

And, blended with that blessed beam,
  Behold the brightness fair,
The light of pure evangel-dream,
  That, on the wintry air,
Pours from its starry halo-gleam
  Celestial glory rare.

The peerless ray that shineth now
  Where white-robed legions wait,
Where angel-subjects lowly bow,
  To own her royal state,
Crown-jewel on that virgin brow,
  The gem immaculate.

Lo! these the treasures thou dost shrine
  Amid thy realm of snow,
These are thy rays that far outshine
  The summer's golden glow;
That shed a radiance divine
  O'er wintry gloom below.

And when the Christmas chimes shall ring
  Through blest December's air,
And when the Christmas garlands fling
  Their festal brightness fair,
Lo! 'mid the glory of the King,
  His Mother's jewel rare,

Two matchless beams, till time is done,
  Shall chase the clouds of hate;
Two wondrous rays shall blend in one,
  That earth, with joy elate,
May hail the Mother and the Son,
  The gems immaculate.

OUR PATRONESS.

FOR THE FEAST OF THE IMMACULATE CONCEPTION.

A PEERLESS privilege is thine,
   O favored Western land !
Unfading halos round thee shine
Of matchless radiance benign,
   Celestial brightness bland.

Ay, heaven hath sent its fairest dower,
   Its starlight cheers thy gloom ;
Its royal rose, its lily flower,
Sheds o'er thy lone, sin-blighted bower
   Transcendent balm and bloom.

Our only boast and pearl of worth,
   Our one unsullied gem,
Sole treasure of our stricken earth,
One jewel meet, amid its dearth,
   For heaven's diadem !

The royal maiden, full of grace,
   In robes of dazzling white ;
Fair daughter of our fallen race,
The beauty of whose queenly face
   No blemish dared to blight,—

She is the guardian of our land,
　　Our starbeam, bright and blest;
Our patroness, whose bounty rare
Sheds benisons and graces fair
　　O'er all the favored West.

Hail, holy morn! with hearts elate
　　We greet thee, day of joy!
And hail, enrobed in regal state,
　Heaven's Lily-Queen, immaculate,
　　Our gem, without alloy.

Lo! framed in drear December skies,
　　Apocalyptic dream!
While far the shadowy monster flies,
We see the star-crowned figure rise,
　　Enthroned on crescent beam.

Sancta Regina! at thy feet,
　　In homage fond we bow—
Thy subjects pay thee tribute meet,
And own the diadem complete
　　That decks thy queenly brow.

Immaculate! O title fair!
　　Crown-jewel, all thine own!
Ah, well may earthly echoes ring
The joy the seraph-courtiers sing
　　Around thy dazzling throne!

One gleam we crave, one beam benign,
    From thy imperial crown,
One priceless ray of light divine,
Upon our darkened souls to shine,
    When tempest-shadows frown.

And though thy pure and perfect grace
    Can ne'er, alas! be ours,
One ray reflected from thy face
Hath potent influence to chase
    The gloom that darkly lowers.

And, mirrored in the sin-washed soul,
    The "swept and garnished" shrine,
Though clouds enwrap and thunders roll,
That ray shall keep its bright control,
    Till dawns the day divine.

CORNELIA'S JEWELS.*

THEY sat within a stately hall,
  A proud, patrician home,
Those daughters of a lordly line,
  The race of regal Rome;
And on their robes of Tyrian dye,
  And in their shining hair,
A flood of living glory streamed
  From jewels rich and rare;
And, clasped within each snowy hand,
  The costly casket shone,
Where dazzling splendor sat enshrined
  Upon its golden throne:
Gems from the far-off Indian mine,
  And crested Persian wave;
The diamond from the foeman's crown,
  The pearl from ocean cave.
Red burned the ruby's bleeding heart,
  The topaz glowed like flame,
And from the smiling skies, I ween,
  The sapphire's azure came.
The emerald's verdant lustre seemed
  From grassy meadows caught,
And one might deem each flashing ray
  With dewy odor fraught.

---

* Some ladies of ancient Rome were one day displaying their jewels
and rare ornaments, when Cornelia, mother of the renowned Gracchi,
being asked to add her gems to the glittering store, led forw'rd her
young sons, saying, "Behold Cornelia's jewels!"

And on the blended glories there,
    As bound by magic spell,
The burning glare of envy dwelt,
    The glance of triumph fell.
Uprose each fettered look at last,
    Uprose each haughty head,
For, lo! within that sculptured hall
    A new and stately tread:
The presence of a queenly form,
    A calm, majestic face,
With shining eyes and noble brow,
    And smile of winning grace.
No gems that peerless stranger wore,
    No wealth of jewels shed
Their rainbow light o'er arching neck,
    . And proudly lifted head.
All unadorned her matron's robe,
    With woollen girdle bound;
Ungemmed the simple fillet-band,
    About her temples wound.
Yet, 'mid that fair and high-born throng,
    She stood, a very queen,
Unrivalled in her quiet grace,
    Her majesty of mien.
Two children fair beside her stood,
    Of princely lineage high;
Bright flashed the future hero's look
    From dauntless brow and eye.
The mistress of that palace proud
    Bent low her lofty brow:
"Cornelia, hail! our treasures wait
    Thy added tribute now."

Her matchless sons the matron clasped :
 " My only gems are these—
My treasures, fairer than the wealth
 Of richest mines or seas.
Nay, tell me not of priceless pearls
 In glittering diadems,
Or robes resplendent with the sheen
 Of countless flashing gems.
No casket's store can match *my* wealth,
 No diamonds can compare
With blest Cornelia's boons divine,—
 A mother's jewels rare."

* * * * * * · * *

O thou who guard'st the glorious shrine
 That holds a ransomed soul,
Who keep'st the young immortal mind
 Within thy fond control !
If the proud pagan mother deemed
 That gift of priceless worth—
A prize, a treasure, far beyond
 The brightest gems of earth ;
What, Christian mother, should'st thou place
 Above thy jewels fair ?
What scene could bid thine eye relax
 Its sweet, maternal care?
Oh ! if, amid the mire of earth,
 Thou castest idly down
The jewels formed to shed their rays
 Around a Saviour's crown,
When He shall count His fadeless gems,
 What shall thy answer be,
If thou hast lost the precious boons
 He gave in charge to thee?

THE SUMMER QUEEN.

In summer time, sweet summer time,
The young year's glad and golden prime,
With rosy crown and robe of green,
Lo, on the hills a fairy queen!
How beams her smile in sunset's gold!
How floats her song o'er vale and wold!
" I give the bleak and barren plain
Its precious store of golden grain;
With magic hand I sow the seed,
And deck for man the grassy mead,
And well I love, when earth is gay,
The pleasant smell of new-mown hay.
The ploughman whistles o'er the lea—
His merry tunes are sweet to me;
The reaper whets his gleaming scythe,
His arm is strong, his step is blithe,
And gayly go the laughing train
Beside the laden harvest wain.
In gleaner's dance and vintage song
I meet the glad and grateful throng;
And leal and trusty are, I ween,
These courtiers of the Summer Queen!
The ripened apples softly fall,
The peach is blushing on the wall,
Bright berries hide in leafy lane,
The currant's heart is rich again,

And south winds gather, as they rove,
The odors of the orange grove.
The lemon tells of nectar-draught,
And ruddy cherries gayly laughed,
When, yester-even, wand'ring free,
I plucked them from the bending tree.
O rare and dainty is, I ween,
The banquet of the Summer Queen!
Fair flowers bloom o'er field and hill,
A pearly crest bedecks the rill,
The dewdrops glitter on the leaves,
Rare gold illumes the banded sheaves,
And sunlight crowns, with rosy glow,
All heaven above and earth below.
Ah, rich and radiant are, I ween,
The jewels of the Summer Queen!"
And thus, with smile and ringing lay,
The sovereign treads her sunny way;
Behind her dance the glowing hours,
O'er velvet moss and damask flowers.
They pass, they float in brightness on,
Softly as glides the snowy swan,
'Mid murmured song and starry gleam,
Upon the lily-laden stream.
Too soon the fairy pomp will fade
From emerald vale and leafy glade,
But earth shall hail again, I ween,
The bright reign of the Summer Queen.

"HE WHO GIVETH TO THE POOR, LENDETH TO THE LORD."

Ay, happy he whose Christ-like pity lends
   Unto God's poor—who makes their wants his
      own!
He hath the fairest gifts our Father sends,
   The brightest rays that sparkle from His throne;
He hath sweet knowledge of all blessed things,
And walketh safely, clasped by angel wings.

Ay, and his shining path is paved with prayer—
   A golden stairway to the home of love;
The balm of benisons doth freight the air,
   And seraph eyes smile softly from above;
And heaven's own music, grand, triumphant,
      clear,
Falls ever on his rapt and favored ear.

Each smile he bringeth to the tear-dimmed eye,
   Each joy he lendeth to the grief-worn breast,
A star-beam is, set in a fadeless sky,
   A rare crown-jewel for his reign of rest:
Bright are those beams upon the heavenward
      road,
Countless those gems in love's fair realm be-
      stowed.

For " cup of water " gladly, kindly given
   To earth's poor pilgrims, parched with noontide
     heat,
From golden chalice he shall drink, in heaven,
   A nectar-draught, rich, bounteous, complete ;
And e'en the " widow's mite " shall be restored,
Exhaustless wealth, a vast, unmeasured hoard.

Search not alone amid the worthless dust
   For gold that perisheth, for gifts that fade,
But seek the wealth undimmed by earthly rust,
   And unto charity be tribute paid—
A hundred-fold shalt thou receive again :
Man lendeth not unto the Lord in vain.

———

SONG OF THE DAWN.

A WELCOME, glad mortals, a welcome for me,
I have painted the cloud, I have gilded the sea ;
From his glorious dreams I have summoned the day:
He cometh in beauty—sad sister, away !
Away to thy caves, on the wings of the gale—
I have broken thy spells, I have lifted the veil !
Hence, sable-robed queen ! Thou art conquered,
    O Night !
And thy shadows have fled at the coming of light.
Lo! the sheen of my armor, the gleam of my lance,
The flash of my swiftness, the might of my glance !
One look o'er the landscape—lo ! darkness is gone,
And earth rises fair in the glory of dawn.

Then give me glad welcome, O children of men!
As I glide o'er the meadow, and light the dark glen,
While my banner of brightness is gayly unfurled,
And my largesse of sunshine is shed o'er the
    world,
How lavish its bounty! it dowereth all,
It gilds the rough hovel, it lights the gay hall;
It smiles on the blossoms, and hides 'mid the leaves,
With the vine's fairy shadows rare tissues it weaves.
On the mist-mantled mount, and the spray-crested
    stream,
How the gold of the dawning doth sparkle and
    gleam!
Earth haileth my coming with shout and with song,
With the carolling glee of her joy-laden throng;
From hill, vale, and wildwood float greetings to me,
From gay, laughing childhood, from bird and from
    bee.
'Mid music and gladness, I glide on my way,
Yielding place to the king of the summer's rich ray;
In glory perfected light springs o'er the lawn,
And the day-god hath followed his herald, the dawn.

THE CHURCH TRIUMPHANT.

WRITTEN FOR THE FEAST OF ALL SAINTS.

HAIL, princes, enthroned in the court of the Lamb!
Hail, conquerors, crowned with the blood-tinted
    palm!
White army of martyrs, glad throng of the just,
Pure flowers that grew in earth's foulness and dust!
Rare jewels, whose lustre for ever shall shine
In a diadem matchless, unfading, divine!
O beauty eternal, that reignest on high!
O splendor, concealed from the sin-clouded eye!
The ransomed are clad in thy garments of light,
They wear thy bright laurels who toiled in the fight.
Thy treasures uncounted their guerdon shall be,
Whose faith-lighted footsteps have crossed the dark
    sea,
Who have passed through the thorns of the desert
    of woe,
To the gladness above, from the sadness below—
For well the enraptured evangelist paints
The joy of the Lord in His blood-purchased saints!
From the crowded arena, where pagan hate yelled
And the martyr's glad pæan of victory swelled;
From dungeon and gibbet, from rack and from
    wheel,
From the torturing flame, and the pang-laden steel,

On pinions of light, lo ! the Christian hath flown
To the realm of the King—to the martyr-God's
    throne.
From caves of the desert, from lone forest cells,
Where the hermit afar in his solitude dwells;
From the cloistered retreat, where the dim arches
    rung,
When the prayer was uplifted, the canticle sung;
Where the learned recluse o'er his manuscripts
    pored,
Till the casket of truth with his wisdom was stored;
From the fair lighted altar, the flower-decked shrine,
Where the priestly hand offers the Victim Divine;
From highway and hovel, where charity's voice
Bids the penitent weep, and the mourner rejoice,—
The stewards have passed to their priceless reward,
The servant hath " entered the joy of his Lord."
O Faith ! let thy vision behold the bright throng,
Let thine ear catch the tone of their jubilant song.
Earth's children, the lofty and lowly, are there—
One bliss they enjoy, and one glory they share;
For the king and the peasant, the noble, the slave,
Were one in His service who suffered to save.
Fair Church, thou dost link, in one mystical tie,
Thy children below with thy children on high,
For a holy alliance and union of love
Binds thee militant here, and triumphant above.
O Christians, who faint ere the battle is done,
Look up to the guerdon your brethren have won !
Ah ! theirs were your sorrows, your trials, your
    woes,
Yet they ceaselessly toiled till the glorious close.

Lives wondrous, heroic, lives simple, obscure,
Lives of sinners repentant, lives stainlessly pure,—
There are models for all, there are copies most fair,
And those who " do likewise," one glory shall share.
O courtiers, that dwell in the realms of the Lamb!
O conquerors, crowned with the blood-tinted palm!
By the union that binds, in one mystical chain,
The slaves and the ransomed, and gladness with
    pain,
Let your influence aid, let your sympathy cheer,
The pilgrims that toil in the wilderness drear;
Let your pleadings give strength to their agonized
    wail—
Lo! the promise: " The prayer of the just shall
    avail."
Ye who treasured the faith, ye who "fought the
    good fight,"
Aid the searcher for truth, aid the strife for the
    right,
Till victory blesses the magical sword,
Till the jewel of price to its Lord is restored;
Till cleansed is the robe from each blemish that
    taints,
Till the list is complete of the legion of saints.

THE TRUCE OF GOD.*

SIR GUY DE COURCY,—braver knight
    Ne'er laid a lance in rest,
Or wore, undimmed, amid the fight,
    A prouder, statelier crest.
De Montfort was his bitter foe,
    A warrior dear to fame,
For mighty hosts had felt his blow,
    And trembled at his name;

---

* The sacred compact, styled the Truce of God, was instituted by the
Church to lessen the fury of the feudal strife that, from the ninth to the
eleventh century, raged continually among neighboring lords and petty
chieftains. "Experience," says the historian Fredet, "having already
shown the impossibility of stemming the torrent at once, prudent
measures were taken gradually to diminish its violence. Several bishops
ordered, under penalty of excommunication, that every week, during the
four days consecrated to the memory of our Saviour's passion, death,
burial, and resurrection, viz., from the afternoon of Wednesday until
the morning of the following Monday, whatever might be the cause of
strife, all private hostilities should cease. Shortly after, the same pro-
hibition was extended to the whole time of Advent and Lent, includ-
ing several weeks after Christmas and after Easter Sunday. Thus, by
the exertions of ecclesiastical authority, the horrors and calamities of
feudal war began to be considerably lessened and abridged. Its ravages
were restrained to three days in the week, and to certain seasons of the
year; during the intervals of peace there was leisure for passion to cool,
for the mind to sicken at a languishing warfare, and for social habits to
become more deeply rooted. Such was the splendid victory which the
religion of Christ won over the natural fierceness of the ancient tribes of
the North,—a victory whose completion was also due to her influence,
when the Crusades obliged those restless barbarians to turn against
invading hordes of Saracens and Turks those weapons they had
hitherto used against their fellow-Christians."

Yet they who crushed invading band,
　And triumphed side by side,
Clasped ne'er the kind, fraternal hand,
　Nor shared the victor's pride.
Ay, they were foemen—fiercest hate
　Burned in each haughty breast,
And deadly strife alone could sate
　The fiend that each possessed.

*　*　*　*　*　*　*

The shadows crept across the plain,
　And lengthened o'er the lea,
For day had wellnigh ceased to reign
　O'er castled Normandy ;
Sir Guy, exultant, homeward went
　From well-won border fray,
De Montfort rode from tournament,
　Bedecked with guerdons gay :
They met where, draperied with moss,
　And clasped by clinging vine,
The pilgrim's guide, the wayside cross,
　Told of a woe divine.
"Hold! hold!" De Montfort fiercely cried,
　" We pass not now, Sir Knight ! "
" Pause then, " his foeman stern replied,
　" And nerve thyself for fight."
The fiery steeds impatient prance,
　Awaiting fierce command,
Gleams now each tried and trusty lance
　Within each mailclad hand.
" On ! on ! " and forth their chargers rush—
　Ha ! is it coward fear

That brings the strange and sudden hush
 Upon that mad career?
Nay, list! from yonder convent tower
 Rings out the solemn bell:
Its echo hath that magic power,
 That strange and soothing spell.
Ay, it could ban the deadly flow
 That else had drenched the sod,
And bid each warrior murmur low,
 "Stay! 'tis the truce of God!"
Now first they raised the startled look
 Where stood redemption's sign,
And now each haughty spirit shook
 With thrill of awe divine.
Outspoke the brave De Courcy then:
 " Here let our combats cease,
Nor bring the fiendish strife of men
 Beneath the sign of peace."
" Nay, heaven forgive our hatred-sin,"
 His softened foeman said;
" Here shall our truce of love begin,
 Where demon hate hath fled."
Each from his prancing steed descends,
 Each flings aside his brand,
And 'neath the cross, as faithful friends,
 Each clasps his foeman's hand;
And, shaded by the draping moss,
 There, on the dewy sod,
They bowed beside that sacred cross,
 And blessed the Truce of God.

A DREAM OF THE SNOW.

OLD Winter hath no frosty frown
  For thee, O favored land!
He weaves thy sunlight's golden crown
  With soft, caressing hand;
He brings no chilling robe of snow,
  To shroud thy vestures green;
No chains to bind thy brooklet's flow,
  No veil to dim its sheen.
Though clouds may gather, 'tis to hide
  The soft, benignant rain,
That bids the rose of Christmas-tide
  A dewy brightness gain.
No icy blasts thy ruin mourn
  In blighted valleys drear,
But fragrance on thy breeze is borne
  Through all the blooming year;
Yet, as I greet thy glowing skies
  With glad, responsive smile,
Strange memory-pictures meet my eyes,
  Strange visions rise the while:
Again within the wintry gloom
  A dreaming child I stand,
And see the snowy garlands bloom
  O'er all the Northern land;
Where lately hung the verdant leaves,
  The pendent jewels shine,
And snow-wreaths o'er the cottage eaves
  Replace the clinging vine.

O sweet to watch the soft flakes fall,
 Like gentle doves of peace,
And greet, with smile and merry call,
 My lambs with downy fleece;
My elves that danced in joyous glee,
 Like happy living things,
My plumes descending noiselessly
 From shining angel-wings.
And sweet o'er silent roads to hear
 The sleigh-bells' merry ring,
Or catch the tones, in echoes clear,
 Of skaters' revelling;
Till paled above the hillock's crest
 The Winter's sunset glow,
And moonlight's silver halo blessed
 Earth's bridal robe of snow.

* * * * * * * *

The dream is o'er; and glancing down
 From heights serenely bland,
I see thy sunlight's golden crown,
 O favored Western land!
I smell the sweet aroma-breath
 Of many a dewy flower,
And find no trace of blight or death
 Within the rose's bower.
But from thy charms I turn me now,
 And yearn, with fond regret,
To gaze on Winter's rugged brow,
 With icy jewels set;
To watch my angel-plumes again,
 As in "the long ago,"
And calm life's weary fever-pain
 With visions of the snow.

CONSECRATED CALIFORNIA.

SHE hath bowed at the shrine of eternal love,
And the snowy wings of the Sacred Dove
Are softly folded her heart above.

She hath brought the tribute of gems and gold,
Like the star-led kings to His home of old,
And hers shall be guerdon of wealth untold.

She hath offered the smile of her sunny skies,
And forth from her cloudland of rainbow dyes
The shadowless day of her peace shall rise.

She hath given the stores of her wondrous bowers,
The balmy bloom of perennial flowers;
And love with the beauty of Eden dowers

Each dewy meadow and bright parterre,
Till the robe of our beautiful land shall **wear**
The radiant bloom of His kingdom fair.

She hath woven the links of a spousal chain,
And the night of ages shall strive in vain
One link to rust, or to rend in twain.

And light is that band on her blissful breast—
'Tis a burden sweet, 'tis a slavery blest,
'Tis the bond that bringeth eternal rest.

'Tis a ladder of light, 'tis a mystic stair,
'Tis the pathway blest for the angels fair,
That for ever shall float through her charmèd air.

Be true, dear land, to thy plighted vow.
At the sacred shrine thou hast chosen now,
Still bend thy shining and spotless brow ;

And the worldly sword and the demon art
Can never sunder thy bands apart,
O beautiful spouse of the Sacred Heart !

THE GUARD OF HONOR TO THE SACRED HEART.

THEY come in still succession to keep the hour of
  guard,
Around His throne they linger, in silent watch and
  ward ;
They bear His badge of service, as at His feet they
  bow,
To pledge their fond submission, to breathe their
  solemn vow ;

---

* The guard of honor is the beautiful title of an association formed in
Europe to honor, in an especial manner, the Sacred Heart of Jesus.
This devotion is most appropriate for the month of June, the lovely
season so fittingly consecrated to that tender and compassionate Heart.
Each member chooses an hour of guard, during which he or she remains
in silent adoration before the Sacred Heart.

While in His audience-chamber He keepeth kingly
    state,
His chosen guard of honor in ranks unbroken wait.
Swift fly the summer hours, soft dies the rosy day,
And still His kneeling subjects their eager homage
    pay.
Ah! why that waiting legion? And whose the
    royal throne,
So hid in crowded cities, to countless throngs
    unknown?
O worldling-throng insensate! O fettered slaves of
    pride!
They come to "watch one hour," the Victim-God
    beside.
That hidden throne is canopied by angels' tender
    wings,
That still, secluded temple conceals the King of
    kings;
In heaven's fondest worship earth takes her eager
    part,
When mortals bow before Him, to guard His
    Sacred Heart.
With spotless lilies blooming before their type
    divine,
With roses pouring incense upon His holy shrine,
With tapers sending steadfastly their upward-
    pointing flame,
With bells that hail His coming in silv'ry, soft
    acclaim,—
With all that nature offereth, with all that earth
    can bring,
Each heart its worship blendeth, low bowed before
    its King.

Love's bloom and blest aroma, love's shining altar-
    flame,
Love's soft and silv'ry utterance that chimes His
    sacred name,
The sweet soul-flowers that charm Him with fresh,
    unfading grace,
Before His sacred portals His guarding legions
    place.
They proffer fond atonement for hearts unkind,
    untrue,
They sigh, " Forgive them, Father, who know not
    what they do ; "
They bring the glad thank-offering for Love's re-
    deeming birth,
They hail the boon celestial of blessed " Peace on
    earth."
They sound the ceaseless echo of heaven's eternal
    psalm
Of " Praise and benediction, and glory to the
    Lamb ! "
O heaven on earth reflected by heav'nly watch
    and ward !
O servitude seraphic ! O grand and glorious guard !
Be faithful, blessed legions, and may the band ye
    bear
Of spirit-service loyal be still the symbol fair.
Within your hearts imprinted by fond, celestial art,
'Keep e'er, in sweet similitude, your Sov'reign's
    Sacred Heart:
The thorny wreath, the crowning cross, the flames
    that soar above,
The glowing hue, the open wound, the life-blood of
    His love.

The mystic signs thus bearing upon your pilgrim-
 path,
Ye shall escape the angel sword of stern, relentless
 wrath;
And in Love's fadeless kingdom His guard shall
 claim their part,
And draw sweet waters from the fount of His
 exhaustless heart.

THE TREASURES OF THE CHURCH.

"BRING forth the Deacon Laurence!"
 And at the mighty tone
Low bowed the servile lictors
 Before the prefect's throne;
And on their guarded captive
 The rabble gazed with awe—
Was this the hated Christian,
 The foe of Roman law?
He stood, a young Apollo,
 A form of godlike grace,
While beams of lambent glory
 Seemed circling round his face;
And yet no haughty flashing
 Of fierce, rebellious eye
Bespoke defiant scorning
 Of Roman majesty.
Ah, no! his look reflected
 His Master's gentle mien,

The calmness, meek and lowly,
　　That marked the Nazarene;
But in his eye's soft beaming,
　　And on his placid brow,
They read the hero-firmness
　　To duty's sacred vow.
　　*   *   *   *   *   *

"We hear of priceless treasures
　　That Christians dare to own—
Of jewels meet to glisten
　　On regal brows alone;
Of wealth of shining silver,
　　And store of gleaming gold,
Which thou, the foe of Cæsar,
　　Dost in thy caskets hold."
The Christian's brow was lifted,
　　And new, celestial grace
Enrobed that matchless figure,
　　And crowned that seraph face.
" 'Tis true, O mighty prefect!
　　A store of priceless gems,
Of jewels meet to glisten
　　In regal diadems—
A wealth of shining silver,
　　Of bright, uncounted gold,
The Christians, friends to Cæsar,
　　As peerless treasures hold."
"Ha! say'st thou so? then listen:
　　Nor rack, nor scorching flame,
Shall crisp thy flesh to blackness,
　　Or rend thy writhing frame;

Nor fear of shrine polluted
  Shall haunt thy visions more,
If thou in safety hither
  Wilt bring the Christians' store."
" Thanks, O most gracious prefect!
  And when three days have flown
My treasures shall be gathered
  Before thy lofty throne."
    *   *   *   *   *   *

On sandals, winged with swiftness,
  Have sped the days of grace,
And Rome's exultant minion
  Sits eager in his place;
And round him throng the rabble,
  Impatient to behold
The store of shining jewels,
  The wealth of gleaming gold.
Again that steady footstep,
  Again that noble form,
Have hushed to awesome silence
  The gath'ring murmur-storm.
" But where the priceless treasures?"
  They ask in whispers low,
"And who are these that follow,
  With feeble steps and slow?"
Sooth, 'twas a vision wondrous
  The blind, the mute, the lame,
A throng of squalid paupers,
  Along the forum came.
Their youthful leader heeds not
  The idlers gathered there,

But calmly guides them onward,
   Before the curule chair.
" Behold the Christian treasures,
   Behold each living gem,
More fair than fairest jewels
   In proudest diadem ;
More bright than sheen of silver,
   More rich than gleaming gold,
Are these, the Master's dear ones,
   The Church's wealth untold."
   *   *   *   *   *   *

O Christians! through the ages
   Love's legacies descend,
The store of gems uncounted,
   The wealth that cannot end.
" The poor ye still have with you,"
   The jewels of His crown,
To mirror heaven's glory,
   And shed its peace adown.
O guard His treasures fondly,
   And bid them ceaseless shine,
In love's resplendent setting,
   In mercy's golden shrine !
So shall ye enter boldly
   The palace of your King,
With wealth eternal laden,
   As royal offering.

THE HOLY FATHER'S SILVER JUBILEE.

HAIL, golden year of benison and jubilee sublime!
Hail, brightest of the gems that deck the jewelled
    zone of time!
O well may glad *Te Deums* ring through many a
    holy fane,
Where faith's enraptured children wake the clear
    triumphal strain,
Till hearts, o'erfraught with happiness, shall mur-
    mur, 'mid their glee,
" Ah! *'nunc dimittis!'* we have seen our Father's
    jubilee!"
Exult, O nations, halo-crowned! with loud evvivas
    ring!
Hail, Pio Nono, pastor true! all hail, our Pontiff-
    King!
Hail to the brow that yet doth wear its glorious
    triple crown!
Hail to the hand that would not lay its ancient
    sceptre down!
Hail to the form that ne'er hath quailed before the
    tempest-shock!
Hail, faithful feet, that firmly stand on truth's eter-
    nal rock!
O wonderful pontificate! O glory-circled reign!
When memory wakes thy golden years to life and
    light again,

Swift gliding o'er that shining path, what scenes of
  magic hue,
What fair, celestial pageants pass before her.dazzled
  view !
Lo, shrined amid the mystic stars that shed their
  wondrous gleam,
The brightest form in all the blest apocalyptic
  dream !
Low bowed before that figure fair, thus throned in
  royal state,   •
We fondly breathe her fitting name, our Queen Im-
  maculate !
Behold the pontiff hand that writes, in lines of fade-
  less flame,
Above her starry diadem, that pure and peerless
  name ;
List to the voice resounding clear, amid our earthly
  din,
Immaculata ! Snowy bloom, unstained by primal sin !
  *   *   *   *   *   *   *   *   *

Borne on the breath of spicy gales, across a sunlit
  sea,
Comes now in clear and ceaseless tones a matchless
  history,—
A tale that tells, in trumpet notes, of hearts serene
  and strong,
Of hands that bear the mystic palm amid the victor
  throng ;
Of feet that trod the thorny path, and crossed the
  crimson flood,
Of robes that wear the royal hue, bestowed by
  martyr blood.

And once again that potent hand hath traced its
 blest decree,
And lo, the deathless list records that wondrous
 history !
O Christians ! greet the shining throng, and fondest
 homage pay :
Hail, sainted heroes of Japan ! hail, martyrs of Cathay!
 * * * * * * * * *
The golden days are speeding on to join the phantom
 past,
Until the glad triumphal morn in glory dawns at last;
And now the crowning vision wakes at mem'ry's
 call again,
The wondrous pageant grandly moves, a vast
 majestic train :
A priestly-vestured multitude, a pure, anointed
 throng,
The dauntless soldiers of the cross, the fearless foes
 of wrong.
Why tread they thus thy throughfares, O star-
 encircled Rome ?
Why peal the silver clarion notes within thy mighty
 dome ?
A magic voice from Peter's Rock hath rung from
 land to land,
The legions of the deathless King have heard the
 blest command ;
Their ranks are formed, their voices ring in clear,
 responsive tone,
Their consecrated armies bow before the Pontiff's
 throne.

They gather on that Living Rock, o'er billows tem-
pest-tossed,
And on each sacred brow descends the flame of
Pentecost.
The Council ends, the task is o'er, the work of
triumph done,
And for the signet-ring of Truth its brightest jewel
won.
Sweet promise kept! O star-eyed Truth, thy foes
can ne'er prevail!
*Thy flock shall know the shepherd voice that cannot faint
or fail.*

*   *   *   *   *   *   *   *   *

And now, while still the golden days in swift proces-
sion flee,
Behold! again the pontiff hand inscribes its blest
decree.
And he whose faithful arm sustained the jewel
shrined in clay,
Still shields the casket whence it shed its life-bestow-
ing ray;
The stainless lily blooms beside, and angels bend
above,
*The eucharistic cradle watched by Joseph's matchless
love.*

*   *   *   *   *   *   *   *   *

O glorious pontificate! well may thy shining days
Receive the meed of fadeless fame, the pealing tones
of praise!
Hail, then, bright year of benison and jubilee sub-
lime,
For ever let thy glory light the jewelled zone of time!

For ever let the echoed notes of glad *Te Deums* ring,
And loud evvivas ceaseless cry, All hail, our Pontiff-
    King !
O faithful shepherd ! in thy fold, upon the Living
    Rock,
Still keep afar from wolf and snare thy vast,
    unnumbered flock,
Till, resting safe in pastures fair, their purer
    glances see,
By angel throngs for ever kept, thy fitting jubilee.

THE VATICAN COUNCIL.

UP, princes of a deathless realm !
    Up, soldiers of the King !
Up, in the strength of hands enclasped,
    And ranks that closely cling !
Haste, on the pinions of the breeze,
    From isles of tropic bloom,
From farth'rest depths of desert wastes,
    From lands of polar gloom.
Come from the radiant Eastern climes,
    Come from the boundless West ;
Come with the lance in loyal hand,
    The shield on knightly breast.
Come with your helmets gleaming fair,
    Your banners waving high ;
On ! for the trump of battle sounds,
    The conflict·hour is nigh !

They come, obedient to the call,
 True soldiers of the King;
One aim, one cause, one *soul* is theirs,
 One standard forth they fling.
They gather from remotest realms,
 From regions strange and far,
Yet naught can break their serried ranks,
 Their firm·alliance bar.
Ah! whose the tones of mystic might,
 The fondly answered call—
The voice that rings o'er land and sea,
 To rouse its legions all?
And who are ye who journey far
 O'er mount, and wave, and waste?
Who claims your willing service-vows?
 What strife doth bid ye haste?
Our Father's is the voice of strength
 That sounds o'er land and sea;
He calls his knights, whose order blest
 Arose in Galilee.
The Pontiff-King, the ruler throned
 On faith's eternal rock;
The pastor of one world-wide fold,
 True shepherd o'er one flock;
The Vicar of the Prince of Peace,
 Pure leader of the right;
The chief who rules a bloodless strife,
 'Gainst wrong's rebellious might,—
We are his vassals, vowed, till death,
 To service fond and leal;
Our strength is as the granite firm,
 Our hearts are hearts of steel.

We gather for a just Crusade,
  A contest pure and blest;
The cross our lance and standard fair,
  Our shield for knightly breast.
We battle for the cause of Truth,
  Her shining sword we wield,
And, till her holy land be won,
  We falter not, nor yield.
We haste to bid our helmets gleam,
  Our potent arms be bright;
To make our magic bucklers firm,
  To gird our limbs for fight.
Hail, army of the Prince of Peace!
  Hail, legions of the Lamb!
Bear home the verdant olive-branch,
  And wear the victor's palm!

A RHYME OF CONGRATULATION.

[Respectfully inscribed to His Grace, the Most Rev. Archbishop of San Francisco, on the twenty-fifth anniversary of his consecration as Bishop of Monterey.]

WHILE came the stately vessels fraught, from deck
    to deepest hold,
With Argonautic hosts who sought the fairy fleece
    of gold,
Another pilgrim staff was placed within a steadfast
    hand,
Another pilgrim pathway traced unto the sunset
    land;
But not to seek the treasure fair within the dark-
    some mine,
And bow in blindest worship, there, at Mammon's
    crowded shrine.
No earthly dross that toiler sought, but to the West-
    ern shore
A richer, rarer boon he brought than all its golden
    store:
The pure and priceless gifts of peace, the gems of
    faith and love,
The shining wealth that can not cease, from depth-
    less mines above.

And, crowning all, the gem of gems, the treasure
    sweetly hid

In calm, secluded Bethlehems, the desert wastes
    amid:

Strength for the "burden and the heat" of earth's
    too torrid day,

Rest for the worn and weary feet that falter by the
    way:

Pure manna-bread, bestowing life, and "wine that
    maketh glad,"

That giveth courage for the strife, and comfort to
    the sad.

Lo! this the wealth *that* pilgrim brought from lands
    beyond the sea,

And ah! with ceaseless care he wrought to shed its
    bounty free.

Behold the rich result of toil—the harvest full and
    fair,

That ripened on the barren soil of desert bleak and
    bare;

E'en 'mid the sheen of worldly dross, with pure,
    unfading glow,

The golden glory of the cross transfigures all below,

Where faith's rock-founded temples rise, the earthly
    mists above,

Crowned, in the light of fadeless skies, with halo
    flame of love.

In cloister homes, serene and calm, the vestal fire of
    truth,

Lit by the spouses of the Lamb, illumes the heart of
    youth;

The orphan flocks no longer roam on highways
    bleak and cold,
For theirs is now the peaceful home in mercy's
    sacred fold;
And where the brows of fever burn, sweet watchers
    hover nigh,
And bid the dying glances turn to peace and rest
    on high.
O loved archbishop, pastor true, to thee our thanks
    belong!
O bravest hand to dare and do, O strongest 'mid
    the strong!
Beneath thy fond and fost'ring care the ripened
    harvest shines,
The guarded vineyard gleameth fair with fruit of
    laden vines;
The fount of grace in fulness flows, to cool the
    noonday heat,
"The desert blossoms like the rose," with dewy
    gardens sweet.
Ah! once again, through misty years, we turn the
    backward gaze,
Again, at memory's call, appears the train of "early
    days:"
Again we see the crozier placed within thy stead-
    fast hand,
Again thy pilgrim path is traced unto the sunset
    land;
Again thy wondrous work is wrought upon the
    Western shore,
Until our favored land is fraught with rich, unfailing
    store.

And as these golden visions glide in swift succession
    by,
How swells each heart with grateful pride, how
    glad thy children's cry !
Ah ! bright for us the festal glow of silver jubilee,
For, five-and-twenty years ago, our father crossed
    the sea.

A WELCOME TO
RIGHT REV. BISHOP O'CONNELL.

RIGHT REV. BISHOP O'CONNELL,

ON HIS ARRIVAL AT MARYSVILLE, CALIFORNIA.

[Recited by the Pupils of the Convent of Notre Dame.]

PART I.

The Younger Pupils. Song of Welcome. (Air, " A Wet Sheet and a Flowing Sea.")

(*Solo.*)—We haste, we haste to welcome thee,
    Our humble gifts we bring ;
With voices mingled, glad and free,
    Our simple lay we sing.
These gentle flowers shall sweetly tell
    Our tale of joy and love,
And be the types of flowers that dwell
    In fadeless bowers above.
(*Chorus.*)—And thus we haste to welcome thee,
    Our humble gifts we bring ;
With voices mingled, glad and free,
    Our simple lay we sing.
FIRST SPEAKER.—Mine is a gift of peerless grace
    The fairest flower that grows :
The monarch of a lovely race
    Is she, the regal rose.

And symbol of that perfect queen
  Of sister virtues rare,
Sweet charity ! her type is seen
  Shrined in its bosom fair.
SECOND SPEAKER.—Deep in the moss, a jewel set,
  I found the lowly violet ;
  Its fairest charm I offer thee,
  The type of sweet humility.
THIRD SPEAKER.—On my purple floweret see
  Fair reward of piety :
  Striving God alone to please,
  Thus we find our best *heart's-ease.*
FOURTH SPEAKER.—I chose the flower that loves
    to dwell
  Deep in the verdant mossy dell—
  Forget-me-not ! That tender name
  For us a priceless boon shall claim :
  A constant place and endless share
  In our dear bishop's heart and prayer.

ADDRESS. (*Presentation of Bouquet.*)
Receive, O honored prelate, now,
  The homage fond, sincere,
Which we, with smiles on lip and brow,
  Have come to offer here !
And take our gift—these blossoms bear,
  Upon their petals bright,
Sweet types of graces pure and fair,
  Fit gems for spirits white.
Thou wilt not scorn thy children's love,
  For He, the Saviour mild

Though King of fadeless realms above,
 Became a little child.
Ah! thou wilt guard, with fondest care,
 With watchful tenderness,
From dangers dark and lurking snare,
 The lambs He deigned to bless.
Thy potent prayers will safely shrine
 Each sacred spirit-gem,
Till all shall gleam, with light divine,
 In love's own diadem.

PART II.

SCENE I.—*The Welcome.* (*For the Young Ladies.*)

FIRST SPEAKER.—A gladsome morn is this, sweet
 friends, and joy
Reigns, crowned and smiling, o'er our hearts to-day
The boon we sought—the fair, the priceless boon,
So long the burden of each earnest prayer,
At length is granted: from his distant home,
Across the watery waste, fair angel guides
Have led our honored prelate—he is here!
Here in our very midst! O joyous words!
What power is theirs to thrill each yearning heart!
Safe here at last—our bishop, father, friend!
From his anointed hands how will the balm
Of benedictions, like the dew of heaven,
Descend on worthy brows! Inspiréd words
Will echo, like sweet music, through the depths
Of each enraptured spirit; soothing smiles
Shall light each joy and banish every care.

Belovéd ones, how shall we welcome him?
How give him greeting? In what fitting form
Shall we express the joy, the love, the hope,
His coming bringeth? Speak, O gentle friends.
   SECOND SPEAKER.—Let us prepare an offering
    most meet
To prove our faithful love, and symbolize
The glorious gifts and graces which bedeck
Our prelate's favored soul.
   THIRD SPEAKER.—A happy thought!
But what, sweet friends, shall this fond tribute be?
Where shall we find a fitting gift for him?
   FOURTH SPEAKER.—What fairer gift, O dear ones,
    can we bring
Than those sweet types of ev'ry gentle grace,
Nature's bright gems—the pure, dew-laden flowers:
They breathe in fragrance, and in glowing hues,
Affection's fondest language. One whose soul
Was robed, as with a mantle, in sweet thoughts,
Hath aptly styled these ornaments of earth
" The angels' alphabet," by which they write,
In gleaming words of fragrant syllables,
A glorious poem, that our longing eyes
May read therein the beauty and the bliss
Which reign supreme in dear and distant heaven.
   FIFTH SPEAKER.—A lovely fancy! It doth well
   . befit
A poet's soul. Appropriate gifts, indeed,
Are the sweet blossoms—but thy thought is late;
Already have the lambkins of our flock
Selected and entwined these graceful types

Of virtue and affection, to present
Unto our honored bishop.

SIXTH SPEAKER.—   In that home
Of fadeless bliss and beauty music reigns,
And perfect harmonies and sweet accords
Express the joy and love of perfect souls:
Let us, then, in our gladness, imitate
Feebly, but willingly, the angel choirs—
Ay, let us tell our happiness in song.
In sweet, melodious notes, and gladsome strains,
O let us welcome him!

SEVENTH SPEAKER.— Ay, that is well;
He will not scorn e'en humble lays like ours.
In this, the spring-time of our lives, 'tis meet
That each young heart, like freest woodland bird,
Should warble forth its happiness in song;
And he will listen, with indulgent ear,
To our imperfect notes, for they shall swell,
Like fresh, glad fountains, from o'erflowing hearts.

EIGHTH SPEAKER.—And now, O dear compan-
  ions, let us choose
One from our number, who, in fitting words,
Will speak our joyous welcome, and implore
For us, the youthful members of his flock,
A little share of his paternal love
And tender guardianship. For this sweet task
I here select thee, Mary; and I know,
O sweet associates, this choice is yours.

(*All.*)—It is, it is, our glad, united choice.

MARY.—You have conferred on me, too partial
  friends, .
A dignity, an honor, which, in truth,

I do not merit—I am all unfit
To execute this sweet, but solemn task.
With faltering tongue and words inadequate
How can I well express those glowing thoughts,
Those earnest feelings, with which your fond souls
Are rife on this glad morn?   And yet my heart
Prompts me to make the effort for your sakes,
And for the joy which, with you, I partake.
My greeting shall be uttered from the depths
Of my full heart: 'twill be, at least, sincere.
Now, for a time, a little time, dear ones,
We separate, here to unite again,
To give, with mingled hearts and blended smiles,
Our joyous welcome, our enduring love,
Unto our dear and venerated friend.

[*Exeunt.*

SCENE II

(*Song.*)—We greet thee, we greet thee,
  With smile and with song,
Like fountains, gay, gladsome, and free;
  Joy swells from the hearts
  That have followed thee long,
In thy way o'er the boundless sea.
And now a fond tribute, united, sincere,
  We give thee, our father and friend;
To hail thy glad coming, to welcome thee here,
  Our hearts with our voices shall blend.

(*Address.*)—To thy new home beside the Western
   Sea,
O father loved! we gladly welcome thee,
For eager hearts have watched and waited long
To greet thee here with blended smile and song;
Here, at thy feet, their homage fond to pay,
And bless the dawn of this most gladsome day.
Before thee, now, our reverent heads we bend,
And fondly hail our bishop, father, friend.
Receive our greeting, humble, yet sincere,
To lays unskilled, ah! lend a patient ear.
These joyous smiles are free from guileful art,
These simple strains gush warm from each young
   heart—
Accept them, then, and grant thy children's prayer:
Place in thy heart, and kind paternal care.
Fondly we thank the love, the zeal, that made
Thy willing footsteps quit the classic shade,
And from the pure and peaceful joys that smile
Their benedictions on thy favored isle,
Depart, obedient to thy Lord's behest,
To His new vineyard, planted in the West.
Ah! faithful servant, 'tis a sterile soil,
Yet richest fruit shall bless thy patient toil.
A helpless flock, long pressed by sorest need,
Shall gladly hasten, from thy hand to feed;
And from wolf-haunted paths and mountains cold
Thy voice shall guide each wand'rer to the fold.
Here is proud conquest for thy Lord and King,
A noble empire 'neath His rule to bring;
New lustre here for heaven's fair renown,
New gems to sparkle in thy monarch's crown;

Souls of uncounted value, here, to win
From the vile slavery of sordid sin;
Hearts to be purged from all their worldly dross,
Wills to be vanquished by the saving cross.
Holy thy task, and priceless thy reward
From the rich bounty of thy well-served Lord—
The fairest boon to faithful servants given:
A glorious title in His court of heaven.
Once more we hail thee, conqueror, pastor, friend,
Once more our reverent hearts to thee we bend;
And once again, with smiles on lip and brow,
Our faithful love we fondly proffer now.
And of thy gifts, again we claim our share:
Place in thy heart, and portion in thy prayer;
For well we know that, strengthened, shielded thus,
Thy heaven-sent graces shall descend on us:
Strength to endure the tempest's blighting power,
Light to discern the rainbow through the shower;
Wisdom to count all earthly things as dross,
Courage to glory only in the cross;
Faith for life's noon, and peace to bless its even,
Eternal freedom when its bonds are riven;
And place, with thee, amid the white-robed band,
In the bright pastures of the better land.
　(*Song.*)—Once more we hasten to swell the glad
　　strain,
　　With voices united and free;
Heart-smiles and heart-greetings we offer again,
　　O heaven-sent Bishop, to thee!
And thus our glad tribute, united, sincere,
　　We give thee, our father, our friend;
To swell the glad chorus, to welcome thee here,
　　Our hearts and our voices shall blend.

ADDRESS. (*With presentation of Stole.*)

A duty sweet remains for me—
  A task with purest pleasure fraught,
To offer here, on bended knee,
  The gift which willing hands have wrought.
Accept it now—a wealth of love,
With every shining thread we wove.

Though all undecked with costly gem,
  No jewel from the gleaming mine,
Set in a monarch's diadem,
  With half so pure a ray could shine
As the rich treasure, hidden here:
Affection's jewels, pure and clear.

Thy children's hearts with new delight
  Will throb, when thou wilt deign to wear
Their offering at the sacred rite,
  That so the incense of thy prayer
On fragrant wings may upward lift
Alike the givers and the gift.

Again in gratitude to thee,
  Our loved Archbishop,* here we bow,
For many a priceless memory
  Of thy fond care clings round us now.
May heaven's best gifts, like dew, descend
On thee, our father and our friend!

---

* His Grace the Most Rev. Archbishop of San Francisco.

Thus fond remembrance shall enshrine
  Our faithful pastors, tried and true,
And love, in golden chain, shall twine
  Alike the old friends and the new.
Fathers! its bond can ne'er be riven—
'Tis linked to one dear name in heaven.*

BETHLEHEM AT THE "MATER MISERI-CORDIÆ." †

O SEMBLANCE fair! O scene sublime,
Sweet picture of the Christmas time!
Grouped in the dimly-lighted room,
As in the grotto's mystic gloom,
Once more the sacred scenes I see
Of love's most wondrous history:
The dreary cave, the beasts that fed
Beside their Maker's lowly bed;
The guardian just, the mother mild,
Low bowed before the Holy Child;

---

* The beloved and lamented Father Slattery, late pastor of Marysville.

† The above lines were suggested by a visit to a most beautiful and t uching representation of Bethlehem and the sacred manger, where "Christ the Lord was born." This really wonderful scene occupies the whole of a spacious room at the "Mater Misericordiæ," adjoining St. Mary's Hospital, and, like it, under the charge of the noble Sisters of Mercy. The manger, or grotto, occupies the foreground, and in the distance is a view of Bethlehem, with its cottages and spacious castle. The latter is illuminated by lights placed within, producing a very

The shepherds three—His earthly train,
First subjects, hast'ning from the plain,
To hail Messiah's longed-for reign,
While angel throngs, attendants fair,
Courtiers of heaven, are watching there.
And from its bleak hills, looking down,
Lo. Bethlehem's chill and churlish town,
With spacious castle, fair and proud,
Where splendor shines, and mirth is loud!
And, nestled near that princely dome,
Full many a cheerful cottage home;
Full many an inn, where welcome rest
Was proffered to the wealthy guest:
But, on that night of cold and gloom,
For heaven's King earth had no room;
And earth's first Christmas words of cheer
Were rude rebuff and scornful sneer.
Ah, well that wondrous room portrays
The contrast, to my awe-struck gaze,
'Twixt love divine and human pride—
Meet picture for the Christmas-tide!
And, journeying from the East afar,
Still gazing on their guiding star,

pretty effect. In front of the castle extends a plain, covered with turf
and grass, on which flocks of sheep are seen quietly feeding. Approach-
ing the borders of the plain are the three Eastern kings, or Magi, gazing
steadfastly on the mysterious star. The figures are all life-size. The
kings are richly robed, and bear golden vases and caskets. This beau-
tiful scene has been constructed with no little labor and expense, and is
one of the many proofs of the affectionate solicitude of the kind Sisters
in providing for the pleasure and edification of the truly fortunate inmates
of the "Mater Misericordiæ," or home for virtuous young girls out of
employment, and exposed to the perils of the "wide, wide world."

Again I see the eager kings,
With gleaming gifts of precious things—
Great monarchs, chosen to adore
Where poorest shepherds knelt before!
*   *   *   *   *   *   *   *

O vision fair!   O scene sublime,
Sweet picture for the Christmas time!
Ah, Mercy's home is fitting place
Love's tender story thus to trace!
For, love like His hath labored here
Fair dwelling for " His own " to rear—
Sweet resting-place for weary age,
For homeless youth rich heritage:
And so 'tis meet that unto them
Be shown blest dreams of Bethlehem.
And they, too, that from worldly din,
From care and strife, from pride and sin,
Come up, as pilgrims, to the shrine
Of lowliness and peace divine,
To linger " e'en one hour " beside
The crib where God hath deigned to hide,—
Shall learn sweet lessons, holy themes
For musings blest and sacred dreams;
And thence shall bear full many a gem
Of graces, won from Bethlehem,
And fondly hail love's ceaseless birth,
Where heaven descends, each day, to earth,
In Mercy's home, serene and fair,
'Neath " Mater Misericordiæ's" care.

THE CHRISTIAN BROTHERS BURYING THE DEAD ON THE BATTLE-FIELD OF CHAMPIGNY.*

[An incident of the Franco-Prussian War.]

A SNOW-HEAPED plain—a grim and ghastly sight,
With crimson stains o'er all its gleaming white ;
And stark, still forms death's dreary harvest yield,
In dread abundance, on that frozen field.
Night brooding near, and torches' lurid glow
Shedding weird lustre o'er the place of woe,
Yet weaving wreaths of radiance, rich and rare,
Round love's brave legions, calmly gathered there.
How gleams the halo o'er each hero-head,
Serenely bowed above the stern-faced dead !
How, framed in splendor, shine the figures brave,
That tireless bend, till ev'ry soldier's grave,
By steadfast hand, by firm, unceasing toil,
At last is conquered from the churlish soil ;

---

* For three days after the engagements of November 29th and 30th,
sixty Brothers of the Christian Schools were occupied in that noble
work of mercy—the burial of the dead. "Some" (I quote from a work
entitled, "The Brothers of the Christian Schools, during the war of
1870 and 1871," "attacked, with spade and shovel, the frost-hardened
ground; others, carrying stretchers on their backs, went into the
Prussian lines. On the third morning, when the Brothers return to
complete their mournful. task, they find the trenches half filled with
snow. The first thing to be done is to shovel out the snow : which done,

And reverent hands uplift the valiant dead,
And lay the warrior in his earthly bed!
And when the grave has ta'en its solemn trust,
And dust is given to its kindred dust:
When the last sod each sepulchre hath sealed,
And iife's fair germs rest in their "Holy Field,"
Then the brave hands that wrought the work of
    love
Are fondly raised those hills of death above,
And on the still and star-illumined air
Floats the sweet incense of the toilers' prayer.
Their *De Profundis*, in its solemn strain,
Bindeth the dead with love's eternal chain,
And weaves fair wreaths of heaven's blest renown—
The Christian Brothers' amaranthine crown.

---

they proceed to the burying of the last bodies. At evening, there were
still some bodies at the edge of the trenches; the shovels rattled on the
hard earth with a dull, sullen sound, and the torchlight flickered
drearily. The last corpse was at length buried, and the Brothers knelt
together on the earth, and recited the *De Profundis,* the final bene-
diction and last farewell of the Christian to those that are no more "—
Noble soldiers of the Prince of Peace! Glorious sons of De La
Salle! Worthy companions of the saintly, the heroic, Brother Philippe!
Eternal honor to the Brothers of the Christian Schools!

THE "MATER MISERICORDIÆ." *

THE world doth rear its stately domes,
    Its palaces of pride,
Where art and beauty find their homes,
    And pomp and power abide;
There rank and wealth full proudly reign,
    There pleasure keepeth state,
There gathers oft a goodly train,
    The lofty and the great.

---

* The "Mater Misericordiæ " is the beautiful and appropriate name
for the home for females of good character, who are out of employ-
ment, or deprived of the safe shelter of home. This noble institution
is under the charge of the Sisters of Mercy, and is situated between the
St. Mary's Hospital building and the " Home for Aged and Infirm
Females," corner of First and Bryant Streets, San Francisco. The above
lines were written with the object of· aiding, as far as the writer's
humble ability will permit, this truly noble and praiseworthy under-
taking of the devoted Sisters of Mercy. The Home is a spacious build-
ing, containing sewing-rooms, dormitories, dining-rooms, kitchen, etc.
Here the inmates are taught dressmaking, plain sewing (both by hand
and machine), ironing, and indeed all kinds of housework. A quantity
of ready-made clothing and articles of needle-work are kept constantly
on hand, and offered for sale at very reasonable prices. Orders for
work are earnestly solicited. A visit to this noble institution will be
found sufficiently interesting to repay the journey thither; and the least
assistance, either by purchasing articles, bringing work, or inducing
others, by a "word in season," to give orders for work, will be remem-
bered most gratefully by the good Sisters, and will merit the rich
recompense promised by the God of mercy to those who give even "the
widow's mite " or the "cup of cold water " in His name.

But I have seen a grander hall,
 A mansion fairer far,
Where fadeless beauty decks the wall,
 And rarest treasures are :
'Tis " Mater Misericordiæ's " home,
 'Tis Mercy's hall of state,
Where reign, beneath its shelt'ring dome,
 The rulers truly great.

The lowly handmaids of the King,
 The spouses of the Lamb,
Their sweet dominion hither bring,
 Their sway benign and calm.
Sisters of Mercy, rulers sweet !
 Your gentle realm is here,
Where virtue finds its safe retreat
 From peril and from fear.

Ay, here the precious charge ye take,
 The tender watch and ward,
And fondly, for the Master's sake,
 His treasures here ye guard.
Home for the homeless ! blest repose
 For weary pilgrim-feet !
Safe shelter when the desert glows
 With fiercest noontide heat !

Sweet words of comfort, teachings fond,
 To guide through life's dark way ;
Blest glimpses of the rest beyond,
 The bright, eternal day,—

These are the priceless boons ye bring,
  The treasures ye bestow,
O gentle handmaids of the King,
  His ministers below !

Ah ! richest benisons shall fall,
  In softest manna-rain,
On Mercy's heaven-guarded hall,
  On Mercy's subject-train ;
'Neath " Mater Misericordiæ's " love,
  Your realm shall e'er be blest,
And peace shall brood, as snowy dove,
  Within her quiet nest.

ST. IGNATIUS.

[Written for his feast.]

SOUND the glad pæans o'er wave and land!
  Hail to the chieftain's name !
For valiant heart, and for dauntless hand,
  Honor and endless fame!
Honor to him who hath won the strife
  Over the hydra foe !
Honor to him who hath brought to life
  Hosts by the fiend laid low !
Honor to him who hath conquered *self*,
  Crushing it 'neath the cross,
Scorning the world and its worthless pelf,
  And its fame's corroded dross !

Honor to him for the conquest made,
  When glory's songs were sweet—
For the soldier's fame and the shining blade
  Offered at Mary's feet!
Honor to him who was nobler far
  In his pilgrim robe of gray,
Than when he shone as the courtly star,
  Or rode in the war array!
Honor to him for the conquest grand,
  With fiend of pride still waged,
When he wrought, with willing and tender hand,
  Where the plague triumphant raged!
Honor to him for a valiant host—
  His glorious subject-train,
Who bravely fight where the need is most,
  In the deadliest battle-rain!
Ay, honor to him for the gift he gave
  The glorious rock-built throne:
For a knighthood grand, for an Order brave—
  Hath earth a braver known?
Then sound his triumph o'er wave and land;
  Loyola's sons, arise,
And waft your pæans, O dauntless band,
  E'en to the sunlit skies!
Legions, who bow at the throne of the King,
  Echo that leader's name!
Blessed Ignatius! e'en heaven shall sing
  Thy fitting and endless fame.

THE FRANCISCAN MARTYR.*

REJOICE, rejoice, O hero-band, that bear the purpled
palm !

Rejoice, O victor-throng, that wear the livery of
the Lamb !

Another hand hath plucked the branch from tri-
umph's mystic tree,

Another royal robe is dyed in suff'ring's crimson
sea :

Room 'mid your shining ranks for him, for him who
well may claim

The hero's halo-circled crown, the martyr's match-
less name.

---

* Father Francisco De Bassoste, one of the exiled Franciscans, who,
banished from their convent and country by the tyrannical revolutionary
government of Guatemala, sought refuge in our city, and received from
the generous Fathers of St. Ignatius' College a cordial welcome and
hospitable shelter after their weary wanderings. Their tale of suffering
and persecution is touching in the extreme, and bids one exclaim, with
Madame Roland: "O Liberty! what crimes are committed in thy
name!" But the consecrated servants of Christ bore their frightful
sufferings with angelic patience. For their cruel enemies they had only
words of pardon and peace, and even their own scanty supply of food
was gladly shared with the soldiers who were driving, like criminals,
those meek and patient followers of Jesus. Father Francisco, aged and
infirm, sank under the fearful weight of his sufferings, and, soon after
his arrival here, his singularly holy and grace-fraught life was fitly
terminated by a martyr's glorious and triumphant death. Ay, a
martyr's death! Not indeed by sword, or flame, or rending wheel, but
none the less a death of martyrdom, for it was the result of frightful per-
secution, gladly borne for the sake of His divine Master and Model.

Within his peaceful cloister-shade, in contemplation
    sweet,
He learned the lesson of the cross, e'en at his
    Master's feet.
He clasped the nail-rent hand that led along the
    path of prayer,
He trod where wounded feet had made the ways of
    duty fair;
He shared the Master's sacred thirst, as for His
    sake he wrought,
He hailed the penitent's return, the straying sheep
    he sought.
Within His pure anointed hand the Lamb was
    " lifted up,"
He broke the blessed Bread of Life, he poured the
    mystic cup;
He fed the famished multitude with manna from on
    high,
He taught the living how to live, the dying how
    to die.
The day of darkness came at last, the evil hour of
    night,
And, 'neath the iron heel of wrong, low lay the
    victim Right;
And in the name of Liberty, that meek Franciscan
    band
Were torn from out their cloister-homes, from out
    their native land.
Through serried ranks of cruel foes, beneath the
    drenching rain,
Across the rugged mountain-top, along the dreary
    plain,

The heroes of the cross went on, rejoicing as they
    trod
The " Via Crucis," traced for them e'en by a
    martyr-God.
And guiding angels led them on, along that thorny
    way,
And Faith was still their star by night, their
    pillared flame by day,
Till, where their own Saint Francis gave his sweet,
    seraphic name
To stately town and shining bay, his banished chil-
    dren came ;
And there the aged pilgrim laid his weary burden
    down—
Ay, there the martyr left his cross, and won his
    fadeless crown :
The sacred hands are meekly clasped upon his
    pulseless breast,
The sandaled feet are quiet now, in everlasting rest.
O shining band of martyred saints, who bear the
    purpled palm,
Who wear the royal robes of love, the livery of the
    Lamb,
Give place, amid your shining ranks, to him who
    well may claim
The martyr's starry diadem, the martyr's matchless
    name !
O favored city, that received the Soldiers of the
    Cross !
They bring a potent charm to purge thy gold from
    all its dross ;

They bring thee white-winged benisons adown
    celestial stairs,
For thou, in truth, dost entertain the "angels un-
    awares:"
Thy poor and humble guests shall prove a fairer
    boon to thee
Than all the gathered wealth that freights thy
    richest argosy.
And thou art now, O city bright! a casket rich and
    rare,
A reliquary that enshrines celestial treasures fair;
A martyr's sacred bones repose upon thy favored
    shore,
A martyr's guardian glance shall rest upon thee
    evermore.
O blessings on Loyola's sons! within whose calm
    retreat
The fainting exiles found repose and shelter safe
    and sweet;
Around whose altar lowly knelt the persecuted
    throng,
While from their fervent lips arose the blest thanks-
    giving song,—
The glad *Te Deum*, chanted here, because their
    Lord had found
His servants worthy of the thorns that once His
    brow encrowned,—
Ay, worthy of the mocking sneer, the insult and
    the blow,
The cruel scourge, the path of pain, the likeness of
    His woe.

O blessings on Loyola's sons! bright benisons to
    rest
On those who see the Crucified in each angelic guest;
Who hail the meek Franciscan band as messengers
    that bring
Blest tidings from celestial shores, and tokens from
    the King;
Who know how sweet to faithful ears the Master's
    voice will be:
" Whene'er ye ministered to *these*, ye ministered to
    me."

THE ORPHAN'S HOME.

[Suggested by a visit to the Boys' Orphan Asylum, at San Rafael,
July, 1871.]

O EDEN-NEST among the hills,
    Where orphaned birdlings cling
Beneath the shelt'ring tenderness
    Of love's protecting wing!
A pilgrim sought thy peaceful shade
    Amid the summer heat,
And found, within thy leafy bowers,
    Refreshment cool and sweet;
And 'mid the pictures, pure and fair,
    Which memory's hand doth trace,
That glimpse of paradise shall keep
    Its fond, unfading place.

Again the sunset glory shines,
　With soft and tender gleam,
On quiet vale and purple hill,
　And smoothly-gliding stream ;
The poplar rears a stately brow,
　To meet its regal glow,
And meekly, 'neath that veil of gold,
　The willow bends below ;
And, grateful for the " ring of flame,"
　That crowns her blooming fair,
The rose, from out her fragrant heart,
　Sheds incense on the air.

　　＊　＊　＊　＊　＊　＊

The night is o'er, the day of rest
　Awakes serene and still,
And sweetly sounds the summons blest
　From yonder sacred hill ;
And, list ! a tread of countless feet
　Along the hallowed road
That leadeth to the " Mount of God,"
　The Monarch's pure abode !
They enter now the sacred fane,
　And, 'mid that childish crowd,
Each guileless heart is lifted high,
　Each knee in rev'rence bowed ;
For there submissive heaven obeys
　Earth's softly-breath'd command,
And Faith beholds her hidden God,
　Within His creature's hand.
Ay, Love hath found His Bethlehem,
　And, from His earthly shrine,

He sheds upon the orphan's path
  His benisons divine.
And there a mother claimeth all
  Of mother-love bereft,
And Joseph guards the fatherless,
  To his sweet guidance left.
Fair Eden-nest among the hills,
  All blessings rest on thee,
Thou pure domain of dove-eyed Peace,
  And white-robed Charity !
All blessings light the pastor's way
  Who guards the peaceful fold,
And gathers here the lonely lambs
  From weary waste and wold !
Meek daughters of Saint Dominic,
  Yours be each priceless grace,—
Sweet guardians of the "little ones,"
  Whose angels see His face !
O blest archangel, as of old,
  Guide safe the youthful feet,
And whisper to the guileless heart
  Thy counsels pure and sweet !
And, sheltered by thy snowy wings,
  The orphan band shall dwell
Within their peaceful Eden-home,
  The realm of San Rafael.

SONG OF THE NEW YEAR.

GIVE me gay and gladsome greeting, O ye busy sons
    of earth!
In the gleeful gush of music sing the New Year's
    mystic birth;
With the deftly woven garland let the blooms of joy
    entwine,
And the heart's own sunbeams glisten in the smiles
    that fondly shine;
For a worthy guest ye welcome, e'en the herald of
    a King,
And a boundless store of blessings to His favored
    realm I bring:
Fadeless wreaths of hope eternal, founts of joy that
    cannot cease,
Richest boons of royal bounty, sent ye by the Prince
    of Peace.
He whose fiat woke from chaos glowing land and
    shining sea,
Sowed the star-blooms in the heavens, and the
    " earth-stars " on the lea;
He who spake, and through the darkness of the
    long, mysterious night
Shone the soft and quivering splendor of the pure,
    primeval light,—
He hath crowned me with His glory, He hath sent
    me forth to bear
Heaven's message, as I journey o'er the sunlight's
    golden stair;

And adown that path of brightness angels follow
    where I lead,
Shedding, from their shining pinions, manna for the
    pilgrim's need.
When the midnight chime hath sounded o'er the
    sleeping vales of earth,
Robed and wreath'd with light celestial, sprung the
    New Year into birth;
And the way is traced before me where my vanished
    sisters trod,
O'er the mountain and the valley, o'er the streamlet
    and the sod;
Where the dreamy Syrian starlight waves its soft
    memento-crown
O'er the meadows where the shepherds saw the
    glory floating down;
In the lonely olive garden, where Love drained
    His bitter cup,
On the mount where "all was finished," when His
    cross was lifted up,—
Unto all the holy places where the Christian's vows
    are paid,
And a sacred silence lingers, shall my pilgrimage
    be made;
And my golden days of sunshine and my wintry
    beams shall shine
On the vast and stately minster, and the lonely
    forest shrine.
From their "rising to their setting" they shall
    shed a ceaseless flame
On the "clean oblation" offered in Jehovah's
    mighty name;

And my feet shall wander, noiseless, o'er the haunts
    of worldly fame,
Where the hero won his laurels, while he wrote in
    sand his name ;
Where the ruins sit like Sphinxes, 'mid their deserts
    drear and wide,
Mocking still, in stony scorning, all the fallen pomp
    of pride ;
Through the streets of busy cities, throned beside
    the billow's crest,
Where the boastful voice of progress ringeth
    through the boundless West :
And my cheering rays shall glisten, and my gentle
    dews shall fall
On the lofty and the lowly, bringing benisons to all.
Lo ! the treasures ye may gather in the shining
    path I tread,
If ye pause not by the wayside till the swift-winged
    year hath fled :
Seeds of virtue, firmly planted, works of duty nobly
    wrought,
Hours of blest, heroic toiling, days with holy
    fragrance fraught,—
Worthy harvests for the reaper, fruits of rarest
    vines are these,
Gather, then, O mortal workers ! linger not in
    slothful ease.
Unto ye, unfalt'ring servants, lo ! I bring a rich
    reward,
Sent to cheer the patient toilers in the vineyard of
    the Lord :

Quiet hearts and tranquil spirits, days of joy and
    nights of calm,
Thoughts that swell, in birdlike carols, gratitude's
    unceasing psalm.
And though clouds may hide the sunshine and the
    blessed stars from view,
Turn ye still your heavenward glances, till the glory
    shineth through ;
Though ye bear, in sultry noontides, weary load of
    pain and loss,
Ye but grasp a seeming burden,—'tis the shadow of
    the cross.
And remember, though I scatter tears with smiles,
    and grief with joy,
All are Love's most precious jewels, *all* His gems
    without alloy.
Give me, then, your gladsome greeting, O ye
    favored sons of earth !
In your carols, gay and gleeful, sing my bright and
    blessed birth ;
Hail me, then, as guest most honored, with a wealth
    of festal cheer,
Bring your stores of spirit-sunshine, tributes to the
    glad New-Year !

OUR FATHER'S PORTRAIT.*

In the bright "empire of the sun"
　　The gifted hand of genius wrought,
Till many a glorious type was won
　　Of scenes with matchless beauty fraught;
Till many a fair, celestial dream
　　In hues of magic brightness came
To bid his favored canvas gleam,
　　And crown him with its halo-flame.
A foreign clime the artist sought,
　　Far from his violated Rome;
And to our Western land he brought
　　Rare treasures from his sunny home.
Entranced, I saw his wondrous store,
　　I gazed on works of varied grace,
But each bright vision paled before
　　The charm of *one* majestic face:
Our Father's face, sublimely calm,
　　The loftiness of strength divine,
The meekness of the victim Lamb,
　　United on that brow benign.
The potent peace that seemed to shed
　　The balm of benediction bland
On the enraptured gazer's head,
　　From tranquil eye and lifted hand;

---

* These lines were suggested by a portrait of Pius IX, the work of
Signor Tojetti, a distinguished Roman artist, now a resident of this city.

. The smile that lights, with wondrous glow,
    Each lineament, reflected fair,
Of that loved face, enshrined below
    The nimbus-wreath of silver hair,—
Well hath the hand of genius caught
    Each detail of that perfect whole.
O semblance clear, divinely wrought,
    True mirror of a matchless soul!
Thanks that our favored Western land
    This treasure henceforth shall enshrine;
For, bowed beneath that lifted hand,
    That tranquil eye and brow benign,
The hearts that keep their loyal place,
    Submissive to the Pontiff-King,
Thus gazing on that sacred face,
    Around his throne shall closer cling.

SAN FRANCISCO.

O FAIR queen city of the wondrous West,
    The sunset glory is thy crown of state!
The sea thy slave, that, on his foaming crest,
    Leads the white ships within thy Golden Gate.

Thy temples rise where shining treasures dwell,
    Where throngs are bowed, and Mammon sits
        enshrined;
Where, dread Calypso! in thy golden spell
    Full many a brave, heroic heart is twined.

Ah, bright enchantress! cease thy woesome wiles,
  A halo-glory shines above thy crown;
With holiest light thy glowing sunset smiles,
  The hills are blest from whence thou lookest down.

A glorious legacy, O queen! is thine,
  Pure hands were laid, in blessing, on thy brow;
Ah! spurn thou not that heritage divine,
  And cast not off that consecration now.

Seraphic Francis gave his holy name
  To thy proud hills and to thy shining bay,
When, years agone, his faithful children came
  Within thy heart to light the sacred ray.

How hast thou quenched that bright, benignant
    beam!
  How hast thou dimmed the halo o'er thy crown,
Till lurid glare and false, delusive gleam
  Mock the pure smiles that shine from heaven
    adown!

Ah! turn thee now from demon gods aside,
  And light again the purifying flame;
Put off the purple of thy pomp and pride,
  And robe thy form in garb of grief and shame.

So shalt thou claim thy heritage of old,
  The nimbus-wreath thy drooping brow shall
    twine,
And foul idolatries of guilt and gold
  No more pollute thy seraph-guarded shrine.

THE BANQUET OF THE KING.

[Suggested by witnessing the first communion of one hundred and
ten children in the Sacred Heart Presentation Convent, on the feast of
the Annunciation.]

I KNELT within a " garnished room,"
  Where shone the banquet fair,
I saw the festal garlands bloom
  In fragrant beauty there.

I heard the glad, triumphant strain
  In clearest chorus ring,
Of hymns that hailed, in fond refrain,
  The coming of the King.

He came adown His path of light, ·
  To keep His royal feast,—
A Monarch, hid from human sight,
  The Victim and the Priest.

In bridal robes and garlands fair
  The favored guests I saw,—
Bright youthful forms assembled there,
  And bowed in love and awe.

A happy multitude they knelt
  Beside that table blest :
'Twas o'er ; in each pure heart He dwelt,
  Their King, their Food, their Guest.

How blest each soul wherein He found
   A " swept and garnished shrine !"
How sweet to know His peace profound,
   His happiness divine !

O radiant morn ! O blissful day,
   When heaven descends to earth !
And Love doth hide, in homes of clay,
   His gems of priceless worth.

O guests of God ! keep watch and ware
   Around your treasure fair,
And day and night His temples guard
   With fond, unceasing care.

On altars decked with fragrant bloom
   Keep bright the vestal flame,
And close from earth the " upper room, "
   Wherein the Master came ;

That so, enrobed in bridal white,
   And crowned with festal flowers,
Your souls may tread the aisles of light
   That lead through fadeless bowers. .

There, decked and wreath'd, the temple stands
   Of heaven's eternal Priest,—
His banquet hall, where angel hands
   Shall spread your nuptial feast.

THE ALTAR AND THE OFFERINGS.*

EARTH rendered up her richest store,
　Her treasured marbles rare,
And Art her magic chisel brought,
　To carve an altar fair.
O precious gift! O wondrous work!
　From out the shining stone

---

* The subject of the above lines is the magnificent altar, lately erected in the chapel of the Sacred Heart Presentation Convent, Taylor Street. This rare and costly shrine, formed of the most richly variegated marbles, was the gift of the late Mr. J. C. Conroy, of the firm of Conroy & O'Connor, of this city. This altar was purchased in Rome, and was first opened on the occasion of the reception of four novices. Thus the splendid shrine before which were breathed the vows of the consecrated ones, who have chosen the Immaculate Lamb as their King and Spouse, was truly rendered an "altar of privilege."

But a sad offering was soon destined to be placed there. The prayers of the community were requested for the generous donor, who had been attacked with sudden illness. Fervent petitions ascended in his behalf, and a general Communion was offered for him, but the pure spirit of the devout and resigned Christian had taken its flight, even while the sweet incense of prayer arose for him; and thus, from the altar his zeal had erected, was formed a path over which the white-winged angels carried potent supplications for the spirit then passing to its eternal home. The wreath and cross of loveliest flowers, which had lain on his coffin, were afterward placed on his beautiful altar: a touching memento of the lamented one, whose singularly pure and pious life was richly adorned with rarest blossoms of grace. The ornaments of the above-described magnificent shrine, including the monstrance, chalice, paten, and cruets, are of solid gold and silver, of the most exquisite workmanship, and were the truly princely gift of D. J. Murphy, senior partner of the firm of Murphy, Grant & Co., of this city (San Francisco).

Was hewed Love's fitting sepulchre,
  Was reared His mystic throne :
A bounteous hand that boon bestowed
  Within a cloister calm,
Where dwell, in sacred solitude,
  The spouses of the Lamb.
Earth sought again her hidden store,
  Far in the darksome mine,
For gleaming gold and silver rare
  To deck that stately shrine ;
Another gift-conferring hand
  These peerless boons bestowed,
And bade their blended glory shine
  In Love's serene abode.

First on that fair and fitting shrine
  The "clean oblation" shone ;
First offered, lay the Victim-Lamb,
  On that pure altar-stone.
A chosen band, in bridal robes,
  Here breath'd the sacred vow,
And bowed before their King divine
  The meek, adoring brow.
Here offered, lay the willing heart,
  The consecrated soul ;
Here courage broke the gods of clay,
  And spurned their base control,—
Sweet offering for that altar fair,
  Pure gems to deck the shrine
Where gleams the jewel earth hath won
  From heaven's courts divine !

While yet its Summer's early glow
  With promise sweet was rife,
The bloom of glad completeness crowned
  A rare and glorious life:
And so the swift-winged angel sped
  Adown his path of gloom,
To treasure, in his Master's sight,
  That fair, perfected bloom.
And he, whose generous bounty gave
  The rare and costly shrine,
To guard the gracious holocaust,
  The sacrifice divine,—
While yet his early Summer shone,
  With earthly promise rife,
Gave sweetly to the Giver's hand
  His pure and perfect life.
They twined the fair and fragrant crown,
  They wove the cross of flowers,
And strewed upon his sacred bier
  The gems of earthly bowers;
They brought the deftly-woven cross,
  They brought the blooming crown,
And, at the shrine his zeal bestowed,
  They laid the off'ring down.
O touching tribute, fondly placed
  Before the captive King
Enthroned upon that altar fair,
  His servant's offering!
There soon shall speed your fragile life,
  O frail and fleeting flowers!
But fadeless are the spirit-blooms
  Of glad, immortal bowers.

Grow there, O pure and generous soul!
  Amid the joys Elysian,
To bloom at Love's eternal shrine,
  To "gladden in Love's vision;"
For sweetly thou hast heavenward sped
  Upon the path of prayer,
Traced by the consecrated band
  Beside thy altar fair.
And still for thee the incense-breath
  Of supplication sweet
Shall rise and wreathe, a fragrant cloud,
  Around the mercy-seat.
No fairer monument to thee
  Can fond affection raise,
No truer epitaph can trace
  Thy well-earned meed of praise,
Than the pure altar thou hast reared
  Within the cloister calm,
Where dwell the chosen brides of Christ,
  The spouses of the Lamb.
There shall the Victim offered be,
  The "clean oblation" shine,
There shall the vestal band be brought
  To serve the King divine.
And while the hosts of Israel strive
  With Canaan throng of sin,
There lifted hands shall aid the right
  Its victory to win;
And justice, when the pure shall plead,
  Shall sheathe its vengeful sword,
And stay the whelming tide of wrath,
  That chafeth to be poured.

Thus shall the grace that saves a world
  Around that altar cling,
And heaven uprear its earthly throne
  On the blest offering.

·THE BISHOPS OF GERMANY.

TWINE the fairest wreaths of glory,
  For each brow a fitting crown ;
Waft their names, in song and story,
  To the latest age adown ;
Give the meed of fame eternal
  To the soldiers of the right,
For, with might of faith supernal,
  They have waged a noble fight.
Unto Cæsar they had given
  What to Cæsar could belong ;
But, when bonds divine were riven
  By the brutal force of wrong,
When religion's haughty hater
  Claimed the tribute due to God,
Then they braved the fierce dictator,
  And they scorned his tyrant rod.
Hail, thou true Archbishop, chosen
  Prussia's victim first to be !
Grand, heroic Lord of Posen,
  Yield we homage first to thee !
Fondest tribute next we render
  Unto him whose righteous scorn

Showed religion's brave defender
  In her Prince of Paderborn.
Crown we, too, the faithful pastors
  Who would ne'er allegiance own
To the sway of tyrant masters
  Over Mayence and Cologne.
Well they bear the " heat and burden,"
  Well they brave the tempest-shock,
Well they earned the worthy guerdon
  Sent from Peter's royal Rock.
Even in his gloomy prison,
  In his dungeon dark and lone,
One to proudest place hath risen,
  At the universal throne.*
And from earth's remotest nations,
  Promptly haste the prelate throng,
Off'ring fond congratulations
  To the dauntless foes of wrong ;
While around each faithful pastor
  Closer cling the subject-train,
Though the rule of tyrant master
  Binds them in its galling chain.
And the exiled ones that wander
  Proudly hail the prelate band,
Guarding faith and freedom yonder,
  In their stricken fatherland.

---

* While the venerable Archbishop of Posen was immured within the walls of a prison by the tyrannical and sacrilegious government, in its fiendish attempt to set up its idol of political pride, and to make the Church of God subservient to the State, the glorious Vicar of Christ, recognizing the worth of the faithful servant of truth, and as a compensation for the indignities to which he was subjected, promoted him to the Cardinalate.

THE ORPHAN'S PRAYER FOR BENE-
FACTORS.

O KINDLY hearts, that freely gave
   Your loan unto the Lord!
The orphan's grateful prayer shall crave
   Your limitless reward ;
The orphan's potent voice shall win
   Rich " measure, running o'er,"
For charity, that covers sin,
   And blesses evermore.

O Father, to whose tender love
   The lonely lamb is left,
Whose pity shields the unfledged dove,
   Of parent care bereft!
We call Thee by Thy dearest name,
   For we are truly Thine,—
Ours is the orphan's sacred claim
   To father-love divine.

And by that name we fondly plead,
   Bestow Thy blessings fair
On those who heard our cry of grief,
   And raised the weight of care.
O give our benefactors, Lord,
   Thy smile of love benign,
Bid angel hands their names record,
   Their wreaths immortal twine !

Shed o'er their earthly days the balm
  Of sweet and soothing peace—
Glad foretaste of the fadeless calm,
  The joy that cannot cease.
O may each father's life be filled
  With blessings from above,
Each mother's tender heart be thrilled
  With duteous children's love!

And in the home-nest, safe and warm,
  O keep each childish band,
Still guarded by the father's arm,
  The mother's gentle hand!
O bless alike the stately dome,
  The lowly cottage roof;
From ev'ry love-illumined home
  Keep cloud and care aloof!

The hearts that gave a willing heed
  To want's distressful cry,
And they who felt the bitter need,
  Meet in Thy realm on high.
There, wandering feet shall cease to roam,
  And mercy find reward
In Love's own fair, eternal home,—
  The kingdom of the Lord.

THE NEW TRIUMPH OF ROME.

THE NEW TRIUMPH OF ROME:

A DRAMATIC POEM.

TRUTH (*solus*).—A new adornment for the Spouse
    of Christ!
Another gem to deck her royal brow,
And shed its light athwart the gloom of time!
O matchless triumph!—treasure proudly won
Amid the darkness of these latter day,
And brightly set within her starry crown,
Safe from the fury of a fiend-led world,
That sought to tear it from its sacred shrine,
And cast it in the mire of contempt.
O Lord of hosts! Thy promise hath not failed—
The gates of hell prevail not o'er Thy Church;
And I, Thy handmaid, I, Thy deathless Truth,
Still teach, unharmed, the sacred lore of heaven.

Enter FAITH.

FAITH.—Immortal sister! lo! I bow to thee,
And share thy triumph! Happy, happy age,
That wins such glory for the brow of Truth,
And proudly giveth to my guiding hand
The staff of strength and signet-ring of love.

Enter ROME.

ROME (*kneeling*).—O guardians blest! in lowly
 homage here
Behold your vassal, heaven-favored Rome!
 TRUTH (*raising her*).—Hail, holy Rome, bright
 capital of Truth!
City of God, and mistress of the world!
All titles fair that tell of triumph blest,
Loved realm of Truth, are thine.
 FAITH.—   All hail, all hail,
Daughter of Faith, arrayed in regal hues,
With robe "washed white" in Love's redeeming
 tide,
And mantle purpled by thy martyrs' blood!
Lo, thine the right to deathless royalty!
Behold thy sceptre, Faith's all-conqu'ring cross,
And lo! thy throne, by Love's own hand bestowed.
Rule here, imperial Rome.
 TRUTH.—   Yet first receive
Thy well-earned meed, sweet sign of queenly state,—
The shining crown by Truth immortal twined.
        [*They crown her.*
Rise, child of Faith, and best-beloved of Truth,
Rest on thy lofty, angel-guarded throne!
   [TRUTH *and* FAITH *seat* ROME *on her throne.*
 TRUTH (*advancing*).—O haste thee, Earth, thy
 homage fond to pay,
And hither bring thy ransomed daughters fair,
That ye, with soulful gratitude, may bless
The royal realm who gave her mighty name
To love's unfading and unsullied spouse,
The deathless Church of Christ!

Enter EARTH, *with* EUROPE, ASIA, AFRICA, *and*
AMERICA.

EARTH.— O blessed Rome,
Eternal queen! behold thy subjects true!
Earth and her children at thy royal feet
In sweet submission kneel. Lo! Europe fair,
And star-crowned Asia, hiding in her heart
Love's mystic cradle and His rock-hewn tomb,
With sun-bright Africa, His refuge safe!
And, youngest daughter of thy favored Earth,
America, the consecrated child
Of Mary blest, the stainless Queen of Heaven!
 EUROPE.—O royal Rome! beneath thy sceptre
  bright,
The sacred cross, salvation's blessed sign,
I haste to kneel. Its magic strength has won
Freedom and light unfading for the race
That dwells, blood-ransomed, in my spacious realm :
Thus Europe hails thee, Empress of the World!
 ASIA.—With breath of incense shed from
  Sharon's rose,
That blooms perennial on my Syrian plains;
With shining skies that keep, reflected fair,
The glory of those starry beams that led
The Magi safely to their new-born King,—
With ev'ry charm that sweetly lingers yet
Around the land a Saviour's presence blessed,
Lo! Asia hastes to own thy holy sway,
O heaven-guarded Rome!
 AFRICA.— Before thy cross
Let dark-eyed Africa in homage bow,

For o'er my dreary deserts it hath cast
The soothing shadow of the Rock of Life;
And all the splendor of my tropic bloom
Doth form an altar of its rainbow hues
To shrine the emblem of all-conqu'ring Faith,
The sacred sceptre of eternal Rome.

    AMERICA.—O sovereign fair, what gratitude is
      mine!
What boundless love to bless thy tender care,
That sheds the splendor of the noonday beams
Across the darkness of my forest gloom!
From Southern realm, the fair and fragrant home
Of Lima's rose, "first flow'ret of the wild,"
To where the icy monarch of the North
Sounds his defiant tocsin through the pines,
Thy love hath sent the sweet celestial ray,
The sun-bright beam of Faith.   Hail, holy Rome,
Columbia's beacon, day-star of the West!
O bright for ever be the crowning gem,
The fair, new jewel, treasured for the Church
By him who ruleth o'er the world-wide realm,
Our holy Pontiff-King!

    ROME (*rising*).—   Thanks, loyal ones.
My glad, new triumph thrills my grateful heart
With ceaseless pride and joy.   In those dark days
Of pagan glory many a gleaming train
Swept proudly onward through my crowded streets,
And flashed the splendor of the sunlight back
From victor lances and the golden spoil
Of conquered cities.   But for this fair age
Was kept the splendor of a matchless scene,—
The bright, triumphal pilgrimage of Faith:

In shining robes the princes of the Church,
A glorious multitude, a peerless host,
From farthest realms, from stranger lands remote,
Passed on in bright procession, summoned here
By him whose throne is on the Living Rock,—
By him who bears, on consecrated hand,
The fisher's signet-ring. Majestic band,
In solemn conclave gathered ! Round them throng
Exulting spirits of the martyred saints,
Enshrined within my blest basilicas ;
And, as of old within that "upper room,"
Above the chosen, lo ! the flaming tongues
Of inspiration, with the magic gifts ·
Of a new Pentecost, again bestowed
Celestial light on that vast multitude.
And now 'tis meet that she whose potent voice
Again doth bid eternal love convert
The worthless fountains of an evil age
Into a boundless store, a living stream,
The magic wine of life-bestowing grace, —
'Tis just that she, the Mother of our Lord,
The Virgin Queen, the light of Israel,
The pure protectress of the world-wide Church,
Should claim the ceaseless gratitude of Rome.
This shining crown, a tribute sweet and fond,
I yield to her, the Queen of earth and heaven.
Ay, this fair garland, twined by holy Truth,
And the bright sceptre, love's eternal cross,
Faith's precious gift, I offer at thy feet,
O peerless Lady of the Sacred Heart !

> [*She places her crown and cross at the feet of the
> statue of our Blessed Lady.—Exeunt omnes.*

ADDRESS FOR WASHINGTON'S BIRTH-DAY.

[Written at the Convent of Notre Dame, Marysville, California.]

CHILDREN of Freedom's land, rejoice! rejoice!
Swell the glad shout in one united voice!
Let strife be hushed, and saddened hearts be gay—
Lo! 'tis the Pater Patriæ's natal day!
Shall not *his* land her eager joy proclaim,
To celebrate her noblest hero's name?
Yes, fair Columbia! hasten now to show
To him the gratitude thou well may'st owe;
Thy faithful love let pomp and pageant prove,
Bid the bright throng, the proud procession, move.
Up! freeman, up! unfurl the flag of stars!
That beacon cheered him through his night of wars.
That cherished flag he risked his life to save,
Unfurl it now! O bid it brightly wave!
Round the proud arch the graceful garland twine,
Spread the gay feast, and pour the ruby wine.
Rouse thee, O poet! from thy fairy dream;
For glowing verse behold the noblest theme!
And thou, whose burning eloquence can thrill
The list'ning throngs, and sway them at thy will,—
O let not now that magic voice be still!
Strike the bold chord, O sweet-voiced sons of song!
To him this day your noblest lays belong.

Your grateful country bids the glorious strains
Ring proudly forth o'er all her smiling plains,
And echo far, o'er mountain, forest, sea,
To bless his name whose valor made her free.
Let party strife and civil discord cease—
To nestle here, he brought the dove of peace;
Cast her not forth o'er the ensanguined flood,
To die in storms, to stain her wings with blood.
O ne'er let furious hate and baneful pride   ·
Sever the Gordian knot his hands have tied;
Through storm and fear he wove the sacred chain—
Ah, never break that holy bond in twain!
United, seek Mount Vernon's peaceful shade,
At that sweet shrine let freemen's vows be paid,
And there resolve that union's blessed band
Shall firmly girdle Freedom's favored land:
Preserving thus the peace he bravely won,
Thus will ye honor best your Washington.
We, too, will join the glad and grateful throng,
Each youthful voice shall swell the noble song,
Each willing hand shall add a shining leaf
To the proud wreath that decorates our chief;
And from the shelter of our dear retreat
Shall cast its tribute at the hero's feet,
And, honoring thus fair Freedom's purest son,
We thank the God who gave us Washington.
But let us not, while lauding man, forget
The bounteous hand which claims our deepest debt
Of endless gratitude, and praise, and love.
Then, 'neath Thy heaven, that fondly smiles above,
We thank Thee, Lord, who armed the patriot's hand,
And poured thy blessings on our ransomed land:

For, vainly strive the noble and the brave,
If Thou, Omnipotent, will not to save.
Hear, God and Father! hear our earnest prayer,
Still let this land Thy richest blessings share;
Bid demon strife and dark dissensions flee,
Let peace and love her guardian spirits be;
Let virtue be her children's highest aim,
Their proudest boast, a pure, unsullied name:
Thus, basking sweetly in Thy smile serene,
Approving nations long shall own their queen.
Thus, free from guile, her children well may pay
A fitting homage to his natal day,
For, keeping pure the legacy he won,
They best fulfil the hopes of WASHINGTON.

———

THE SPOUSAL SACRAMENT.

[Suggested by a most edifying and truly Christian marriage, which
it was lately my privilege to witness in this city.]

IT was a sweet and solemn scene,
    That Christian spousal rite,
Amid the blossoms' dewy sheen,
    The tapers' starry light;
Within the home of faith divine,
    The garnished banquet-room,
Where Love lies in His earthly shrine,
    His angel-guarded tomb.
Upon that "holy ground" they stood,
    The bridegroom and the bride,

While, 'mid the sacred quietude,
  The heavens opened wide;
And from the shining heights above
  Soft fell the manna-dew,
And sweetly sought the Sacred Dove
  Its Eden-home anew.
In faithful hearts, by love entwined,
  In union pure and blest,
Ah! safely there, where love is shrined,
  The dove of peace may rest.
O Christian rite! again I see
  Thy picture, pure and fair,
In village home of Galilee:
  As now, the Lord was there;
As now, beside her Son divine,
  The Maiden-Mother blest!
Lo! water turned to rarest wine,
  At her low-breath'd behest!
Behold! with wine of graces rare,
  At her benign command,
He blesses *now* a spousal fair,
  With glad, submissive hand.
O nuptial rite! O mystic chain!
  Securely forged for ever,
No force that bond may rend again,
  No art its links dissever.
Ah, holy chain of plighted hearts!
  Eternal band of love!
For e'en when death its union parts,
  'Twill re-unite above,
If with that spousal link ye twine
  Faith's altar-garlands white,

And in your guarded souls enshrine
  Remembrance, pure and bright,
Of sacramental banquet fair,
  And of the Saviour guest,
Who gave your feast unbounded share
  Of manna-graces blest.

SAINT DOMINIC.*

DOST sing the fame of the ages past,
  And tell proud tales of the days of yore?
Ah, pageant-glory, too bright to last!
  Ah, hero-days, that return no more!
Dost vaunt the skill of the knightly lance,
  And paint the pride of the war array?
'Tis the boastful dream of a dead romance,
  'Tis a lance long sheathed in the rust's decay.
Thy heroes fought for an earthly fame,
  For the lurid flash, and the lightning's glow;

---

* Among the glorious names that "shine as stars" in the clear firma-
ment of the ages of faith, surely none gleams with a purer lustre than
that of the saintly founder of the noble Order of the Friars Preachers.
His life was an unbroken reflection of that of his Divine Master and
Model; his every thought, and word, and deed, the faithful echo of His
of whom he had indeed learned to be "meek and humble of heart." And
the invincible strength and courage of the "Lion of the tribe of Judah"
were his also. He was ever the fearless defender of truth, the undaunted
foe of wrong and error; but his contests were the bloodless battles of
the Prince of Peace, and his numberless victories, those over which
"the angels rejoice," for they rescued countless sinners from the dark
dominion of evil. And well has his noble Order continued the work

And the trumpet's vaunt of the victor's name
  Is lost in the wail of his battle woe.
But I sing of a fame that shall ne'er decay,
  Though its dawn-light rose in the gray old past;
But its source was the light of an endless day,
  Through the " vast for ever " its beams shall last
Dost thou show the castle of stately stone,
  The turrets proud, and the bannered height?
Dost thou boast of the conqueror's lofty throne,
  Of his boundless realm and his kingly might?
But the ivy hangs on the ruined wall,
  And the moss is green on the mould'ring tower;
And years have fled since the kingdom's fall,
  And earth is thronged with the tombs of power.
I paint the pride of a conflict blest—
  'Tis an olden strife, but it rageth yet;
I sing of a bright lance still in rest,
  But its edge was ne'er by a blood-drop wet.
My stately tower was builded fair
  In the golden days of " the long ago,"
But its banners wave in their beauty there,
  And its walls are white in their first fresh glow.

---

of their holy founder. Through long ages they have toiled, and their
bond of brotherhood is as firm now as in the faith-illumined days when
its sacred links were first united. In every age the starry names of
its heroes gem the azure sky of truth. Centuries ago, the angelic han l
of a Thomas Aquinas lighted the pure flame of Christian philosophy,
that still sheds its guiding light and beacon ray of warning where
the shoals and quicksands of error are hidden by the shining foam of
sophistry. And, in our own days, the heaven-inspired eloquence of a
Lacordaire, and a Father Burke, has seemed to countless listeners even
as echoes of the voice of God, resounding from cloud-encircled Sinai.
Honor and eternal fame, then, to the glorious work of a glorious
founder, the holy Order of Saint Dominic!

I sing of a kingdom grand and vast,
   It lies at the foot of a rock-built throne,—
That realm first rose in the far-off past,
   And its strength is great as in ages flown.
And I tell of a founder brave and strong,
   A hero-arm, and a lance well tried,—
The fearless foe of the hydra wrong,
   The mighty slayer of serpent pride.
His field of fame is the lowly cell,
   His coat of mail is a monk's robe white;
And the magic arms he hath used so well
   Are the word of truth, and the voice of right.
An Order noble, and brave, and true,—
   This is the realm he hath founded fair;
The stately tower, so old, yet new,
   That gleams in its earliest freshness rare.
The saving cross is its banner bright,
   Where the face of the conquering Victim pleads;
And the hosts are linked with a chain of might—
   'Tis the rosy wreath of the mystic beads.*
O wondrous Dominic! leader strong!
   O king of a glorious subject-train!
The future's centuries, bright and long,
   Shall see no end of thine ancient reign;
Shall see no pause in thy olden strife,
   The hero-work by thy hand begun,
Till thy hosts are crowned with eternal life,
   The guerdon fair of the deeds well done.

---

* We are indebted to St. Dominic for the beautiful and efficacious
devotion of the Holy Rosary.

"THERE STOOD, BY THE CROSS OF JESUS, HIS MOTHER."

WITH a weight of grief o'erladen,
　Weary, helpless, and forlorn,
Stood a sweet and sinless maiden,
　Close beside the tree of scorn.
Ay, while He, our God, our Brother,
　With His life redeemed our loss,
Bravely stood His Maiden-Mother
　By His blood-empurpled cross.

Silent, meek, and uncomplaining,
　By that cross whereon He hung,
From all coward grief refraining,
　Till the end that Mother clung.
Learn, O heart with grief o'erladen,
　Weakly fainting 'neath the rod!
Patience from that mourning maiden,
　From the Mother of your God!

THE ROCK OF GUADELOUPE.

ONCE it cast a cold gray shadow
  O'er a desert bleak and bare,
Now, a grand and stately temple
  Stands in sunlit beauty there.
Now the fairest smiles of heaven
  Fling their glory o'er the gloom,
Now a wealth of lily-graces
  Fills the waste with balm and bloom.
Who hath wrought this transformation?
  Who hath blessed the barren wild?
Wondrous Rock of Guadeloupé,
  Hath a seraph on thee smiled?
Nay, a splendor far outshining
  Brightest beam of angel wing,
O'er that brow of rugged bleakness
  Heaven's glory deigned to fling.
'Twas the pure, celestial day-star
  That hath chased the desert's gloom:
From the royal Rose of Sharon
  Came its store of balm and bloom.
As an Indian, simple-hearted,
  Passed at daybreak through the wild,
Lo! a wondrous apparition
  Blessed the forest's favored child!
On the rock of Guadeloupé
  Strangest vision met his view

Of a sweet and gracious lady,
  Clad in robe of azure hue;
And in tones of silver sweetness
  Thus that royal lady spake:
"Quickly seek thy lord the bishop,
  And to him this message take:
Straightway must he build a temple,
  In my honor, on this rock,
And from thence, as patron tender,
  I will shield his land and flock."
    *   *   *   *   *   *

Twice, in vain, her royal mandate
  To the prelate's door he brought:
Sneering servitors received it
  As a dream of one distraught.
"Hence!" at last they cried, "and come not
  With that wondrous tale of thine,
Till thou bringest from the lady
  Of its truth the certain sign."
Then upon the rock she showed him,
  Where no blossom ever grew,
Verdant bushes, thickly laden
  With a bloom of richest hue;
And he gathered, at her bidding,
  All that bright, abundant store,
Hid it in his coarse serapé,
  And the bishop sought once more.
Sneered the servitors no longer,
  For, upon his mantle shone
Europe's white and crimson roses,
  To that Western land unknown!

And they twined, in dewy garland,
  Round a picture pure and fair,
Round a radiant vision gleaming
  In celestial beauty there!
Ay, upon that coarse serapé,
  Imaged in her royal state,
Guadeloupé's gracious Lady,
  Heaven's Queen Immaculate!
So that lone rock of the desert
  Won its fair and stately shrine,
Where the hidden bloom of heaven
  Sheddeth benisons divine.
O thou, favored Guadeloupé!
  Only wastes like thine have seen
Bright and blessed apparition
  Of the pure celestial Queen.
Lourdes, that dry and dreary desert,
  With a fount of grace was wet,
And the glory of her presence
  Lit the gloom of La Salette;
But the princes clad in purple
  And the wise of earth she shuns,
And she gives her royal message
  To the least and lowly ones.
On our desert hearts, O Lady!
  Shed thy manna-dews of grace,
Build in each a worthy temple
  For thy sweet abiding-place;
Make us meek and poor in spirit,
  From the guile of worldlings free,—
Worthy followers of Jesus,
  Worthy messengers for thee!

THE POISONED CHALICE.

[A Legend of Saint Louis Bertrand, Apostle of Panama.]

I HEARD, from ancient pages, rife
  With holy legends rich and quaint,
This story of a hero-life,
  That knew nor guile nor worldly taint.
A hero? Ay! as brave and grand
  As e'er this world of combat trod ;
A wonder in a wondrous band,
  A star amid the knights of God.
And yet no clanging mail he wore,
  No haughty plume adorned his crest,
That dauntless arm no buckler bore,
  No lance victorious laid in rest ;
A woollen robe of purest white,
  A simple cross in steadfast hand,—
This was his armor for the fight,
  His magic shield, his mighty brand.
He conquered? Ay! but not by blood
  From gaping wound of prostrate foe ;
No crimson sea, no fatal flood,
  Swept o'er his path in ceaseless flow.
His strife was won by holy art,
  With potent prayer his triumph gained ;
His battle-field the savage heart,
  In pagan bondage foully chained.

He marched, undaunted, o'er the wild,
  Through tropic rain and torrid heat,
To bless the forest's roving child
  With tidings of salvation sweet.
Ah! wildly mourned the demon foe
  His dark defeat, his ut.er loss,
And planned to crush, with fiendish blow,
  The conqu'ring soldier of the cross.
He filled with hate a human soul,
  He wove his wiles with malice fraught;
And by that tempter's dread control
  A matchless sacrilege was wrought:
Within the sacramental cup
  Was poured, one morn, a poison-draught,
That, e'en in Life, there offered up,
  Death agonizing might be quaffed.
But when the saint's anointed hand
  Made there the consecrating sign,
When, at His servant's blest command,
  To earth descended Love Divine,
Afar the baffled demon fled;
  For swiftly, from that mystic flood,
A writhing serpent darkly sped,
  And left unharmed the Sacred Blood!
O blessed Louis! bid us learn
  Sweet lesson from thy legend fair,
That from our life-cup we may spurn
  The venom-death and demon snare.

THE TRUE TALES OF CHIVALRY.*

In his ancestral castle,
  With stately turrets crowned,
Where banners floated haughtily
  O'er walls that grimly frowned,
Within a spacious chamber
  A wounded warrior lay,
The bravest of the knights that led
  In Pampeluna's fray.
Ill brooked that restless spirit
  Thus indolent to lie,
And watch the weary hours pass
  In slow succession by ;
While golden dreams of glory
  Trooped ever through his brain,
And Fancy led new legions forth
  Upon her phantom plain.
" Ho ! bring the volumes olden,
  The tales of weird romance,
That boast of dauntless chivalry,
  And skill of magic lance."

---

* St. Ignatius, then an officer in the Spanish army, being ill of a wound received at the siege of Pampeluna, requested his attendants to bring him some old romances of chivalry, in order to beguile the tedious hours of convalescence. None, however, could be found, and they brought him, instead, the Lives of the Saints. So struck was he with the holy heroism displayed by those true soldiers of Christ, that he determined to follow their glorious example. Accordingly, on his recovery, he abandoned the army, devoted himself to God, and became the illustrious Founder of the Society of Jesus.

And forth to do his bidding
　The willing vassals leap,
They search the grim old castle,
　From tower to donjon keep;
And yet (and much they marvel)
　They find no musty store
Of tales of knightly prowess,
　The quaint chivalric lore.
They bring, from dust and silence,
　One volume, worn and old,
But 'tis no legend fanciful
　Of knighthood proud and bold;
No scene of joust and tourney,
　No pomp of pageants gay,
No ghastly rhyme of goblin grim,
　No tale of greenwood fay.
He turns the pages listlessly,
　The pages old and quaint,
That tell the simple history
　Of many a hero-saint;
But, lo! his languid glances
　Are waxing eager now,
A flush spreads o'er his pallid cheek,
　And mantles on his brow.
Well may that volume olden
　Enkindle his proud eye:
The noble deeds he readeth there
　Are registered on high.
And well the truth-inspiréd scribe
　In simple language paints
The prowess of those knights of God,
　His self-subduing saints.

O'er that ancestral castle
　His banners flaunt no more,
And rusted lies the gleaming lance
　Its master proudly bore;
He leads a nobler chivalry,
　A brighter, braver host,
His name becomes the Christian's joy,
　The Church's proudest boast.
On heaven's deathless tablet,
　Lo! angel hands record
Another soldier of the Lamb,
　A servant of their Lord;
And earth, from farthest regions,
　In tongues of every land,
Still hails, with glad, united voice,
　Loyola's sacred band.

HEAVEN'S HERO, ST. FRANCIS XAVIER.

THE world doth hail her heroes and her sages,
  The sons of might and fame;
Their names are wafted down the ringing ages,
  In jubilant acclaim.
The world doth weave, in ceaseless song and story,
  The garlands of their praise:
The victor's wreath, the laurel crown of glory,
  The poet's glist'ning bays.
And who are they to whom the nations render
  Rich tributes of renown?
Whose brow is wreathed with coronal of splendor,
  Earth's fairest halo-crown?
Ambition's slave, his Gordian knots untying
  With reeking, ruthless sword,
Red with the blood that feeds his thirst undying,
  Libations foully poured.
He of the voice whose ringing intonations
  The spellbound spirits thrill,
Yet serving oft, with servile adulations,
  Corruption's demon will.
And he whose pen on fair soul-tablets traceth
  Its lines of lurid light,
Whose serpent-trail from sullied shrines eraseth
  The golden laws of right.
The bard, alas! from seraph ranks descending
  To sin's discordant throng,
His lays divine, his notes celestial blending
  With pleasure's syren song.

But what, O world, shall be his fitting guerdon,
 Who, battling for the right,
Undaunted bore the conflict's " heat and burden,"
 And won the lifelong fight?
Whose magic tones could win a mighty nation
 To truth's serene control?
Whose accents woke the "new song" of salvation
 In many a silent soul?
Whose hand unsealed the error-guarded portal,
 And traced, with golden pen,
Love's precepts pure, in lines of light immortal,
 Upon the heart of men?
Behold, proud world! the tributes thou dost offer
 For hero-toil like this:
Thy children's scorn, the sneer of smiling scoffer,
 The sceptic's serpent hiss!
Ah, senseless world! he spurned thy homage fleet-
 ing,
 Thy frail and fading crown,
Thy empty praise, thy sycophantic greeting,
 Thy pomp of vain renown.
For fadeless fame, for recompense eternal,
 He, ceaseless toiler, wrought;
Through wild and waste safe led by strength super-
 nal,
 A worthy prize he sought.
Ay, noble Xavier, true and faithful pastor,
 Thou led'st the flock forlorn
Safe to the fold, back to its home and Master,
 From crag and path of thorn.
Angelic hands inscribe thy blessed story
 On heaven's page of fame,

And seraph voices chant thy deeds of glory
  In echoing acclaim ;
And heaven's King doth give thy guerdon royal,
  Thy radiant reward :
"Share now, true knight, for service fond and loyal,
  The glory of thy Lord."

THE KNIGHT'S VIGIL.*

THE abbey towers stood gray and tall
  Against the moonlit sky,
And the soft light played o'er massy wall
  And sculptured turret high ;
But the chapel arches rang no more
  To the sweetly-chanted hymn,
For the vesper's holy rite was o'er,
  And the aisles were still and dim.
The fadeless lamp of the sacred shrine
  Still shed its tender ray

* When the hero of Pampeluna, Saint Ignatius of Loyola, resolved to consecrate himself to the service of the meek and lowly Jesus, he left his castle, and proceeded to the abbey of Montserrat. On his way he gave his rich apparel to a beggar, assuming the mendicant's humble garb, over which he wore a coarse gray tunic, with a cord about his waist. Arriving at the abbey, he passed a night in prayer before the holy shrine ; then leaving in the sacred temple his glorious sword, he went to the hospital of Manresa, and employed himself in attending to the sick and afflicted, adopting the title of the " Unknown Pilgrim." He afterward journeyed to Palestine, converting infidels and ministering to the distressed. Worthy preparation for the noble work for which he was destined—the founding of that glorious soldiery of Christ, the Jesuit Order !

Where the priceless gift of love divine
   In its hidden glory lay ;
But the heavy portal op'ning swung
   To a stately form at last,
And the echoing cloister softly rung
   Where a reverent footstep passed.
'Twas the vigil of arms for a coming fight,
   For an hour of triumph nigh,
For the dauntless sword of the belted knight,
   And his spirit brave and high ;
But the warrior wore no coat of mail,
   No proudly waving crest,
No flashing helm, no visor's veil,
   No shield for the knightly breast.
A pilgrim's garb was the robe of gray,
   With its hempen girdle bound—
Is this a theme for the minstrel's lay,
   Or the trumpet's vaunting sound ?
But his step was firm, his bearing high,
   As he trod the lonely aisle,
And the lamplight shone in a fearless eye,
   Though moist with tears the while.
A bright blade flashed in his stalwart hand,
   A lance well-tried and true—
No arm e'er poised a stronger brand,
   A goodlier falchion drew.
He bowed him low at the altar fair,
   And kept his watch till day,
And the sword of a hero glittered there,
   When the pilgrim went his way ;
For he laid his lance on the sacred shrine,
   And he breathed a solemn vow :

"To the holy cause of a King divine
    I give my service now."
Where the fever burns in the throbbing vein,
    And the pestilence wastes at noon,
The knight hath been, at the couch of pain,
    As heaven's brightest boon.
Where the faithful feet of the pilgrim band
    Toil on in their weary way,
At the shrines of faith's own Holy Land
    Their homage fond to pay;
Where the loathsome leper croucheth low
    At the sacred entrance-gate,
A Christ-like love hath soothed his woe,
    And eased his anguish-weight.
O dauntless knight of the saving cross!
    O spirit of quenchless flame!
Thou hast changed the glitter of worldly dross
    For the gleam of eternal fame.
Loyola, chief of a wondrous host,
    Till the journey of Time is done,
The rock-built city of Truth shall boast
    The triumphs thy band hath won;
Shall tell thy vigil of arms, brave knight,
    Thy watch at the sacred shrine,
Where strength was won for a worthy fight
    In the service of love divine.

THE MARTYR'S TWOFOLD OFFICE OF ALTAR AND PRIEST.

THE noise of festal riot had died at last away,
And silence held the city at early dawnlight gray,
Save where the watchful warden still paced in
    arméd state,
With slow and ringing footsteps, before the prison
    gate.
Within that dismal dungeon no sleeper lay, I ween,
The captives kept their vigil in wakefulness serene;
For death they calmly waited, yet not in still despair,
For parted lips were smiling, and eyes were shining
    there.
It was their festal morning, and lo! the board was
    spread
With sacred wine of gladness and store of manna-
    bread.
But where the garnished altar—the vested priest?
    behold
That fettered form extended upon the pavement
    cold!
It is the priest, thus fastened by many a cruel band,
One limb alone hath freedom—the pure, anointed
    hand.
And, lo! the wondrous altar! Upon that prostrate
    breast
Is laid the mystic off'ring, for "clean oblation"
    blest.

The captive's head is lifted, the consecrating word
The martyr's lip hath spoken, and list'ning love hath
heard;
The hand yet left unshackled hath made the sacred
sign,
And, lo! a God reposes upon that sacred shrine,
Above that pure heart's throbbing, above that puls-
ing stream,
That soon, in blest libation, shall shed its crimson
gleam.
To share the sacred banquet the guests are gathered
now,
And round their living altar the glad adorers bow;
Again that hand is lifted, and to the kneeling
throng
It gives the Bread of Angels, the wine that maketh
strong.

That wondrous Mass is over: from ruder pagan
sight
They take the altar vessels, the cloth of snowy white.
And when, at golden noonday, the fierce and
fiendish cry
"Of Christians to the lions!" reëchoes wild and
high,—
And when, in dread arena, beneath the summer ray,
The monarch of the desert is roaring for his prey,
The nuptial guests are ready—exultant, calm, and
strong,
Go forth the willing legions, the manna-nourished
throng.

And he, the martyrs' chieftain, who walks with firm-
    est tread,
Lay fettered, in the dawnlight, upon his dungeon
    bed;
Ay, there, in twofold office, he shared the daybreak
    feast,
And offered love's oblation, its altar and its priest!

THE VISION OF SAINT DOMINIC.

WITHIN their silent cloister
    The wearied brethren slept,
Save one, that, in the midnight lone,
    His tireless vigil kept:
It was their saintly founder,
    That, lowly kneeling there,
Sent upward, from his heart's pure vase,
    The incense-breath of prayer,
And as that snow-white garland
    Rose through the midnight lone,
His spirit, on its fragrant cloud,
    Ascended to the throne,—
The "great white throne" eternal!
    And ah! what bliss to see
His wreath of prayer entwining there
    Its shining canopy!
The royal-robed Redeemer
    Upon His servant smiled,
The Maiden-Mother's outstretched hand
    Gave welcome to her child;

Before their Monarch bending,
  Close wreath'd around His throne,
Bright saints of every Order blest
  He greeted, save his own.
Then wept that saintly founder,
  In agony of woe.
The Queen, with tender glance, beheld
  His sorrow's bitter flow;
With kindly hand she beckoned,
  Yet still he shrank in fear,
Till, at his King's benignant sign,
  He drew, yet weeping, near.
"Why flow thy tears of sorrow
  At joy's immortal throne?"
" Dear Lord, I see, before Thee bowed,
  Each Order save my own."
Then to His royal Mother
  The King of glory turned:
"Behold, O son, the blessed sight
  For which thy soul hath yearned:
Sweet Mother, ope thy mantle."
  Ah! blest, ecstatic view!
O'er heaven's realm extended wide
  Her cloak of azure hue!
How thrilled the saint with rapture
  Of joy, and love, and awe,
For, gathered 'neath that wondrous robe,
  His white-robed sons he saw.
Soon fled the glorious vision;
  But ah! what joy to tell
The story to his children dear,
  When rung the matin bell.

And as the thronging brethren
  That tale of rapture heard,
With glad, ecstatic gratitude
  Their very souls were stirred;
And fervent vows ascended
  Of loyalty and love
To her whose boundless mantle guards
  Their white-robed band above.

SAINT VINCENT FERRER.

O SAINT of God, successor true
  Of blest apostle-band!
Bright bearer of the " tidings glad "
  From land to eager land!
Ah, parents wise, that could discern,
  On noblest heights of fame,
The tablet clear, where angel hands
  Inscribe each hero-name!
Ye gave your child without a sigh,
  An off'ring, glad and free,
To serve where glory's worthy prize
  Is immortality.
Sweet garden of Saint Dominic!
  This lily-bloom of grace
Soon found, within thy peaceful realm,
  His fair and fitting place:
And so he came, a Samuel vowed
  To temple-service blest,
With " holiness unto the Lord "
  Borne ever on his breast.

And when to toil the Master called,
    Quick rung his glad reply—
Where'er must turn his herald steps—
    " My King! lo, here am I!"
Then forth he went o'er land and sea,
    True soldier of the cross,
Accounting, as the Master bade,
    All earthly things as dross.
To hear his voice of strength divine
    The eager nations throng,
And hail him truest friend of right,
    And sternest foe of wrong.
Within his land of sunny Spain
    A wondrous work he wrought,
Rich harvest, then, of ransomed souls,
    In stranger lands he sought:
A peaceful Hannibal, he crossed
    The Switzer's Alpine height,
And e'en on Albion's snowy cliffs
    Upreared his standard bright.
O'er Cambrian mounts and Scottish hills
    The sacred toiler trod,
And found, in Erin's favored isle,
    Full many a flow'r of God.
Throughout the smiling land of France,
    All-conquering, journeyed he,
And gathered rich, unfading store
    In blooming Italy.
Proud unbelievers heard his voice:
    For e'en the Moorish king
Within his fair Granada sought
    Christ's messenger to bring.

And soon the haughty Moslem saw
  His Crescent's lurid glare
Grow dim, when holy Vincent showed
  The Cross of Jesus there.
But, saint of God! my simple rhyme
  Essays in vain to trace
The record of thy hero-life
  Of blest, supernal grace.
Thy history is fitly told
  By seraph scribes alone,—
Thy deeds they write, in living light,
  O'er Love's eternal throne.

SAINT AGNES.

VIRGIN AND MARTYR IN THE REIGN OF DIOCLESIAN.

CHILD-MARTYR! noblest heroine
  That earth had ever known,
With heaven's own majesty of mien,
  And firm, unfalt'ring tone;
Before the judge I see thee stand,
  Thy dauntless words I hear,
I mark thy upward-pointing hand,
  Thine eye serene and clear.

Clad in thy robe of spotless white,
  Heaven's glory on thy brow,
Thou speakest of thy mystic plight,
  Thy solemn nuptial-vow;

I hear thee name a kingly spouse,
  When they would bid thee wed :
They marvel who hath claimed thy vows,
  And, then with lifted head,

And radiant eyes upraised to heaven
  In ecstasy of love,
Thou say'st thy youthful heart is given
  To One who dwells above.
They deem thee crazed : in dungeon dim
  . Thy tender limbs are bound,
Still thy lips to the Christian's hymn
  Make the dark vaults resound.

They drag thee forth, the cruel sword
  Gleams o'er thy dauntless head—
One stroke, and to its Spouse and Lord
  Thy stainless soul hath fled.
'Thus, watered by thy martyr-blood,
  The seed so lately sown,
Laved by its pure and strength'ning flood,
  To fadeless bloom hath grown.

FATHER JUNIPERO SERRA.

THROUGH the sounding ages wafted,
   Still the lofty pæans ring,
Of the mighty chiefs who conquered
   For a transitory king—
For the glory of a nation,
   Darkly shrouded in decay,
'Neath the ivy-mantled ruins
   Of its evanescent sway.
Let us vaunt a nobler triumph,
   And, in sounding chorus, sing
Of a chief who led the banners
   Of the everlasting King;
Who hath added new dominions
   And a countless subject-train
To the crown that, through the ages,
   Still unconquered shall remain.
Lo! that valiant chieftain battled
   In the fair and fadeless West—
To our own bright El Dorado
   Came his legions, brave and blest;
Through the Golden Gate they entered
   Of our still and shining bay—
E'en our royal-vested city
   Meekly owned their peaceful sway.
Peaceful! ay, no mail-clad legions
   Clanked along the sunset shore;

On the sand-hills lay no death-heaps,
   Poured no tide of ghastly gore.
Not one blood-drop of the vanquished
   Stained your wreaths of victor-palm,
Brown-robed sons of sweet Saint Francis,
   Blessed legions of the Lamb!
Only from the fiendish armies
   Rose the wail of woe and loss,
For your weapon, world-subduing,
   Was the demon-dreaded cross.
Hail to thee, O valiant leader!
   For that brave and dauntless band
Guided was to deathless conquest
   By thy firm, anointed hand.
Earthly glory shall be given
   To thy sweet and saintly name,
And our golden land shall echo
   With thy pæan-notes of fame,
While the pilgrim, gazing fondly,
   Sees the sunlight's tender ray
Light the cross of Padré Serra,
   On the shore of Monterey.
And while, in our verdant valleys,
   Priceless vestige yet remains
Of thy quaint adobé temples,
   Of thy ruined mission-fanes;
And within the courts of heaven
   Seraph hosts shall sing thy fame,
Bidding endless ages echo
   With the glory of thy name;
For, amid the white-robed subjects,
   Bending at " the great white throne,"

Stand thy pure and priceless trophies,—
  Blessed conquests, all thine own.
Ay, the forest's countless children,
  Freed from demon-thrall by thee,
Weave thy crown of fadeless laurels,
  In their glad eternity.

THE LILY OF QUITO.

In a garden of the Southland
  Once a matchless lily grew,
That, through all its earthly blooming,
  Kept its white, unsullied hue—
Kept its first celestial fragrance,
  For its heart was e'er the shrine
Of the brightest beams of heaven,
  And the balm of grace divine:
Though it shunned the glare of noonday,
  Where the worldly flowers fade,
Yet it could not hide the brightness
  That illumined e'en the shade.
Purest eyes that gazed upon it
  Saw, serenely mirrored there,
All the sweet and smiling graces
  That the blooms of heaven wear.
Sinful eyes that gazed upon it
  Veiled their glances in affright,
For the awful flame of Sinai
  Darted thence its angry light;

But repentant eyes that sought it
    Through the tempest-rain of woe,
Saw the blessed bow of promise
    Arched within its cheering glow.
Stainless lily! sister blossom
    Of the fair and fragrant rose,
Whom the walls of favored Lima
    With a tender care enclose!
Brightest treasures of Columbia,
    That in mingled wreath entwine
Round the royal Rose of Sharon,
    Round the lily-flow'r divine,—
In that coronal of splendor
    Shine for e'er, in blended hue,
Blessed lily-bloom of Quito,
    Saintly rose of fair Peru!

SAINT ALOYSIUS GONZAGA.

O HEART detached from toys of earth!
    O spirit-gaze uplifted high
    From dreams that fade and joys that fly,
From rank, and pomp, and pride of birth!

No worldly scene could win thy soul
    That mirrored heav'n serene and clear.
    No earthly echoes charm thine ear,
Where seraph strains unceasing stole.

The flow'r supreme, the fairest star
  Of blest Loyola's knightly band!
  From age to age, from land to land,
Thy hero-deeds recounted are.

Yet throngs saw not thy labors done,
  For, in the mystic life of grace,
  'Tis from the least and lowliest place
The victor's loftiest meed is won.

O may our lives thine image be!
  May each young Christian heart possess
  Thy royal robes of lowliness,
Thy lily crown of purity!

THE CHRISTIAN BROTHERS' GOLDEN MINE.

FAR down within the dismal mine,
  Where fragrant breezes never blow,
Where genial sunbeams may not shine,
  Or crystal brooklets flow,
There gleams the wondrous gold amid
  The shrouding granite's dark disguise,
And there, in deep oblivion hid,
  The shining silver lies.
Far, far below the verdant soil,
  So soft with dew, so bright with bloom,
The miners dig, with weary toil,
  In dread, eternal gloom.

What seek they?—wealth that taketh wings,
　Delusive treasures, set in rust,
The gods where worldly worship clings,
　The idols of its trust;
The mocking gleam that falsely leads
　Through stagnant marshes, foul with sin;
The demon bribe that darkest deeds
　And deadly wiles may win.

*　*　*　*　*　*　*　*

Within a rich, exhaustless mine
　The Christian Brothers fondly toil:
There blessed sunbeams ever shine,
　And bloom bedecks the soil;
There gleams the wealth that fleeteth not
　On restless pinion, swift as light;
There shine the gems no rust can blot,
　No blemish e'er may blight.
Within the fruitful heart of youth
　These willing miners long have wrought,
For there the stainless gold of truth
　Their patient toil hath sought.
From foul alloy of guilt and vice
　They free the wealth of silver ore,
They set the wondrous "pearl of price"
　Within that shining store.
Ah, saintly toilers, not from earth
　Your labors claim a scant reward!
Look upward! lo, your task is worth
　The guerdon of your Lord!
" Come, blessed ones, and with each gem
　Your hands have freed from earthly leaven,
In love's eternal diadem
　Be fitly shrined in heaven."

THE BIRDS OF YO SEMITE.*

THE seething torrent writhed and roared
  Adown its dizzy path,
And o'er its rocky barriers poured
  The white foam of its wrath;
It burst at last its granite cage,
  It leaped from out its lair,
And ceaseless thunders of its rage
  Crashed through the quiv'ring air.
Yet firmly, at that torrent's foot,
  The forest monarchs grew;
Its foam-wreaths laved each sturdy root,
  And gemmed each leaf with dew.
O fearless oaks! the wrathful storms,
  The cataract's endless frowns,
Could never bow your stalwart forms,
  Or dim your leafy crowns.
And safe within your verdant shade,
  E'en o'er its angry crest,
The merry minstrel of the glade
  Had built his humble nest;

---

* The above poem was suggested by a prose description of Yo Semite, in which the writer enthusiastically and charmingly expresses the emotions awakened in his heart by the majesty of the mighty cataract, and the exquisite melodies of the mocking-birds, warbling fearlessly, even amid the angry roar of the waters, their songs of gratitude to Him whom the Germans, with sweet, childlike simplicity, style "the dear God."

Ay, there the gleeful warbler sang
  His joyous matin lay,
And there his vesper carol rang
  Sweet farewells to the day.
A pilgrim, rapt in rev'rent awe,
  Stood on that giddy verge,
And, spellbound by its tumults, saw
  The torrent seethe and surge ;
And, as its ceaseless thunder-tone
  Fell on his shrinking ear,
His spirit quailed : "A Monarch's throne
  And awful voice are here.
Thou King of kings! Thou God supreme !
  How weak the tones of praise !
How rash the trusting glances seem
  That mortals dare to raise !
For here, upon the torrent's path,
  Thy boundless power I see,
And own, amid its mighty wrath,
  Thy awful majesty."
But whence that burst of joyous song,
  Those carols sweet and clear ?
O wildwood birds ! O minstrel throng !
  Your voices knew not fear.
High o'er the angry storm that smote
  The rock with ceaseless blows,
The echoes of each gleeful note
  In purest cadence rose :
"Praise to the dear all-Father's name ! .
  E'en to Thy throne above
We waft the meed Thy mercies claim,
  O God of light and love !

List to the birdlings' simple song,
  Clear ringing through the morn !
Though round Thee chant the seraph throng,
  Our lays Thou wilt not scorn.
The torrent's deep, resounding tone
  Proclaims Thy boundless might;
It bids a world its Sov'reign own,
  And tremble in Thy sight.
But our unceasing carols suit
  Our fonder, sweeter theme—
We sing Thy crowning attribute,
  Thy mercy's fairest gleam.
O shrinking human heart ! be calm !
  Look upward from the dust,
And wake a new, unfalt'ring psalm
  Of perfect love and trust ! "
So, on the pilgrim's dreaming heart
  Those sweet bird-voices thrilled,
Their music's soft and soothing art
  Its terror-tumult stilled.
Dear messengers ! till life shall cease,
  My grateful heart shall bless
Your melodies of love and peace,
  Your tones of tenderness.
O maddened waters ! wildly dash
  Adown your rocky path,
And, in resounding thunder-crash,
  Peal out your mighty wrath :
Type of the terrible ! sublime
  And awful voice of power !
Yet blending sweetly with the chime
  Of birds in leafy bower.

O cataract roar and forest lay!
  To heedful heart and ear
Your blended tones have brought to-day
  A twofold lesson dear.
Then bow, my soul, in reverent awe
  Creation's God before;
Submissive own His kingly law,
  His Majesty adore.
Yet cast thy trusting glance above,
  Where Mercy's smile is bland,
And rest, in confidence and love,
  Beneath a Father's hand.
And while affliction's torrents pour
  In madness o'er thy way,
And claim, with wild, discordant roar,
  An unimpeded sway,
Still keep love's birdlike notes within
  A consecrated bower;
And high above the tempest's din
  And fierce, despotic power,
Shall ring their carols sweet and calm,
  Their chorus glad and clear,
That gratitude's unceasing psalm
  May reach the Father's ear.

THE VISION OF CONSTANTINE.

Forth came the countless legions,
  By vile Maxentius led,
With shining spears, and bucklers bright,
  And royal ensigns spread;
There gleamed the conqu'ring eagles
  Beneath the noontide ray,
And there the sheen of armor flashed,
  Proud challenge to the day.
High dreams of matchless triumph
  Smiled on the tyrant's sight:
No marvel—for a world was won
  By Rome's resistless might.
Forth marched, to meet her legions,
  A band as brave and true.
But match with countless forest boughs
  A sapling's branches few,
Then may ye dream of conquest,—
  Ay, then securely hope
To see the band of Constantine
  With serried legions cope.
E'en while their noble leader
  His troops unfalt'ring led,
Within his dauntless heart awoke
  This agony of dread.
He knew how vain the struggle
  Against such fearful odds,

Yet scorned to seek the augurs false,
  Or bend to demon gods.
The one Almighty Ruler, .
  To whom the Christians bowed,
Who led His chosen o'er the sea,
  And guided from the cloud,—
To Him that leader lifted
  His eager anguish-cry:
" Help! Christian God of armies!
  Send vict'ry from on high! "
Upon the shining heavens
  He turned his pleading eyes,
And, lo! the sign of hope and strength,
  Emblazoned in the skies!
The standard of the Christians,
  The cross whereon was won
The man-God's matchless victory,
  Shone fair above the sun:
" By this sign shall ye conquer,"
  O words of magic might,
Upon that sacred emblem traced
  In lines of living light!
         *   *   *   *   *   *

The Lord of Hosts hath triumphed,
  The battle-toil is o'er,
And potent was the standard pure
  That valiant army bore.
O'er Rome's resistless legions
  Proud victory was won,
The sacred sign of Constantine
  A wondrous work hath done:

The gleam of golden eagles
　Grew dim as worthless dross;
An army, countless as the leaves,
　Was conquered by the cross.
O Christian heart, that wagest
　A wild, unequal strife
With hosts that crowd, in fierce array,
　The battle-field of life!
Faint not amid thy peril,
　But turn thy glance above,
And thou shalt see, beyond the sun,
　The sign of hope and love:
" By this sign thou shalt conquer!"
　The words of strength shall win
Proud triumph o'er the countless hosts,
　The myriad throng of sin;
The gleam of pride's fierce eagles
　Shall pale as worthless dross,
And demon legions fly before
　The standard of the cross.

THE LORD'S ANOINTED.

[Suggested by witnessing an Ordination in the Church of St. Ignatius.]

NAY, tell me not of tinsel pomp,
  Of glory false and frail,
Of pageants bought with heroes' blood,
  Death-moan, and widows' wail;
Of kingly crowns, whose flashing gems
  The thorny anguish hide,
Of regal robes, by tyrants worn,
  In palace halls of pride:
For I have known a fairer scene,
  A triumph that shall last
When worldly honors withered fly,
  Like leaves before the blast.
Beside the hidden Monarch's shrine,
  Where bowed the pleading throng,
Where tapers glowed, and flowers bloomed,
  And pealed the holy song;
Where incense bore, on wings of balm,
  Contrition's fervent sigh,
And softly came, like evening dew,
  The manna from on high,—
At blest Redemption's nuptial feast,
  In Faith's bedecked abode,
There was the fadeless triumph won,
  The title fair bestowed;
There were the mystic robes put on,
  There breath'd the solemn vow,

And there the oil of strength was poured
 Upon a warrior's brow.
A warrior! ay, yet not of those
 Who wade the crimson sea,
And, ruthless, bid the captive foe
 Their car of triumph be.
To battle 'gainst the tempter's wiles,
 To crush the mighty wrong,
To cope with evils, fierce and dread,
 The demon's hydra throng;
To heal the bruised and broken reed,
 To soothe the stricken heart,
To bid the leprous soul be clean,
 The freed in peace depart;
To carry through the desert wild
 Salvation's tidings blest,
To bring the wand'rer home again,
 To bid the pilgrim rest;
To cheer the lone, plague-stricken bed,
 Unshrinking, to the last,
To nerve the faint and parting soul,
 Until the strife be past;
To preach, to teach, to " bind and loose,"
 To fast, to watch, to pray,
To tread, with firm, unwearied feet,
 Privation's rugged way;
To spurn the cup of worldly joy,
 Earth's fondest ties to break,
To cast aside her golden gifts,
 Her paths of peace forsake;
To toil in drear and distant lands,
 The noontide heats to bear,

That bloom may bless the wilderness,
  And vineyards ripen there,—
This is his task, for this he counts
  Earth's fairest boons as dross,—
Ay, this the field where nobly strives
  The soldier of the cross.
Yet O, what privilege is his !
  At altars fair he stands,
And holds his hidden God and King
  In consecrated hands ;
His voice the mystic summons speaks,
  When heaven descends to earth :
And Pyx and chalice cradles are
  For Love's new, wondrous birth.
The pure baptismal tide that laves
  The smiling infant's brow,
The sweet absolving sentence breath'd
  When contrite sinners bow ;
The strength the dying pilgrim wins
  By blest, anointing rite,
Fresh girding for the journey dread,
  The last mysterious flight,—
These are the treasures he bestows,
  The glad commissions given,
To him whose sacred footsteps bear
  The messages of heaven.
Hath earth a dignity like this ?
  Can proudest monarchs claim
His priceless privilege who wears
  The glorious priestly name ?
The harvest rich, the garnered sheaves,
  The overflowing net,

The flock secure within the fold,
  The jewels safely set,—
These are the fruits that bless his toil,
  And, lo! his fair reward:
" Well done, thou good and faithful one!
  True servant of thy Lord!"
An honored guest, for evermore
  He shares the Bridegroom's feast,
And seraphs hail, with joyous song,
  Their Lord's anointed priest.

SOBIESKI'S SONG OF TRIUMPH.

HOSANNA to the Crucified, who bade the Crescent's
  dross
Grow dim before the matchless light of His trium-
  phant Cross!
And honor to Our Lady blest, whose potent aid
  hath won
Proud conquest for their arms who bore the stand-
  ard of her Son!
Hail, Lily-bloom of Israel! Hail, Maiden, full of
  grace!
The might of Moslem hosts hath quailed before thy
  royal face;
Thine image decked the banner fair that flung its
  folds on high, *
Thy badge was on each warrior's breast, thy name
  his battle-cry.

The Paynim hosts came proudly on, a dread, exult-
ant throng,
Like to the venomed blasts that swept the desert
wastes along ;
Fierce flashed the cruel scymitar within each ruth-
less hand,
And wild the shout, "In Allah's name we claim the
Christian land."
And forth, to meet that mighty host, a little army
came,
Armed with the sacred sword of truth, the Chris-
tian's cherished name ;
Strong with the mystic wine of love, the Bread of
endless Life,
As from the holy feast they rose, fresh girded for
the strife.
" For God, Our Lady, and the Cross !." outrang
the dauntless cry ;
Each heart beat proudly at the sound, each glance
was lifted high ;
While on their banner, brightly stamped, a mother's
image shone,
And, far above, a mother watched, and pleaded for
her own.
O potent pleading ! faithful watch ! all-hail, our
peerless Queen !
For ne'er on earthly battle-field such victory was
seen.
As onward, in the fearful fight, the Christian soldiers
sped,
Like leaves before the wintry blast, the Paynim
legions fled,—

Ay, fled before the feeble few, the scorned, the
pigmy band,
The handful they had sworn to crush with *one*
Damascus brand !
Their haughty crescent sunk in gloom before Our
Lady's glance—
The scymitar hath failed to match the Christian's
sacred lance.
Hosannas to the Crucified, O rescued nations, sing !
Let vaulted aisles and cloisters fair with glad *Te
Deums* ring !
Let light and bloom, and jewels rare, bedeck the
holy shrine,
Where lies our sweet thank-offering, the Victim-
Lamb divine ! .
From demon hand of sacrilege is saved the Christian
fane,
The peaceful homes of sanctity know not the lawless
train ;
The priceless gems of art and love will light no
Moslem fire,
No Christian cities whet the sword of Moslem hate
and ire.
Sing, then, your glad and grateful joy, ye favored
sons of art !
Breathe now, O child of eloquence ! the rapture of
thy heart ;
And, pale-browed scholar, let thy fair, illumined
pages tell
How Sobieski's Christian band hath checked the
infidel.

O holy city of our love! O heaven-guarded Rome!
Let ceaseless pæans grandly ring within thy mighty
    dome:
The feet of ruthless Saracens pass not within thy
    gate,
Thy martyrs' dust is unprofaned, thy shrines in-
    violate.
Hosanna to the Christians' God, who armed our
    swords with might!
And praise to her, whose potent aid hath blessed the
    Christian knight!
Mater Immaculata, hail! the Crescent's sheen is
    dross,
Thy smile hath dimmed its haughty ray, and crushed
    it 'neath the Cross!

CALIFORNIA'S RELICS: THE MISSIONS.

FULL many a theme of twilight song and story
    Yet lives in elder lands,
The stern-eyed Sphinx uplifts her forehead hoary
    Above the desert sands;

And Greece still holds, with firm, defiant power,
    From Lethe's dread abyss,
The ruined walls that yet so richly dower
    Her proud Acrópolis.

The castled height, of "legends quaint and olden"
    The fierce and fitting shrine,

Still darkly frowns within the sunset golden
   That lights the mystic Rhine.

But these are records of a clouded glory,
   When wrong o'ermastered right;
One burden dread fills all their sounding story,—
   The ruthless rule of might.

Ah! fairer far the relics thou enshrinest,
   Bright sovereign of the West!
O'er sacred walls a fadeless wreath thou twinest,
   The amaranth of the blest.

Nor Egypt's fanes, nor stately domes enclosing
   The sculptured gods of Greece,
Can match the homes of love divine, reposing
   Beneath the wings of peace.

No feudal halls, no banner-flaunting tower,
   Frowned grimly o'er the land;
Nor vassal-trains, nor mail-clad hands of power,
   Enforced a stern command.

Humbly they stood, yet crowned with sunny
   splendor,
   Those wondrous walls of clay;
A power benign, an influence sweet and tender,
   Held there its potent sway.

The gray-robed monk, the messenger of heaven,
   There ruled his willing band:
No blood-spot clung, nor taint of worldly leaven,
   To that anointed hand,—

That steadfast hand, to truth securely leading
   The forest's wayward child,—
That tender hand, that tamed, with silent pleading,
   The savage nature wild.

There docile hearts bowed low in adoration,
   When, 'neath that humble dome,
In sacred rite, in endless " clean oblation,"
   Love sought His earthly home.

And knees were bent, when rang the angel-story
   From out the mission-tower,
While gleamed its cross, with halo-crown of glory
   Twined by the sunset hour.

And so when crime, with trail of serpent, blighted
   The sheen of stately halls,
The tender beam of Eden-blessings lighted
   Those rude adobé walls.

O golden land! thy richest, rarest treasure
   Dwells not in darksome mines;
Still prouder wealth thou hast in countless measure,
   Thy holy mission-shrines.

Let Eastern lands yet vaunt, in song and story,
   Their ivy-mantled halls;
A halo-flame, a nimbus-wreath of glory,
   Encrowns *thy* sacred walls.

THE MOST HOLY ROSARY.

O ROYAL road, that heavenward leads
Along the chain of mystic beads!
O lily-chaplet, sweetly hid
The blood-empurpled thorns amid!
O rose-wreath, twining, pure and fair,
Around the holy heights of prayer,
Where love's bright cross begins and ends
The pilgrim-path that faith ascends!
Blest garland! on each shining bead
A rare and wondrous tale I read:
The life that rose in Bethlehem
Is traced on every sacred gem;
I see *her* sweet and sinless face,
Hailed by archangel, " full of grace!"
How gently falls each answ'ring word,
" Behold the handmaid of the Lord!"
I catch the gleam of angel wings;
Again their Christmas carol rings,
As on that eve when love began
The history of the God made man.
I follow all that childhood fair,
O'erwatched by Mary's tender care;
I feel the balm of incense-breath
His fair youth sheds o'er Nazareth,
And 'mid the lily's gleam I read
A joyous tale on every bead.

But shadows fall on balm and bloom
Amid the olive garden's gloom,
When o'er the Victim's spirit flow
The surging waves of human woe,
And on His sinless heart is hurled
The anguish of a guilty world.
The night of darkness shades the morn,
The Monarch wears His crown of thorn,
And mortals throng, with shout and sneer,
His royal pathway, strange and drear.
Nailed to His throne, the Martyr-King
Completes His reign of suffering;
A God redeems His creatures' loss
On the dread altar of the cross!
So, 'mid the blood-dyed thorns, I read
A doleful tale on every bead.

But lo! upon that weary way
Immortal Love's triumphal ray!
The tomb is rent, the night is gone,
And brightly breaks the Easter-dawn!
I see the risen Saviour stand
Amid His chosen awe-struck band;
I see Him fondly linger where
The flock still claims the Shepherd's care,
Until His promise sweet is given
Of comfort blest, and strength from heaven.
Then, from that heaven's opened doors,
A matchless flood of glory pours.
Love's prize is won! Love's labor ends!
The Victor to His throne ascends!

Yet Truth's assurance is not lost,
For, lo! the boons of Pentecost!
With tongues of flame and unction sweet,
Behold the promised Paraclete!
Bright visions bless inspiréd sight,
Unsealed is wisdom's fount of light,
For, heaven's own messengers must be
The fishermen of Galilee.
The Maiden-Mother, full of grace,
Again I greet her queenly face,—
She o'er a Saviour's childhood hung,
And to His cross unfalt'ring clung;
She in each sorrow bore her part:
The sword of grief had pierced her heart.
Now, in that Saviour's triumph fair,
The Mother claims her royal share;
New gladness thrills the angel throng,
New rapture swells the seraph's song.
The pain is past! the bliss is won!
The sinless Mother greets her Son!
And lo! the handmaid of the Lord
Receives her radiant reward,
And on her bright, unsullied brow
The peerless crown is gleaming now:
And so, 'mid regal gems, I read
A glorious tale on every bead.
O wondrous privilege to see
The visions of the Rosary!
To hear the mystic voice that reads
Redemption's story from the beads;
To linger, rapt in holy dream,
Where Israel's lily sheds its gleam;

To tread the peaceful path of prayer,
To mount o'er heaven's shining stair,
To clasp the bright, rose-jewelled band
That leadeth to the better land!

THE SHADOW OF THE CROSS

WEARY with the world's unrest,
  Blinded by its glare,
Gone devotion's holy zest,
  Gone its soothing prayer.

So I passed, with footsteps slow,
  Through the sunny street,
Shrinking from the summer-glow,
  Drooping in its heat.

Bitter wailing of despair
  Rose within my heart:
"Why," it moaned, "this cark and care?
  Why this anguish-smart?

"Why these weary burdens borne
  Through life's torrid day?
Why the pangs that make us mourn
  O'er its desert way?

"What can bid the torture cease?
  What can heal its pain?
Where the spell to bring ye peace,
  World-sick soul and brain?

"What, O Life! canst thou bestow
  For thy grief and loss?
Shadowed on the path below
  Saw I, then, a cross."

And a "still, small voice" arose
  Silenced heart within:
" Cease thy plaint of earthly woes,
  Cease thy thought of sin.

"Said He not, ' Take up the cross,
  Ye who follow Me :'
So the gain for every loss
  Limitless shall be.

"Ask'st thou whence thy sorrow's cure?
  Where the healing blest?
Lo! the promise, sweet and sure,
  ' I will give thee rest.' "

Then I raised my weary eyes
  Where the saving sign,
Pointing upward to the skies,
  Crowned the sacred shrine.

As a rock in desert land
  Cooling shadow throws,
Bringing to the pilgrim band
  Shelter and repose ;

So that shadow o'er my path
  Wrought its soothing spell,
When, 'mid noontide's fiercest wrath,
  Tenderly it fell.

And I went, with humble tread,
  From earth's blinding glare,
Where the lighted altar shed
  Radiance soft and fair ;

There my fainting spirit found
  Shelter and repose,
Resting, on that holy ground,
  From her weary woes.

And remembering One forlorn,
  That she might be free,
Toiling, crowned with cruel thorn,
  On to Calvary.

Ceased she then her sad complaint—
  Seeing woe and loss
But the shadowed image faint
  Of her Master's Cross.

THE PASSION FLOWER.

I GAZE with trembling awe and fear
  Upon thy purple glory,
Thou strange, mysterious souvenir
  Of earth's most wondrous story!

Weep, human eyes! ay, weep to read,
  Enshrined in nature's jewel,
Dread record of a direful deed
  Of sacrilege most cruel.

When to His death the Victim-God
  Toiled, anguish-worn and weary,
Didst rise, sad blossom, where He trod,
  To deck that path most dreary?

Ay, fancy sees thy petals shine
  Where His faint footsteps falter,
Until thy clinging tendrils twine
  Round Calvary's blood-stained altar.

And from that scene of woe and scorn
  Thou bring'st the fearful vision
Of purple robe and crown of thorn,
  His creatures' blind derision.

I trace each emblem, strangely clear,
  Amid thy mystic glory:
The nails, the gall-soaked sponge, the spear,—
  Types of that mournful story.

'Tis well the record thus to see,
  That each regretful dreamer
May shrine, in tender memory,
  Thy love, O sweet Redeemer!

O martyr-God! O Lamb Divine!
  If earthly blooms that perish
Form of their purple leaves a shrine
  Thy matchless woes to cherish,

How meet that human blossoms fair
  Those blessed types should borrow,
And through our blighted Eden bear
  The likeness of Thy sorrow!

That so, beside the living stream,
  In heaven's unfading bowers,
Our souls may wear the royal gleam
  Of Love's own passion flowers.

MAPLE LEAVES.

O CHILDHOOD'S home across the sea!
　O sweet and sunny past,
By dream-light guided back to me
　O'er waters wild and vast!
O'er wintry wastes of grief and care,
　O'er desert paths of pain,
In glowing freshness, pure and fair,
　The bright scenes throng again ;
And Memory's fond and skilful hand
　Full many a vision weaves,—
Each bright with tints of Fairy-land,
　And crowned with maple leaves:

A country home, with velvet lawn,
　And fields of golden grain
And fragrant meadows stretching on,
　Beyond the grassy lane ;
With garden wealth of glowing flowers,
　With orchard treasures rare,
With vine-wreath'd porch, and trellised bowers,
　O'erhung with blossoms fair ;
Yet o'er the winding lane I rove,
　Beyond the golden sheaves,
For, yonder waves the maple grove,
　Enrobed with glossy leaves.

What joy beneath those leaves to sit,
  In Summer's softened glow,
And watch the fairy shadows flit
  O'er mossy dells below!
O wondrous books of ancient rhyme!
  How oft your magic words
Were blended there, in tuneful chime,
  With songs of woodland birds!
And many a tale of sylvan fay,
  Which childish faith receives,
Was learned where morning's glory lay
  Upon the maple leaves.

The picture fades—another dream
  Shines on my spellbound sight,
And village walls of whiteness gleam
  In Summer's rosy light;
And o'er the wide and silent street
  Fair trees for ever bend,
And twined, as in communings sweet,
  Their whispering branches blend.
Bright maple boughs, my casement's shade!
  Weird Fancy fondly weaves
Her dreams, in rainbow hues arrayed,
  Amid your graceful leaves.

O fair, lost home beyond the seas!
  Through tear-drops falling fast,
I see your softly waving trees,
  And greet the risen past.
In green and glossy robes of Spring
  Those stately guardians stand,

And sigh their tender murmuring
　To Summer's breezes bland ;
And Autumn's mellow sunlight glints,
　And Autumn's sad wind grieves,
Where brightly gleam the gorgeous tints
　Of dying maple leaves.

And Winter drapes, in fleecy snow,
　The branches brown and bare,
And leafless stems in brightness glow
　With icy crystals fair ;
And so, the charms that cannot fade
　Upon those maples nest,
And Peace, within their magic shade,
　Has built her Eden rest ;
And I, in visions bright and calm,
　Gaze on, while Memory weaves
And dowers, with sweet and soothing balm,
　Her crowns of maple leaves.

ADELAIDE ANNE PROCTER.*

PEACE warbled through her poet-life
    Its strain of magic sweetness,
And every golden day was rife
    With Summer's glad completeness.

An English landscape, fair and calm,
    Greets now her grateful vision,
And now Italia's bloom and balm
    Bring happiness Elysian.

And shores of blest enchantment smiled
    Where'er her life-bark drifted,—
Meet pictures for a poet's child,
    Rare glories for the gifted.

---

* Adelaide Anne Procter was the eldest child of Bryan Walter Proc ter, best known, as a poet, by his *nom de plume* of "Barry Corn-wall." His glorious gift was inherited by his sweet and gentle daughter, the character of whose poetry is best described by a quotation from an article in the *Catholic World*, entitled, "The poems of Adelaide Anne Procter." The writer says : "Their simple, delicate beauty appeals alike to men and women, and to the soul of the young child; their transparent clearness is that of an unusually lucid intellect; their profoundness is only that of a believing heart." Her conversion to the Catholic faith took place when she was about twenty-four years of age. Her life had ever been peaceful as a summer day, and her death was tranquil as its close. On the Feast of the Purification the heavenly messenger came, and, amid the prayers of the Church, whose faithful child she was, her gentle spirit passed away. *Requiescat in pace!*

Yet, though she trod a sunny way,
  No idler may we deem her,
No laggard through the busy day,
  No self-indulgent dreamer.

Her glowing pen, her ringing song,
  Ceased not its earnest labor
To plead the right, to crush the wrong,
  To soothe her woe-worn neighbor.

And in the fragrant Southern land,
  With Truth's white garment o'er her,
She knelt, with Faith's illumined band,
  A fervent, rapt adorer.

Ah! well she loved the gleaming shrine,
  Home of the man-God hidden,
Where to the Bridegroom's feast divine
  His faithful ones are bidden.

And sweet her song of chapels, where
  The Maiden-Mother holy
Smiled gracious answer to the prayer
  Of hearts sincere and lowly.

And on that Mother's festal day
  The lights that graced her altar,
Shone softly o'er the heavenward way
  Of feet that would not falter;

For then that fair life reached its close,
  And death's calm angel sought her,
To bring the better land's repose
  To Poesy's sweet daughter.

So passed she to its blissful rest,
   And lay, a tranquil dreamer,
Close clasping to her pulseless breast
   The cross of her Redeemer.

Bright flowers! lend your fragrant bloom
   To grace that grave-bed lowly,
And, sunlight! let no shadow-gloom
   Bedim its brightness holy ;

For, the dear dust, so treasured there,
   Held once a sweet soul-flower—
Transplanted, lo! it bloometh fair
   In amaranthine bower.

O happy lot, a poet-life,
   Kept free from earth's vile leaven !
A " grand, sweet song " to calm its strife,
   And ring fore'er in heaven.

THE LESSON HEEDED *

THE sounds of festal music rose within a stately hall,
And garlands shone, and banners waved, upon its
gilded wall ;
A gay and goodly company were brightly gathered
there,—
The youthful and the nobly born, the valiant and
the fair.
Unheeded fled the smiling night amid the tumult
sweet,
The strains of witching melody, the tread of dancing
feet ;
Nor faintest note of graver thought could sound
its warning knells,
Where rang the tones of pleasure's lute, the clang
of folly's bells.
And, 'mid the proud and jewelled throng that
graced that festal scene,
One peerless star serenely shone a fondly wor-
shipped queen :

---

* These lines were suggested by an incident in the life of Nano
Nagle, foundress of the Presentation Order. This lady was one of the
brightest ornaments of the French Court. Returning one morning
from a royal ball, she saw a crowd of people waiting at a church door
for early Mass. So deeply was she struck with the contrast between
their self-sacrificing piety and her own life of vanity and frivolous
pleasure, that she immediately formed the resolution of casting off the
livery of worldly pride, and consecrating herself to the service of the
"meek and lowly Jesus." How perfectly she fulfilled this glorious
intention, let the noble Order she founded, and its beautiful work
among the children of the poor, bear witness.

O'er all the gleaming galaxy of brightest beauty
    there,
That high-born maid of Erin reigned the fairest of
    the fair.

   *   *   *   *   *   *   *   *   *

A murmur of the coming morn dissolved the spells
    of night,
And through the shadows dimly peered the herald
    beams of light;
And as the day its throne upreared within the
    golden East,
An eager throng thus early came to share a nuptial
    feast.
A grand and goodly company had fondly gathered
    there,
Yet not in silken raiment clad, nor decked with
    jewels rare;
In mean and tattered drapery they braved the
    wintry cold,
And oft the thin and pallid cheek its dismal story
    told.
Yet grand were they, those heirs of heaven, those
    children of the King,
And goodly was the company o'erwatched by
    angel wing;
Nor proud heraldic blazonry, nor wreath'd and
    gilded wall,
Could match that Monarch's matin feast, that Bride-
    groom's banquet-hall.
And while they humbly knelt beside the yet un-
    opened door,
The worldly revel hushed its strain, the stately
    dance was o'er.

And now from worship false and vain, from gods
    of frailest clay,
The star of courtly splendor turned, in weariness,
    away ;
And as she sought her regal home, a strange,
    unwonted scene
Met, on her way, the startled gaze of pleasure's
    petted queen :
She saw the lowly band that knelt beside the temple's
    gate,
She saw the " meek and humble " ones their matin
    feast await ;
And lo ! the Master seemed amid His chosen flock
    to stand,
With dust upon His tattered robe, and blood-drops
    on His hand :
" Behold ! " He cried, " the picture pure, the lesson
    traced for thee ;
Thus early seek thou wisdom's gate, thus early
    wait for Me."
   *   *   *   *   *   *   *   *   *
They gathered in a simple room that knew no carv-
    ing rare,
No banner with its proud device, no festal garland
    fair ;
And none amid that childish band could boast a
    lordly name—
They were the children of the poor, unknown to
    rank or fame.
They gathered fondly, lovingly, around a gentle nun,
And sweetly, for the Master's sake, she gave each
    little one

Pure lessons of the precious love that once on earth
He taught,—

Glad knowledge of the wondrous work their hidden
Saviour wrought.

Thus was the warning heeded well, for, lo! that
gentle guide

Was she who reigned, a royal rose, within the
realms of pride,—

Was she who shone with brightest ray amid the
gleaming train

That glided through the stately hall to music's
witching strain.

Her voice, of softest, sweetest tone, had breathed
the solemn vow,

The sable veil replaceth now the gems that decked
her brow;

The dress of coarsest serge enshrouds the form of
queenly grace

That lately wore the costly robe, the scarf of dainty
lace.

But pleasure's vot'ry never knew, amid the pomp
of pride,

The peace divine that fills the heart of heaven's
holy bride;

For she hath watched at wisdom's gate, hath heard
the summons blest,

Hath cast the worldly burden down, and found the
promised rest.

Sweet is the Master's sacred yoke, His service
maketh glad,

And rare the feast she shareth now, in "wedding
garment" clad;

And oft she sees, in vision fair, the shining jasper
  walls,
The amaranthine garlands twined o'er heaven's
  banquet-halls;
And sweetly falleth on her ear the welcome of her
  Lord:
" Well done, thou pure and faithful one! behold thy
  rich reward!"

THE EARTH-ANGEL.

I GAZED upon the motley throng
  That filled the sunny street,
I heard the din of Babel tongues,
  The tread of busy feet;
I saw the silken robes of pride,
  And all its bright array
Of gems, that flashed, in rainbow light,
  Defiance to the day;
And yet I marked how oft the sheen
  Of trappings, rich and rare,
Still darker showed the shades of woe,
  The clouds of brooding care
How ghastly shone the vacant smile
  On faces wan and worn,
How hollow rang the gladsome words
  From hearts by anguish torn.

How petty spite and secret scorn
   Were hissed in accents bland,
And hidden hatred lurked within
   The clasp of friendly hand.

Ay, mirrored in that shining street,
   And echoed by its din,
Were all a selfish world's unrest,
   And hollowness, and sin.
But lo! upon that busy path
   I saw a gliding form,
That seemed to bear a spell of peace
   To soothe the restless storm;
For, silenced was the Babel tone,
   And, 'mid that motley crowd,
Full many a brow of pride and scorn
   In deepest rev'rence bowed.
'Twas well: that form in coarsest serge
   Outshone, in heaven's view,
The haughty sheen of worldly gems,
   The robes of rainbow hue;
And 'neath its quaint white covering
   How gleamed that gentle face
With halo-light of peace serene,
   And calm, unearthly grace!

How fair her gems,—the mystic beads,
   The rose-wreaths pure and fair,
The sacred chain that sweetly leads
   To sunlit heights of prayer!

Daughter of Vincent, meek and pure,
  'Twas meet to honor thee,
O bride of Christ, and handmaid fair
  Of dove-eyed Charity!
Thou lead'st the helpless orphan lamb
  From weary waste and wold
Safe to the pastures fresh and green,
  Safe to the Master's fold.

Thou shrinkest not from battle-storm,
  Thou tread'st the crimson plain,
Where speedeth Moloch's cruel car
  Above the heaps of slain;
Thou kneelest where the warrior lies
  On that ensanguined sod,
And showest, to his dying gaze,
  The image of his God.
Thou biddest care, and want, and woe,
  Their dread dominion cease,
Thou bringest to the stricken earth
  The blessed boons of peace:
Be honored, then, in highways broad,
  As in thy calm retreat!
Be honored whereso'er shall pass
  .Thy consecrated feet!

A CONGRATULATORY RHYME.

[Affectionately addressed to Mrs. H. D. on the birth of her daughter, at Geneva, Switzerland.]

O NEVER brought the swelling sail
    A richer freight or fairer,
And ne'er of dearer, fonder tale
    Was snowy dove the bearer,
Than when, upon its pinions fleet,
    Beneath the boundless water,
The lightning sent its message sweet,
    That bade us bless thy daughter.
Thy daughter! To the countless hearts
    That hold thee chiefest treasure,
The utterance of that name imparts
    Electric thrills of pleasure,
And bids each grateful spirit be
    A telegraphic station,
Whence love shall flash across the sea
    Its glad congratulation;
And, blended with the words that greet
    Thy pure and priceless treasure,
We waft the prayer, that graces sweet
    Be hers in boundless measure.
Good angels guard her smiling rest,
    And watch her gleeful waking!
Within her soul its sacred nest
    May peace be ever making!

Bright be her life as is the glow
  Of Leman's placid fountain,
And pure as shines the stainless snow
  That crowns her Switzer mountain!
O thus we blend, with greetings fond,
  Unnumbered fervent blessings,
And waft, the restless waves beyond,
  Our countless, glad caressings:
Our kisses for the brow still bright
  With blest baptismal water;
Our smiles, to crown with tend'rest light
  The gem of gems—thy daughter!

BISHOP McFARLAND.

(IN MEMORIAM.)

THE warder stricken from the bannered wall!
  The leader lost amid the battle's heat!
The voice so still, that rang the warning call!
  The arm so numb, that gave the foe defeat!

But Zion's King hath called her faithful guard,
  And bade His warrior in His triumph share:
The loyal servant claims his earned reward,
  The soldier resteth from the battle-care.

O warders, that succeed him on the tower!
  Keep watch like his, around, above, below;
O hands, that grasp his shining sword of power!
  Be strong, like him, to check the daring foe.

And hosts, that miss him from the ceaseless strife!
    Think he awaits you in the home of peace;
Fight till *your day* with noblest deeds is rife,
    Fight till, like him, ye win the glad release.

Ah, valorous chief! the sounding voice of fame
    Hath rung thy glory through the East and West;
The sunset-sea doth sing thy mighty name,
    And climes remote give thee their homage blest.

And now, when tidings of thy loss are borne,
    In wailing tones, across the Western wave,
Our grief doth rise, *our* sorrowing spirits mourn
    The pastor true, the leader bright and brave.

Though fairest garlands deck the sacred shrine
    That holds thee, treasure of the favored East!
May I not add this simple wreath of mine?
    Sincere the tribute, though, in worth, the least.

Take, then, the gift, O spirit pure and blest!
    And, from thy place amid the ever free,
Plead for the flocks, earth-roaming, till they rest
    In " pastures green," by " waters still," with thee.

REV. THOMAS BRIODY.

GONE! ere he reached life's fair, meridian height!
Gone! while his path was bright with summer's
　bloom
And the glad glory of the morning sun!
Why grew his step so weary that he turned
From the white harvest and the vintage fair,
From the dear flocks that knew their shepherd's
　voice,
From the decked altar and the waiting feast,
To seek the silent slumber of the tomb?
Because his work was finished, and he heard
The Master's voice that called him to his rest.
The wondrous echoes of the seraph-song
Fell on his list'ning ear: afar he saw
A radiant multitude, enshrined within
The glory streaming from the "great white throne;"
Then fondly rang his glad, ecstatic cry,
"Here am I, Lord! my Master! lo! I come!"
O faithful pastor! from thy place beside
The "fair, still waters," thou wilt cast adown
Thy guardian glance upon the helpless flock
Still roaming where, across the desert path,
The torrid glare falls fiercely, or the shade
Of the chill cloud conceals the thorny snare.
Ay, thou wilt guide them till the sunset hour;
And, when the night falls darkly, thou wilt call
Each wanderer homeward to the shelt'ring fold,
And the "green pastures" of his rest with thee.

NELLIE.

(IN MEMORIAM.)

[Inscribed to Mrs. R. Finley.]

SOFT, dove-like eyes, and brow serenely fair,
   Crowning a pale, sweet face,
Where the calm strength a martyr's look might
    wear,
   Shines with its saintly grace.

So, through the pain-fraught years that marked her
   life,
   A patient sufferer smiled;
So bloomed a flower, with heaven's own sweetness
   rife,
   Within earth's dreary wild.

So, angel-guarded, in its shrine of clay
   A radiant jewel slept;
Secure, "unspotted from the world," it lay,
   And changeless lustre kept.

But, 'mid the weeds that throng our earthly way,
   Heaven's flow'ret found no room;
Unheeded, shone its pearl's transcendent ray
   Within this prison gloom.

So, on white wings, death's angel floated down—
   A casket earth enshrines;
But, 'mid the gems that light th' Eternal's crown,
   Another jewel shines.

With soft hands folded on the pulseless breast,
  A white-robed figure lies:
A ransomed soul hath found its welcome rest
  In radiant paradise.

Peace, mourning hearts! upon whose household
    light
Death's sable shadow fell ;
With her, whose absence brings the gloom of night,
  Lo! angels say, " Tis well."

Ay, well to know the blest, unbroken sleep,
  To His beloved given,—
The Sabbath peace, the slumber calm and deep,
  The blissful rest of heaven.

MRS. SARAH E. McCORMACK.

O King of Terrors! thou did'st seek
  A fair, transcendent prize:
The glow upon a matchless cheek,
  The light of tender eyes.

The queenly grace, serenely set
  Upon a noble brow,
Life's rare and radiant coronet,—
  This is thy treasure now.

The smile that on a bright lip played
  Like sunlight, soft and warm ;
The majesty whose charm arrayed
  A lithe and stately form,—

These were her gifts, whose cordial hand
   So late was clasped in mine,
When first, within our Western land,
   I saw her clear eyes shine.

Her childhood's home beyond the wave
   For ever dark must be :
Its household light hath found a grave
   Beside the Western Sea ;

And stricken hearts are mourning here,
   Above that lonely bed ;
And heavy sigh, and bitter tear,
   Bewail the cherished dead.

O holy Church ! thy mother-heart
   Still clasps the child of grace ;
And naught its links of love can part,
   Or rend its fond embrace.

Thy potent prayer and sacred rite
   Embalm the precious clay,
That waits the resurrection-light,—
   The fadeless Easter day.

And loving hearts, by faith entwined,
   True to that faith shall be,
And keep the sister-soul enshrined
   In tender memory ;

Shall bid the ceaseless prayer ascend,
   To win her guerdon blest :
The radiant day that hath no end,
   The calm, eternal rest.

MRS. ADA BAINE GUILLEN.

A LILY-BLOOM from life's fair chaplet riven,
  A star-beam quenched in gloom,
A priceless pearl, in purest lustre given
  To deck the dismal tomb;

A precious life, by patient suff'ring brightened,
  And crowned with graces rare,
Whose magic sheen, by anguish-pallor heightened,
  Grew yet more strangely fair,

Till the pure glow, the radiance resplendent,
  Filled that last hour with light,
And left its gleam of loveliness transcendent,
  E'en on the veil of night,—

This was the boon that blessed your earthly bower,
  O hearts by anguish torn!
These were the charms that decked your cherished
    flower,—
  Her graces fitly worn.

Yet, peace! the jewels of her life are rendered
  To Him whose love bestowed;
With added charms, lo! angel hands have tendered
  Gift meet for His abode.

The lily-bloom within His fadeless bowers
  Sheds now its fragrant light,
For the glad beauty of immortal flowers
  Is won by mortal blight.

Rememb'ring earth, with all its sorrows weary,
  How glad the voice of praise
Of that sweet life, that gave its darkness dreary
  For heaven's eternal rays !

Check, then, the murmurs of your human sorrow,
  And hush the wail of woe—
See, stricken ones! the glory of a morrow
  That ne'er can lose its glow :

The shining courts within the pearly portal,
  Where ransomed spirits meet ;
The gleaming throng, where white-robed throngs immortal
  Bow at their Monarch's feet.

There shall the flowers, from love's chaplet riven,
  By love's dear hand be twined ;
And there the gems, to death's cold casket given,
  Each grateful heart shall find.

There shall ye clasp, in tenderest caressings,
  Your lost, restored again ;
And there forget, 'mid heaven's fadeless blessings,
  Earth's weariness and pain.

MRS. MARGARET C. MAHONEY.

TRUE register of Christian grace,
   Fair crown of deathless fame,
And fitting epitaph to trace
   Beneath thy cherished name!
Ay, thou art with the blessed dead,
   Thou claim'st their bright reward
Who follow, with unfalt'ring tread,
   The footsteps of their Lord.
In vain earth showed each golden prize—
   For thee 'twas worthless dross,
And naught could turn thy steadfast eyes
   From truth's unfading cross;
For wisdom lent her aid divine,
   And thy pure glance could see
The motto of that saving sign,
   " All else is vanity."
Rare lessons hath thy precious life,
   By blest example, taught,—
By deeds with duty's fragrance rife,
   With heaven's sweetness fraught.
The stricken hearts in anguish bowed,
   The eyes that weep thy loss,
Yet see the stars within the cloud,
   The halo o'er the cross;

The light reflected from thy crown,
  The pure and peaceful ray,
Sent from thy home of brightness down,
  To guide their upward way.
Sweet memory of thy virtues, shrined
  The pall of woe beneath ;
Bright garland of thy graces twined
  With sorrow's cypress wreath,—
This is thy legacy of love,
  That gladdens e'en the tomb ;
These are the star-beams from above,
  Still shining through the gloom.
And these shall deck the golden stair
  O'er which thy loved shall tread,
To claim, with thee, their places fair,
  Among the blessed dead.

LITTLE BERTHA.

[Inscribed to Mrs. W. H. Gleason.]

A NEW angelic voice
  To swell the ceaseless song!
O white-robed choir, rejoice!
  Be glad, ye seraph throng!
Another shining beam
  Of heaven's fadeless sun,
Another jewel-gleam,
  In spotless lustre won!
An opening lily, fraught
  With fresh baptismal dew,

In primal beauty brought
　To blossom in love's view!
A white lamb, angel-led
　Unto the peaceful fold,
A birdling early fled
　From wintry cloud and cold!
O mourning mother-heart!
　Look upward from thy woe;
Behold, the shadows part,
　The morning splendors glow!
Upon the gleaming skies,
　Lo! visions. glad and fair,
In matchless glory rise,
　To charm thy spirit's care.
The white-robed legions stand
　Before the Monarch's throne,
And, 'mid the shining band,
　Lo! treasures once thine own.
Ay, throned among the blest,
　All earthly fetters riven,
Safe, safe on Jesus' breast,
　Two angels thou hast given.
Two guardians hast thou won,
　For thee to watch, to pray,
And, when the night is done,
　To guide thee to the day.
And though thy path be drear,
　Thy pilgrim journey long,
Unceasing, on thy ear,
　Shall fall their soothing song,
Till, at the " great white throne,"
　Where saints adoring bend,

Thy own triumphant tone
    With seraph strains shall blend ;
And, gazing face to face,
    Where glory's torrents pour,
Thy children's fond embrace
    Shall clasp thee evermore.

MRS. MANUELA T. CURTIS.

Give all your wealth, O balmy bowers!
O choicest store of cherished flowers!
Bring now your fondest tributes here,
The fragrant sigh, the dewy tear.
Let all your hues of light entwine
Around the fair, yet faded, shrine,
The casket frail, the blighted bower,
That held *our* sweet transplanted flower.
Ay, yours will be an off'ring meet,
For ye have lived in kinship sweet.
She ministered, with tender care,
To sister blossoms, pure and fair ;
And, mirrored in your bloom, we trace
Sweet semblance of her spirit grace :
The fragrant charm, the shining dower,
That decked our fair, immortal flower,

O kindly hand, that death hath chilled!
O faithful heart, for ever stilled!
Dread darkness! hast thou kept no ray,
No promise, of a coming day?

Must hope be lost in sorrow's sea,
And love lie mute with agony?
No! shining through the night of woe,
Behold the sweet auroral glow!
Hope on the Living Rock shall stand,
And show its beam with steady hand,
While love shall break the spell of pain
With echoes of her soothing strain:
" The Lord His covenant shall keep,
And give to His beloved sleep.
O sweet soul-flower! securely rest
In verdant pastures, calm and blest.
Lo! where the stainless lily glows,
Where bloometh Sharon's royal rose,—
Beneath life's fair, unfading tree
For evermore thy place shall be;
And there, at last, shall fondly bloom
Thy loved ones, rescued from the gloom—
Transplanted from the earthly sod,
To deck the garden of their God."

GWIN MAYNARD.

O DARK death-angel, messenger of woe!
  The "gleaming mark" thou lovest well is thine!
A bright young life is withered 'neath thy blow;
  The casket pure, the fair and fitting shrine
Of earth's best gem,—a fresh, unsullied heart,—
Lies rent and ruined 'neath thy ruthless dart.

So richly dowered with each youthful grace,
  So bright with promise of a glorious life;
A fair soul mirrored in a fair young face,
  With all the charms of life's sweet spring-time
    rife,—
Could not such bloom the angel-reaper stay?
Alas! alas! it is his best-loved prey.

The reaper's prey! Yet, words with comfort
    fraught!
  'Tis "for his Lord he binds the golden sheaves;"
For heaven's bright bowers the seeming spoiler
    sought
  The bloom, with dewy freshness on its leaves.
That rare soul-flower, that gem of priceless worth,
Was all too bright, too beautiful, for earth.

Swiftly he snatched the blossom from its stem,
  Ere dust could soil, or trailing serpent blight—
Look, eye of faith! in love's own diadem,
  A jewel new, enshrined in living light!
O mourning hearts! behold your treasure fair,
Safe, safe and shining, in the Master's care!

The storms may beat, the winds blow chill and cold,
　　No blast disturbs *his* summer air serene :
Earth's withered leaves may lie on wood and wold,
　　Heaven's stately trees are robed in living green :
While clouds brood darkly o'er earth's frosty sod,
Eternal sunshine floods the fields of God.

E. H. COMERFORD, M. D.

[Died in Kilkenny, Ireland, January 7, 1875.]

SWEET is the memory of the just,
　　And well the bard hath said
Their " actions blossom in the dust,"
　　And sweet aroma shed ;

Each deed, with purest purpose fraught,
　　Shall live in deathless bloom,
Though cold may lie the hand that wrought,
　　Within the silent tomb.

So live *thy* deeds, O healer kind,
　　That soothed with tend'rest art !
So lives thy fragrant memory, shrined
　　In many a grateful heart.

So hath thy life its blossoms won
　　Of sweet, celestial hue,
Thou faithful friend, thou tender son,
　　Thou brother, fond and true !

How shines thy name in letters clear,
  Which angel hands record:
"The soul that knew nor stain nor fear,
  True mirror of its Lord."

Thy Erin, sweetest Isle of Saints,
  Is fair and fitting shrine,—
Where serpent-venom never taints,—
  For sacred dust like thine.

But while, beyond the Western Sea,
  An echo cometh, rife
With true and tender eulogy
  Of thy untarnished life,

Made bold by faith's fraternal band,
  That linketh clime to clime,
Upon thy grave, with stranger hand,
  I lay my wreath of rhyme.

In spirit there I breathe my prayer:
  O may thy soul be blest,
With beatfiic vision fair,
  In glad, eternal rest!

JAMES McNALLY.

[Inscribed to his mother.]

EARTH prisons in her shrines of clay
  Full many a jewel rare,—
Bright gems, resplendent with the ray
  The King's own treasures wear ;
And many a fair and fragile flower,
  For love's own garden meet,
Sheds o'er our lone, sin-blighted bower
  Celestial odors sweet.

So, oft the rare and radiant gem
  From earthly shrine is borne,
And often from its fragile stem
  The stainless bloom is torn.
Thy leaves, O sweet, transplanted flower !
  The Master fain would see
Safe sheltered in His fadeless bower,
  By life's immortal tree.
And thou shalt deck His kingly crown,
  O gem of priceless worth !
And still thy splendor, shining down,
  Shall light the gloom of earth.

O mother-heart ! by anguish riven,
  O grief-rent soul ! be calm ;
And with the blow thy God has given,
  Receive His healing balm.

While many a weary pilgrim-waif
  'Mid earthly snares must roam,
The treasure of thy love is safe
  Within his Father's home;
While darkly rests the serpent-blight
  On many a blossom fair,
Its robes of pure, unsullied white
  Thy lily-plant shall wear.

Ay, twine across his snowy hand
  His chaplet—sacred chain!—
That linked him to the shining band,
  The Queen's seraphic train;
And childish comrades, angel-led,
  With him, through earthly snare,
Glide on, with soft and reverent tread,
  Beside that body fair,

Until, upon its couch of clay,
  That favored form shall rest,
To wait the last, eternal day,
  The summons glad and blest.
For then, within His diadem,
  Love's royal hand shall twine
The blossom and its glowing stem,
  The jewel and its shrine.

HARRY MASSEY.

A FAIR and fragrant memory
  For ever shall be thine,
Full many a heart shall treasure thee
  In sweet and sacred shrine:
Full many a voice shall fondly breathe
  Thy dear and cherished name,
Full many a hand for thee shall wreathe
  The fadeless crown of fame.

The frankness of thy sunny smile
  That mirrored peace within,
Thy glance, undimmed by worldly guile,
  Unmarred by care and sin ;
Thy noble brow, the fitting throne
  Of hopes sublime and high,
The brilliant dreams that brightly shone
  From out thy thoughtful eye;

Thy graceful gifts, thy worship fond
  Of all things pure and sweet,
Thy aim, in higher paths beyond,
  To tread with willing feet,—
These are the relics, sweetly set
  In pictured thoughts of thee,—
The soft'ning shadows of regret
  O'er lights of memory.

And yet, no shadow can enshroud
　　The fair and fadeless ray,
Where love shall trace, beyond the cloud,
　　Thy bright excelsior way ;
And o'er that path of blissful light
　　Religion's hand doth twine
Her mystic chain, serenely bright,
　　Her links of faith divine.

In fond communion, joined for e'er
　　Within that sacred band,
Lo ! heaven doth shed its splendor fair
　　O'er earth's lone desert-land.
Thus linked within one blessed fold,
　　One holy bond of grace,
The mourning mother-heart shall hold
　　Her child in fond embrace.

The loved ones yet in exile left,
　　The sorrow-stricken band,
The household group, of joy bereft
　　By ruthless reaper's hand,—
Shall still in closest union blend,
　　And o'er that path of prayer,
With fearless footsteps, shall ascend
　　The angel-guarded stair,
Until, beyond its golden gates,
　　The gathered flock shall see
The " pastures fair," where love awaits
　　Its glad eternity.

THE ANGEL AND CHILD.

[Translated from the French, for Mrs. A. E. S.]

AN angel passed, on wings of light,
 From out the blest, adoring number,
And softly took his earthward flight,
 To watch an infant's rosy slumber;
And, mirrored in the placid face,
 Thus by his guardian glance protected,
His own pure smile of heav'nly grace
 He saw, as in a brook, reflected.
"Sweet child!" the holy watcher said,
 "Thou angel-likeness, pure and tender!
O come with me, where seraphs tread
 The pathway of celestial splendor!
Fly to thy home of cloudless joy!
 Earth merits not so fair a treasure;
Her golden gifts are base alloy,
 The worthless boons of worldly pleasure.
Here, smiles foretell the weary sigh,
 And sunbeams hide in shades of sadness;
The wail of woe, the anguish-cry,
 Succeed the ringing shouts of gladness.
Grim fear is joy's unwelcome guest,
 Mirth smiles, the messenger of sorrow;
To-day the vales in calmness rest,
 The tempest rules unchecked to-morrow.

Shall terror pale this shining brow?
  Shall grief o'ercloud its smiling sweetness,
And dim those azure eyes, that now
  Are bright with joy's serene completeness?
No! no! thy sunny path must be
  O'er fadeless fields and meadows vernal,
Where star-crowned Peace shall shed o'er thee
  The radiance of a day eternal.
And thou through endless years shalt wear
  The angel garb, the robe of brightness,
And no dark stain of guilt or care
  Can ever soil thy vesture's whiteness;
No grief shall shroud, in midnight gloom,
  Thy soul's serene and smiling splendor,
Nor show the dark and cruel tomb,
  Concealed in bloom and brightness tender.
Then fly, sweet child! away! away!
  Ere time can dim the smile thou wearest:
Earth's parting hour, her latest day,
  Shall be thy happiest and fairest."

The angel, 'neath his wings of light,
  Hath fondly clasped a sinless brother;
To heaven they take their willing flight—
  Thy child is dead. Alas! poor mother!

IRELAND'S CONSECRATION TO THE SACRED HEART.

[None who have read the beautiful and touching descriptions of the Consecration of Ireland to the Sacred Heart, could fail to utter, with heartfelt earnestness, "How sweet and how fitting!" Ay, sweet and holy is the love that prompted that solemn, sacred offering; and most fitting is it that the riven heart of long-suffering Erin should be thus consecrated to the wounded, sword-rent Heart of the King of Sorrows, her Divine Master and Model.]

IT was a worthy offering for Faith's own martyr-
    land,—
Her bleeding heart unto her Lord's thus bound by
    sacred band;
It was a consecration meet for her whose heart
    hath known,
Through ages dread, through ages long, an anguish
    like His own;
But, pierced and wrung, that loyal heart was still
    His truth's abode,
Still clear within its guarded shrine, the sacred
    flame hath glowed
And blended in the weary wail, and wafted with
    the sigh,
The incense-breath of purest praise and love
    ascended high,
And O what manna-stores of grace from out His
    Sacred Heart
Flowed down to bless the stricken land that bore
    her faithful part;

That faltered not, that murmured not, her cruel
cross to take,
That bore the lash, and wore the thorns, and suf-
fered for His sake!
But blessed balm of Gilead, and dew of Hermon
sweet,
Have healed the wound, and cooled the wrath, of
persecution's heat;
Have won for her the magic strength that never
can depart,
For 'tis the blest supernal strength that fills the
Sacred Heart.
And so 'tis meet, O martyr-land! that on one sacred
shrine
Thy bleeding heart should offered be, beside the
Heart Divine,
That, in the shadow of its strength, thou may'st
securely rest,
And trace a truer copy still,—a likeness yet more
blest.
And shall not other lands prepare an offering like
thine?
Respond, Columbia, starry-crowned! respond, O
land of mine!
Wilt thou not deck a worthy shrine within the
golden West,
And offer there the noble heart that beats within
thy breast?*

---

* Since the above poem was written, most of, if not all, the dioceses of
the United States have been consecrated to the Sacred Heart of Jesus.

Wilt thou not clasp the golden links that naught
    can rend apart,
And breathe thy consecration-vow unto the Sacred
    Heart?
O prelates, princes of the realms o'erruled by
    endless Love!
O ye who stand as sentinels on Zion's walls above!
Ah, will ye not within those realms the Sacred
    Heart enshrine,
And trace upon Columbia's heart a likeness all
    divine?
The Heart that throbbed with deathless love in
    Bethlehem's lowly cave,
The Heart that unto Nazareth's cot its Eden-beauty
    gave;
The Heart that pulsed with tenderness, when,
    through the crowded street,
By lonely shore, in desert wild, He walked with
    tireless feet;
The Heart within whose sacred depths the bound-
    less anguish-sea
Surged wildly, on that wondrous night, in drear
    Gethsemane;
The Heart that broke for very love, when rung the
    bitter cry,
That told a world its life was won—its God had
    deigned to die,—
That Sacred Heart, that Sacred Heart, its deathless
    pulses yet
Are throbbing with its mighty love, its yearning,
    fond regret

That they for whom it panteth thus, for whom its
love doth glow,
No answering throb of gratitude, no flame respon-
sive, know.
Then give unto the Sacred Heart the rich and
radiant land,
And bind her heart to endless love in Love's eternal
band ;
Let incense wreathe, let flowers bloom, where hearts
adoring bow,
To breathe before each altar-shrine the consecra-
tion-vow :
And thus unto the Sacred Heart, across the Western
Sea,
One holy chain of love shall bind the fettered and
the free.

THE HOME OF OUR LADY OF THE SACRED HEART.*

THE treeless town a silent captive lay,
  Spellbound by summer-heat;
And dreary dust, in penitential gray,
  Enrobed the shadeless street.
A lone Sahara seemed that weary path,
  By toiling pilgrim trod,
Traced, drear and endless, through a vale of wrath,—
  A desert, banned by God.
The wanderer raised her sad and longing eyes,
  And lo! a vision fair!
Faith's steady symbol, pointing to the skies,
  Encrowned a gateway there.
The pilgrim paused—O scene divinely calm!—
  Within that portal blest!
Fair home of peace! sweet realm of Notre Dame
  Bright paradise of rest!
On dewy leaves, and rainbow blossoms fair,
  A softened splendor hung,
And balmy fragrance filled that bright parterre,
  From blooming censers flung;
And while the wearied day-beams sought repose
  Beyond the purple hill,
Seraphic tones, in clearest echoes, rose
  With sweet and tender thrill.

---

* The above lines were suggested by a visit to the Convent of Notre
Dame, San José, California.

The pilgrim followed where the soft notes led,
  As in a blissful dream:
Had the freed spirit from its thraldom fled,
  With daylight's dying gleam?
A glimpse of heaven hath blessed her longing eyes
  Beyond that cross-crowned gate;
Lo! Sharon's Rose, the sovereign of the skies,
  Throned here in royal state!
Beneath her dome that Maiden-Mother stands,
  And O, the matchless grace,
The tender yearning of her outstretched hands,
  The glory of her face!
Lo! at her feet, in union close and fond,
  A childish figure stands,
Serenely shrined in sweet and mystic bond,— ·
  His Mother's shelt'ring hands.
O likeness fair! that Mother's matchless grace
  Reflected in her Son!
Her tender smile, the light upon *His* face,
  Seemed blending into one!
His gesture fond reveals her gracious part
  In all His life of love:
One hand points sweetly to His Sacred Heart,
  One shows her smile above.
And gently there, on fair and youthful heads,
  Low bowed before the shrine,
That blended brightness of compassion sheds
  A benison divine.
O picture fair! sweet home of Notre Dame!
  On life's lone desert-path
Thy leafy shade, thy light benignly calm,
  Shall soothe the noontide wrath;

And dreary roads, in robes of dusty gray,
   Shall fade from memory's view,
While sweetly gleams, in summer's glad array,
   Thy bloom of rainbow hue.
For ever shrined above the bright parterre,
   Its crowning gems shall shine,—
A child's pure brow reflecting, sweet and fair,
   A mother's smile benign.
And worldly care, exorcised, shall depart
   When memory's echoed hymn,
" O sweetest Lady of the Sacred Heart!"
   Floats through the twilight dim.
While thus is won, from breath of song and bloom,
   Full many a magic gift,
The-pilgrim's voice, from paths of dust and gloom,
   Its grateful tones shall lift.
Hail, sweetest Lady of the Sacred Heart!
   Within thy gleaming dome
All Eden-joys, as royal boons, impart
   To thine own convent-home!

THE TRIAL OF ST. FRANCIS DE SALES.

THE desert waste of worldly care
  Hath spots of verdure blest,—
Oases silent, cool, and fair,
  Where pilgrim-souls may rest;
Pure temples, gardens of our God,
  Heaven's shining entrance-gates;
Its audience-court, by angels trod,
  Where love eternal waits!
Thus blooms, amid a city's dust,
  One ever-bright parterre,
Thus shines, undimmed by worldly rust,
  One jewel-casket fair.
There burns the fadeless lamp before
  The hiding-place of Love,
And there its " Well-Beloved " o'er
  Hovers the Holy Dove;
And near that altar's light and bloom
  The Maiden-Mother stands,
Clasping the Conqueror of the tomb
  Within her sinless hands.

A spectral figure glideth slow
  Through faith's serene retreat,
And sinks, in agony of woe,
  At Mary's sacred feet.

What tortures thrill that prostrate form?
   Ah! whence that anguish-rain?
What power could rouse such fearful storm
   Of wildest woe and pain?
Hath conscience, checked through guilty years,
   Arisen in wrath at last?
Doth sorrow shed its burning tears,
   To mourn the sinful past?
Ah, no! yet near that favored soul,
   All white as lily's bloom,
The Tempter's baneful shadow stole,
   And brought its night of gloom.
Wild was the storm, and dread the spell,
   The king of darkness wrought,
·And ever through that darkness fell
   His hissed and cruel thought:
" Vain is thy vigil, vain thy prayer,
   Hope sheds no ray for thee;
Thine is the blackness of despair,
   Through all eternity."
So passed each anguish-laden day,
   So fled each dismal night,
Till the frail body owned the sway
   That wrought the spirit's blight.
O stricken, crushed, yet faithful soul!
   Thy glad release is near—
Afar the gloomy clouds must roll,
   When faith shall conquer fear.
" Sweet Mother!" thus his anguish-cry
   In sobbing utterance woke,—
" If thus my dearest hopes must die,
   Beneath this fearful stroke;

If, through the dread, eternal years,
  The woful fate be mine,
To curse, 'mid bitter, burning tears,
  Thee and thy Son divine;
If I must hate, in realms of death,
  O let me love thee now,
Still keeping, till my latest breath,
  My holy service-vow!"
Could Mary's heart such pleading scorn?
  O " Memorare " blest!
Thy power unto that spirit lorn
  Hath brought the blissful rest.
Scarce had he breath'd the first sweet word
  When, lo! the spell is broke!
The Queen of Hope her servant heard,
  And slumb'ring joy awoke.
The fiery martyrdom is past,
  The night of trial o'er,
And lo! the sunlight shines at last,
  Whose beams shall pale no more.
O favored Francis! happy saint!
  When storm-clouds linger nigh,
And, battling in the gloom, we faint,
  Hear thou our anguish-cry!
By thy dread trial, lend thine aid
  Until the strife be done,
And peace shall shine, that may not fade,
  By Mary's power won.

A MOTHER'S PRAYER.

THE regent of a goodly realm,
  A sovereign wise and fair,
Gazed fondly on her youthful son,
  And breath'd her earnest prayer,—
The one wish of her loving heart,
  Her ceaseless, solemn thought,—
Sole boon her love had craved for him,
  The only prize she sought.

Was it new conquests? blood-bought gems,
  To deck his kingly hand?
Fair realms, by cruel triumphs wed
  Unto his rightful land?
Rich trappings, robes of royal state,
  A fawning courtier throng?
Or minstrels' ringing lays, to pour
  The flatteries of song?

Nay, nay! no earthly leaven base,
  No worldly dross could cling
Unto that pure, maternal prayer
  For France's youthful king:
" My precious son, more dear than life,
  More prized than aught on earth!
In all this false and fleeting world
  My only gift of worth!

" Oh, loved and cherished as thou art,
   Far rather would I weep
Above the bier where thou wert laid
   In thy last, dreamless sleep,
Than live to know this form of thine
   Held, foully shrined within,
A tarnished gem, a soul defiled
   By e'en one mortal sin ! "

Well answered was that mother's prayer !
   No foul, polluting taint
E'er marred the white and shining soul
   Of France's royal saint :
His pure baptismal robe of grace,
   Unstained, through life he wore ;
The lily sceptre of the just
   King Louis brightly bore.

O Christian matron ! in thy heart
   This lesson fair enshrine,
And let the blest, heroic prayer
   Of holy Blanche be thine.
For, what are all the gifts of earth,
   The charms of form and face,
If the immortal soul hath lost
   Its bright baptismal grace ?

Ay ! what avails the wealth of worlds,
   If, lured by syren vice,
God's heir hath sold his birthright fair,
   His only " pearl of price " ?
In vain may proud ambition grasp
   Vast realms to tyrants given,
If from his guilty hand hath passed
   The heritage of heaven.

SAINT PHILIP NERI'S QUESTION.

O WORLDLY hearts, close linked to gods of clay!
   O foolish feet that chase the flying beams!
O spellbound ears enraptured by the lay
   Ambition sings, in false and fleeting dreams!
Pause in your worship, cease your senseless race,
   List to the voice that drowns the syren's song,
That hurls the idol from its lofty place,
   And stays the tumult of the hast'ning throng!

"Proud plans are thine," the holy Philip said
   To one bowed low o'er tomes of legal lore,—
"Tell them, my son." The student lifts his head:
   "I seek the gems in learning's depthless store;
My hand would grasp the treasures of the wise,
   And seize the wealth fair Science calls her own;
From halls renowned would bear the gleaming
     prize,
   And clasp the crown the victor wears alone."
The student paused. "And then?" still urged the
     saint.
   "Then power, and fame, and honors shall be mine;
Then fairer scenes than fancy's skill could paint
   Of triumphs proud, upon my path shall shine."
"And then?" Again that question, low, yet clear.
   Still proudly shone the scholar's dreamy eye,
Still sung the syren to his spellbound ear,
   And still ambition urged his quick reply:

" Then all that wealth, with magic hand, can give,
  My conquered boons, my boundless store, shall be;
In lofty halls sole monarch will I live,
  King of all treasures of the earth and sea."
" And then ?" A shadow crossed the shining brow
  Yet struggling still to cast its pall aside :
" To death's stern mandate I at last must bow,"
  Forcing a smile, the dreaming youth replied.
" And then? And then ?" The syren song was
    still,
  Dark fell the shade o'er fancy's pictures fair ;
Through that young heart swift sped a swordlike
    thrill,
  And fairy scenes grew dim and blighted there.
" And then, my son, all worldly dreams must fade
  In the dread radiance of an endless dawn.
Where, then, those hopes, in rainbow tints arrayed ?
  Where those proud pageants?—gone, for ever
    gone !
Will the false lustre of a lofty name
  Dazzle His eye who sits upon the throne ?
Canst thou then sound the trumpet-notes of fame
  To awe thy Judge, or still His sentence-tone ?"

O magic words ! Ambition's reign was o'er—
  Its golden chains, as ropes of sand, were riven ;
And the proud heart that sought its fleeting store,
  To holier sway and purer search was given.

THE CAPTIVE'S WELCOME TO DEATH.

My rest draws near,
This weary life has reached its welcome close;
The vast, sad burden of its clinging woes
    I cast off here.

At last, at last,
The blessed hour of sweet release hath come,
When the wild pangs that made these pale lips dumb
    Will all be past.

No more, no more,
For thy frail loveliness, O earth! I pine:
Freedom and light eternal shall be mine,
    Beyond thy shore.

Thou better land!
My soul hath caught the glory and the gleam
I vainly sought in youth's deluding dream.
    Entranced I stand,

And on my ear
Steals the glad rushing of thy rivers free,—
The blissful echoes of thy harmony,
    Remote, yet clear.

Ere long, ere long,
White-robed and crowned, amid the shining band
This weary captive fetterless shall stand,
    And join thy song.

Father, to Thee
I give up all to which my soul hath clung,—
Idols of clay, on whose frail strength I hung,—
        For, unto me,

At length, is given
The eye of faith, clear-seeing and serene;
And not one cloud of earthly love between
        Its glance and heaven.

OUR LADY'S DEATH.

LIFT, radiant East!
Your flaming doors! fling wide your gates of gold!
A Queen would pass beyond your bars to hold
        Her royal feast.

O blissful bower,
Bedecked anew! prepare her shining way;
For brightly breaks the blest transplanting day
        Of Sharon's Flower.

O night of woes!
O drear remembrance of the bitter past!
Your reign is o'er, the glory dawns at last,
        The morning glows.

The selfish town,
The chilly cave, the dreary desert way,
The pagan land, where Love secluded lay
        From tyrant frown.

The pangs, the fears,
That watched the life by pain and peril led,—
His life, who owned " no place to rest His head "
    Through weary years.

    The woful way
With those who watched beside the martyr-God,
Whose fainting steps their blood-decked journey
    trod,
    Our debt to pay.

    The sword that rent
Her mother-heart who fondly, firmly clung
To the dread cross whereon her dear One hung,
    Till life was spent.

    The death-cold face,
The pallid lips, that spoke no soothing tone,
The lifeless arms close-clasped within her own
    In dread embrace :—

    All, all is o'er.
No memory-pang can rend that royal soul,
Where love and joy shall keep their sweet control
    For evermore.

    Her realm is won,
The radiant crown shall wreathe her sinless brow ;
The Mother claims her throne of brightness now,
    Beside her Son.

    No dismal tomb
Held that fair form within its blighting power :
The serpent-trail could leave no venom-dower
    On Israel's bloom.

Nay, stainless Queen!
Thine is the triumph of thy blessed Son:
Corruption foul by thee, thou holy one!
    Was never seen.

When the last sigh
From thy pure lips in peaceful breath had fled,
Thy seraph-train, on swiftest pinions, sped
    From realms on high.

Thy body fair
Through gates of gold, beyond the radiant East,
Triumphant passed—the glad, eternal feast
    Of love to share.

Our sweet release
From clinging bonds of misery and sin,
O Mother pure! O Queen of mercy! win,
    In deaths of peace.

"HERE SHE IS AGAIN."

[The following poem was suggested by an incident which occurred in one of the proselytizing schools in Ireland. A poor Catholic boy, tempted by want, was induced to attend the school. On one occasion, when the Protestant bishop was examining the pupils, he asked the Catholic child to repeat his prayers. Having finished the Lord's Prayer, the boy proceeded to say the Angelical Salutation, or, Hail, Mary, but was instantly stopped by the bishop, who said: "We do not want to hear anything about her. Go on with the Apostles' Creed." The boy accordingly began the Creed; but, after saying, "Who was conceived by the Holy Ghost," abruptly stopped. "Why do you pause?" asked the bishop. "What am I to do now, sir, for here she is again?" replied the boy, alluding to the name of the Blessed Virgin, in the words, "born of the Virgin Mary," which immediately follow.]

AY, she is here! The seamless robe of truth
To her blest name doth owe its wondrous strength.
No change can rend its shining threads apart,
For, woven firmly in its warp and woof,
Ay, broidered there, in chains of priceless pearls,
Lo! these sweet words that angels joy to breathe:
"The Virgin Mary, Mother of the Lord."
She in salvation's gracious plan hath shared,
And Love's sweet sacrifice doth own her aid:
Redemption's work would else be incomplete.
Through all the scenes of that strange history,—
That wondrous life that hid itself in clay,—
One bright companion-figure ceaseless moves.
In the chill cave of churlish Bethlehem
The sinless Mother watched her infant God,
And owned earth's Monarch on His throne of
    straw.

The blissful days fled like a vision by:
In the poor cottage home of Nazareth,
Where the child Jesus grew in age and grace,
Submissive to the gentle Mother-Maid,
Who kept His sayings treasured in her heart,
The hidden God began His work of love
At Mary's potent mandate. Cana's feast
Saw the strange power of those maternal tones,
That won the first sweet miracle of Christ,
When, as the gold-tongued poet chronicles,
" The conscious water saw its God, and blushed!"
And when Redemption's tender story drew
Near its dread close; when all its kindly deeds
And loving toil received His world's reward,—
A thorny crown, a royal garment dyed
In royal blood, a throne enriched with gems
From hands outstretched, and nail-transfixéd feet,—
Here, too, is she co-martyr in His woe.
For, lo! the Gospel, " Now His Mother stood
Beside the cross of Jesus."   Unto death
Faithful and fond!   O tend'rest mother-heart!
And there He gave—ay, listen, scoffer proud!—
To her His last sweet legacy of love:
" Behold thy Mother!" and, " Behold thy son!"
O ingrate heirs of that divine bequest!
Unthankful children!   Can eternal love
Look kindly on rebellion that disowns
The sweet and sinless handmaid of the Lord,
The cherished guardian of His children fair,
The loved co-worker in redemption's toil?
She unto whom the echoing ages breathe
The greeting learned from Gabriel's angel lips,

"The Lord is with thee ! Hail, then, full of grace ! "
O King of Truth ! we praise Thee,—she is here !
O Lord of Love ! we bless Thee,—she is here !
O sweet Redeemer ! bid our tongues be mute,
Our hands " forget their cunning," if we fail
To give Thee thanks.   O joy, that she is here !
Here in the weary desert of our woes,
A shining column o'er the pilgrim path,
A steady star above the crimson sea,
Sure guard and guide unto the " pastures green, "
And the " still waters " of the better land !
How could we tread, without our beacon-light,
This dark and lonesome valley—how escape
The serpent-snares upon that weary way ?
Or how sustain the " burden and the heat "
Of our drear journey?   Mary ! Mother ! hail !
As once thine own prophetic voice did sing,
All generations of the faithful race
Shall call thee blessed—handmaid of the Lord !
We hail thee, Mary ! Maiden full of grace !
Mother of God ! above all women blest !
O leave none orphans ! lead each rebel home,
To the safe shelter of thy mother-love,
That all may join thy children's pæan-tone :
" We thank thee, Lord ! Thy Mother still is here ! "

OUR LADY OF LA SALETTE.

NOT to the purple-robed princes of earth,
    Not to the palace of pride,
Not where the sceptics, with blasphemous mirth,
    Love's pure Evangels deride ;
Not in the capital's echoing street,
    Not where the busy have met
With babel of voices and tramping of feet,
    Came the Lady of La Salette.

Not to the holy and peace-haunted cell,
    Not to the home of the saint,
Not where in cloistered seclusion they dwell
    Who flee from the world's venom-taint ;
Not to the guarded and flower-decked shrine,
    Where the Jewel of jewels is set,—
Not e'en the retreat of her Treasure divine
    Won the Lady of La Salette.

But to the little and lowly of earth,
    Shepherds who "guarded their flocks,"
Simple of spirit, and humble of birth,
    Dwelling content 'mid the rocks, —
Ay, to the children untainted with guile,
    Untortured with care or regret,
With halo celestial, and tenderest smile,
    Came the Lady of La Salette.

Sadly she wept o'er the sins of the world,
  Lifting the dread arm of wrath,
Speeding the judgment, swift to be hurled
  Down on the guilty ones' path;
Pitying promise of mercy she gave,
  Soothing the heaven-sent threat:
Of pardon, that only repentance can crave,
  Spoke the Lady of La Salette.

O beautiful vision! O children more blest
  Than the greatest and wisest of earth!
O fountain, that flowed where the glorious guest
  Hath loosened the spell of thy dearth!
O hamlet so favored! though long years have flown,
  A world gives thee reverence yet;
Sweet spot, that the radiant presence hath known
  Of our Lady of La Salette!

O penitent France! thou hast felt the dread sword
  In the hand of Omnipotent wrath;
The angel-avenger his vials hath poured
  Down on thy sin-sullied path;
But cheer thee! for mercy and peace from above,
  Are won by thy grief and regret:
Dear land! thou art safe in the sheltering love
  Of our Lady of La Salette.

At thy wonderful shrine, O thou Lady most sweet!
  A pilgrim in spirit I bend,
And homage of gratitude, earnest and meet,
  I give for the boons thou didst send,—

For answer so gracious, for healing so swift,
  When lips parched with fever were wet
With health-bringing drops from thy bounteous gift,
  Thy fountain of La Salette.

Poor votive, I ween, is this rude lay of mine
  'Mid costliest tributes to place,
But even the farthing finds favor divine,
  In the coffers of infinite grace;
And O may the dearth of my sin-fevered soul
  With drops from thy fountain be wet,
And healing be won by the tender control
  Of our Lady of La Salette!

———

TRUE HEROISM.

YE weave for the hero bright chaplets of fame,
Ye hail his approach with your loudest acclaim.
What, though the fair flowers are dyed 'neath his
    tread,
And the streamlets flow dark with the blood he hath
    shed!
And what, though the death-shriek and agonized
    wail,
And the curses of stricken ones blend on the gale!
Though the heavens are dark with the storm-clouds
    of wrath,
And vengeance still broods o'er the conqueror's
    path,—

.Ye see but the halo that crowneth his name,
Ye hear but the trumpet that vaunteth his fame.
Ye are dazzled and led by the false lurid glare,
Ye are charmed by the pæans that ring on the air ;
And with song and with shouting the hero ye greet,
And ye twine the fair chaplets to die at his feet.
But soft steps are stealing where fiercely he sped
O'er the battle-field heaped with the dying and
 dead.
Undaunted, unchecked by the war-demon's ire,
They fearlessly glide o'er the pathway of fire,
Unheeding the thunder that thrilleth the plain,
Unheeding the rush of the wild bullet-rain.
And meek faces bend where the soldier lies low,
And kind hands are staunching his life-torrent's flow ;
And soft voices breathe the sweet accents of
 prayer,
To soothe the dread anguish of death and despair ;
And the pitying tone and the bountiful hand
Bring comfort and peace to the desolate band.
To the victims of war to the vanquisher's prey,
To the hearts he has crushed in his conquering
 way,—
Ay, the soft, gliding step, and the delicate form
That scorned the wild wrath of the dread battle-
 storm,
Steals silently now on its mission of peace,
To bid the sad wail of the lone orphan cease.
And when the foul pestilence heareth afar
The music of Moloch—the tumult of war,
And wingeth his flight on the pinions of death,
To scatter the blight of his curse-laden breath,—

Doth the hero who weareth the wreath of your
  praise,
Haste, then, the proud standard of conquest to
  raise?
Doth he meet the dread plague? Doth he hurl at
  the foe
Defiance and death in his terrible blow?
Ah! no! o'er your garlands that shine at his feet
The conqueror speeds in his coward retreat;
And his proud cheek is blanched with the pallor
  of fear,
And faint is the arm that hath lifted the spear.
But a soft step is gliding o'er regions of death,
Where the pestilence scatters his curse-laden breath,
And meek faces bend o'er the plague-stricken bed,
And watch by the couch whence the dearest have
  fled;
And the kind hands will soothe, and the soft voices
  bear
A peace-giving balm on the white wings of prayer.
Who, then, are the brave? Whose the worthiest
  claim
To the pæans of praise, to the chaplets of fame?
'Tis a delicate maiden, who courts not applause,
Who serveth her Saviour, and aideth His cause;
'Tis the Sister of Charity, gentle and meek,—
But the glory of earth is a tribute too weak
For the heroine of heaven, the toiler for fame
With chaplets eternal, and endless acclaim;
Whose glory shall live when the victor's proud
  wreath
Lies faded and trampled the grave-dust beneath;

Whose triumph shall sound when the conqueror's
    song
Hath died in the distance of centuries long.
For hers are the deeds that are worthy alone
The hymns that ascend by the martyr-God's throne
From the white-vestured throng, with the conquer-
    ing palm,—
The numberless legions that follow the Lamb.

ORATE, FRATRES.

"ORATE, fratres !" through the silence solemn
    Rings out the pleading cry ;
On incense-clouds, entwining arch and column,
    Glad answers rise on high :
For, favored throngs, in adoration bending,
    The sweet request obey.
Lo ! countless chains to love's fair throne ascending,
    Where faith-bound brethren pray.

"Orate, fratres !" bond of blest communion !
    O strong and sacred spell !
O magic words ! of highest, holiest union
    Your tender accents tell ;
For, faith divine, and love sublime and holy,
    And truth, with mingled ray,
Illume alike earth's lofty and her lowly,
    When brethren humbly pray.

From desert clime, and region rich and pleasant,
　'Neath fair or frosty skies,
In blended tones of love-linked prince and peasant
　Sweet supplications rise ;
Where'er, beside the "clean oblation's" altar,
　His loved their homage pay,
In ceaseless tones, that cannot faint or falter,
　Adoring brethren pray.

The priestly voice that wins Love's consecration
　In sacrifice divine,
The kneeling vot'ries' whispered supplication
　Before that sacred shrine,—
Each potent tone the white-winged prayer is send-
　　ing
　Upon its heavenward way,
Each earnest voice in magic chain is blending,
　When fervent brethren pray.

The suff'ring soul that burns in blest purgation,
　The earth-bowed heart that faints,
The voice that sings the "new song" of salvation,
　In brotherhood of saints,—

In bond most pure, in true and fond communion,
　To love sweet homage pay ;
And freed and fettered cry, in tend'rest union,
　"Orate ! brethren, pray ! "

THE CHRISTMAS TREE.

THE waving woods of sunny Spring,
  With leaves of living green,
The fairy shade those branches fling,—
  Are fitting themes, I ween,
For artist's skill and poet's lay ;
  For fair it is to see
The spring-tide bloom of orchards gay,
  The vernal forest tree.

And in the Summer's golden prime,
  O sweeter still to lie,
And list the forest's murmur-chime,
  And catch, of cloud and sky,
Fair, trembling glimpses, while the boughs
  Are swaying dreamily,—
Soft answers to the South Wind's vows
  That thrill the summer tree !

And lo ! the gay and goodly sight,
  When Autumn rules the land,
And halo-crowned with mellow light,
  The tinted maples stand.
Ay, when the frost-enchanter weaves
  His first fair tracery,
How rich the robe of rainbow leaves
  That decks the dying tree !

But when, beneath its shroud of snow,
   The silent landscape lies,
And faded is the sunny glow
   From out the winter skies,
Then bright with icy jewel-sheen—
   O wonderful to see!—
The glad, immortal evergreen,
   Hope's never-dying tree!

These are the fresh and favored boughs,
   These are the branches fair,
That Love's benignant hand endows
   With fruitage rich and rare;
Ay, here the gleeful children know
   Are treasures sweet to see,
When hosts of starry tapers glow
   Upon the Christmas tree.

O magic tree, whose branches bring
   The gifts of every clime!
The bloom and brightness of the Spring,
   The fruits of summer-time,
And richest of the gems that glow
   In deathless mine and sea,
Upon thy boughs of beauty grow,
   O bounteous Christmas tree!

Long may those blessed branches spread,
   Long may their shadows fall
Within the simple peasant-shed,
   The stately palace-hall!
Long may the "least ones" of His fold,
   Whose face their angels see,
The Christ-Child's loving smile behold
   Above the Christmas tree.

SAINT PATRICK'S DAY.

"I BELIEVE IN THE COMMUNION OF SAINTS."—*Apostles' Creed.*

RISE, lonely mourner, crouching by the shore,
  O pallid Erin! proudly rouse thee now!
Call back the smile, the joyous smile of yore,
  To thy dim eyes and sadly drooping brow.
For one bright day, O check the rain of tears!
For one bright day, forget the woes of years!

Of the green shamrock clustering at thy feet
  O'er the long-silent harp a garland fling,
And wake once more the tones so wildly sweet,—
  The bold, free strains, thy bards so well could sing
In those proud days, when, emerald-crowned and
      free,
Thou satst a queen, beside the smiling sea.

Island of Saints! why bearest thou that name?
  Faith's holy symbol shines upon thy brow;
Who brought its beam? who lit the sacred flame
  That brightly burns upon thy altars now?
Bethink thee well; up! up! and, for *his* sake,
With hymns of joy the slumb'ring echoes wake.

Ay, she *will* rise! E'en now she proudly stands,
  A holy triumph flashing from her eye;
The bonds are shaken from her royal hands,
  Checked are her tears, hushed is her wailing cry,
The harp is wreathed, and now the noble lay
Rings proudly forth to speak her joy to-day.

Hark! hark! it floats far o'er the Western Sea!
   Her exiled sons have caught the thrilling strain,
And as they list those welcome notes of glee,
   Their palsied hearts awake to life again;
And now they haste, a glad and grateful throng,
To wreathe their lyres, to swell the holy song.

'Waked by those sounds, the glowing dreams of
      yore,
   Like phantoms, glide through burning soul and
      brain;
On Tara's hill her monarch sits once more,
   And round him throng a brave and brilliant
      train,—
The dauntless heroes in the bloody fray,
The mighty chiefs of Erin's war-array.

Lo! 'mid that throng a single form appears!
   Where ring the harps one thrilling voice is heard;
The wild song ends, down fall the flashing spears,
   And savage wills obey the sacred word;
Low in the dust the haughty monarch bends,
And on his brow the saving stream descends.

The perfect day succeeds its dawnings faint,
   Soon Erin basks in learning's beaming smile;
The savage chief becomes the Christian saint,
   And wond'ring nations bless his holy isle.
Fair temples rise—through cloistered arches dim
Floats the pure prayer, and rings the holy hymn.

Night came at last,—the dark and dreadful night,
  How deep o'er Erin's life its shadow fell!
How fiercely clung the Saxon's wasting blight,
  Let ruined shrine and mould'ring abbey tell;
But from her brow the spoiler could not tear
One priceless gem that brightly glistened there.

In vain he doomed to tortures and to death
  The helpless children of that suff'ring isle;
Unquenched, undimmed, the blessed light of faith
  Nerved the racked frame, and lit the martyr's
    smile,
And sweetly burned, with pure, unclouded ray,
To light the exile on his weary way.

Though proudly still the stranger's banners wave,
  Yet once again Faith's temple decks her land,
And he who crouches on his plains a slave,
  Beneath that holy roof may firmly stand:
No tyrant *there* can claim the servile knee—
At God's pure shrine the Christian Celt is free.

Erin go bragh ! * thy children's love shall live
  For thee, fair home of virtue's holy ray!
And grateful hearts shall fondly, freely give
  Cead mille failtha † to *his* natal day
Who brought that beam, who bade them firmly
    cling
To faith's bright cross, the banner of her King.

---

* *Erin go bragh*—Erin for ever.·
† *Cead mille failtha*—Ten hundred thousand welcomes.

THE DAISY.

In quiet paths, with loving grace caressing
　　The weary pilgrim's feet,
There, smiling back his fond and fervent blessing,
　　With dewy eyes so sweet,

Behold the modest daisy!　Rural blossom!
　　It needs no sorcerer's art
To read the motto on thy gentle bosom:
　　"Simplicity of heart."

Thus have I found thee in the golden even,
　　When dewy pearls were set,
To mirror back the radiant smile of heaven,
　　In thy fair coronet.

Fondly I've blessed thy simple charms adorning
　　The grassy altar where,
In the calm splendor of the early morning,
　　Rapt nature knelt in prayer.

And when the spell of noontide's wizard hour
　　Held earth in still embrace,
Oft hast thou roused my spirit's fainting power
　　By thy fresh, smiling face.

To the pure lessons of thy gentle teacher,
　　O listen, heart of mine!
For the sweet glance of nature's silent preacher
　　Hath eloquence divine.

In the soft glory of thy youth's fair morning,
　From pride and art still free,
Be then the daisy's charm thy best adorning,—
　Serene simplicity.

Content to bloom in hidden paths and lowly,
　To shed an influence sweet,
And with thy tranquil brightness, fresh and holy,
　To calm life's noontide heat;

Then, in the silence of its golden even,
　Crowned with the dew of grace,
Thou shalt reflect, in smiling hues of heaven,
　The dear all-Father's face.

TO A YOUNG FRIEND.

I LOOK into thy laughing eyes,
　I hear thy voice of glee,
And only think of summer skies,
　And bird-notes glad and free;
And fondly, from my inmost heart,
　I breathe this fervent prayer:
" Be ever free, as now thou art,
　From sorrow and from care."

Alas! I hear the moaning blast,
　I see the winter rain,
And dream no more of pleasures past
　But wake to present pain;

I think how life is ever made
  Of mingled joy and care,
And of its sunshine and its shade
  Each, each must know a share.

Peace! peace! I turn my weary eyes
  Far onward to the Spring,
I see the future's sunny skies,
  I hear its robins sing;
Sweet thoughts of heaven fill my heart,
  I breathe this better prayer:
"Father! when earthly clouds depart,
  O give her sunshine there!"

———

THE ORDEAL OF QUEEN EMMA.

'Twas done in England's elder days,
  Long ere the curtness quaint
Of Saxon speech and Saxon ways
Had caught the softer style and phrase
  Of courtly Norman taint;

When e'en religion's precepts bland
  Scarce checked the savage mood:
For, though the sceptre of the land
Was held in Edward's saintly hand,
  Full many a custom rude

Around the rock-bound island cast
  Its fierce, despotic thrall.
And of those laws, linked firm and fast,
One relic of the pagan past,
  I ween, o'ermatched them all,—

" The fiery ordeal."   Thus they named
  That strange and fearful test,
Wherein the burning bars proclaimed
If he, of foul transgression blamed,
  Must still be banned or blest.

For, if that fierce and fiery path
  He crossed in triumph o'er,
Then proudly from the road of wrath,
All safe, and free of guilty scath,
  The rescued one they bore.

But woe to him whose heart could yield
  To coward, craven fear,
Or if *one* scar his guilt revealed !
For then his dismal fate was sealed,
  And death came swift and drear.

*   *   *   *   *   *

As 'mid the chosen twelve abode
  A Judas false and vile,
So in the courtly train that rode
Beside the King, Earl Godwin showed
  The traitor's demon-guile.

His tongue of malice e'en could dare
  To cast its slander-taint
Upon the court's queen lily rare,—
The holy Emma, wise and fair,
  Fit mother of a saint.

Alas! the saintly monarch lent
    His too confiding ear
To that false tale, and rashly sent,
To long and dreary banishment,
    His parent good and dear.

Against that verdict's doom unjust
    The stricken queen appealed
To Him in whom the righteous trust,—
Who raiseth virtue from the dust,
    And biddeth falsehood yield.

Then uttered they the stern decree,
    The sentence fierce and dread:
" The fiery ordeal now shall be
Her test of truth and purity.
    Barefooted must she tread

" O'er nine red-heated ploughshares, placed
    Within Saint Swithin's fane.
If safe her steps that pathway trace,
She shall be free from foul disgrace,
    And dark suspicion-stain."

Three days her solemn fast she kept,
    And at Saint Swithin's shrine
One livelong night she prayed and wept,
Then rose, as though in peace she slept,
    And shared the feast divine.

That morn a countless subject throng
    Surged 'neath the sacred roof,
For they had loved her well and long,
And scorned the tale, so foully wrong,
    And blamed that cruel proof.

Ah! sad those hearts assembled there,
  All bowed in grief and gloom;
They sent for her the ceaseless prayer,
From lighted altar still and fair,
  And Swithin's holy tomb.

But forth she came, that lady blest,
  With heavenward-lifted head,
And meek hands folded on her breast,
As onward to the cruel test
  She walked with fearless tread.

Not once her glances sought the floor,
  Her fiery path to see;
She crossed those burning ploughshares o'er,
As though she trod a tranquil shore,
  Or dew-bespangled lea.

Nor knew she when the bound was passed
  Until a wild acclaim,—
Her people's joy,—uprose at last,
All blent with fierce revilings cast
  On Godwin's hated name.

Thus He whose arm upholds the right,
  On that dread pathway traced
A track of pure, celestial light,
A triumph-progress safe and bright,
  For England's lily chaste.

THE SISTER OF MERCY'S CHANGE OF DRESS.

"O SPOUSE of Christ and virgin bride of heaven!
  Arise! arise! the Master calleth thee!
Put on the robes undimmed by earthly leaven,—
  The nuptial robes of immortality!"

Ah! swift she speeds, that welcome call obeying,
  Beyond the golden portals of the East;
And freshly clad in fadeless life's arraying,
  She meets the King, and shares the bridal feast.

But the worn raiment whence her soul hath risen,
  The cast-off garb of earth's poor, fragile clay,
Rests deeply hidden in its dreary prison,
  The "narrow home" of darkness and decay.

Yet not for aye. That mortal robe forsaken
  Shall claim life's boon of beauty ever new,
And to its spirit's dear embrace re-taken,
  Lo! flower and stem shall gladden in Love's
    view.

O willing heart that gave its pure oblations
  Of every throb to Love's sweet service blest!
O faithful hands, in mercy's ministrations
  For e'er unwearied, for a season rest!

O steadfast feet, the narrow pathway heeding!
　Rest till ye tread the fields of fadeless calm;
O voice once raised in pure and potent pleading!
　Peace! thou shalt join in life's eternal psalm.

Dear earth-companion of the bride of heaven!
　Securely rest! the King shall summon thee;
Thou, too, shalt wear, unstained by mortal leaven,
　The nuptial robe of immortality.

THE PRIEST'S FISHING-PLACE—THE CONFESSIONAL.

IN vain the weary fishers wrought
　Beside the shining sea:　.
Still safely swam the prey they sought
　In depths of Galilee.
A voice of strangest sweetness spoke,
　"Let down the net once more!"
And lo! its laden tissues broke,
　O'erfraught with finny store.
Spellbound, that wondrous draught they saw,
　But sweetly rung again　.
The voice that filled their souls with awe:
　"Be fishers, now, of men!"
They left their nets upon the shore,
　And, with their wondrous guide,
They sought a new and nobler store
　In waters wild and wide.

Ah! who shall count their mystic prey,
   Their wondrous draught of souls,
Where, 'neath the skies of gold or gray,
   The restless ocean rolls?
For, when they turned to needed rest
   Beside the " crystal sea,"
Lo! others came, as fishers blest
   Of lost humanity,
As through the vanished ages long,
   They toil unwearied yet,
And ever glide the countless throng
   Within their sacred net.
Ah! blessed shelter on the shore,
   From whence the fisher's gaze
Doth search the turbid waters o'er,
   E'en through their shrouding haze!
But not to death beside the sea,
   He dooms his mystic prey—
In shining rivers, clear and free,
   He guides their gladsome way;
Far from the dark, envenomed tide,
   They sport in waters calm,—
The flood that love hath purified,
   The life-stream of the Lamb;
So, cleansed from slime of guilt and woe
   By sweet absolving hand,
Fit prizes they for waves that flow
   By heaven's shining strand.
From monsters freed, and icy bond,
   Their endless life shall be
Earth's "upper sea" of clouds beyond,
   In glad eternity.

THE ISLE OF SAINTS.

I NEVER saw thy verdant plains,
  Sweet emerald of the sea!
I never heard the wondrous strains
  That tell thy song-birds' glee;
I ne'er inhaled the glad perfume,
  That cheers thy vernal day,
Of hedges bright with hawthorn bloom,
  And meadows " white with May."

No; never o'er thy grassy turf
  Hath yet my footstep strayed,
Nor where thy sands caress the surf,
  Have I in childhood played;
But Celtic blood is in my veins,
  Its faith within my heart,—
And these are links of golden chains
  That naught can rend apart.

A tender voice thy songs hath sung
  Unto my childish ear—
The love that o'er my cradle hung,
  Hath made thy shore so dear;
Ay, *one* was born beyond the sea,
  Upon thy sacred strand,
Who gave my heart its love for thee,
  My mother's native land!

And 'twas not of thy bloom alone
    That gentle voice could sing,
Nor thrush's trill, nor blackbird's tone,
    That hail thy soft-eyed Spring ;
Nor e'en thy royal grace of yore,
    Thy glorious ancient name,
When sages learned thy matchless lore,
    And poets sung thy fame

Before the iron hand of wrong,—
    The hand that holds thee now,—
Could clasp thy chain of ages long,
    Or brand thy queenly brow :—
Not these alone the lofty themes,
    The sounding, sweet refrain,
Of poet's purest, proudest dreams,
    Of minstrel's noblest strain ;

But the stately fane, or lowly shrine,
    The altars bright or bare,
Where offered lies the Lamb divine,
    The " clean oblation " fair ;
The pauseless prayer, the ceaseless rite,
    The faith that faltered not
Through sunny day or cloudless night,
    Though proud or low thy lot.

O sweetest strains that bards could sing !
    O scenes that love still paints!
The deathless echoes fondly ring
    Thy name, sweet Isle of Saints!

Ay, sweeter than the sweetest strain
　Thy wildwood warbler knows,
Is that *one* song, whose glad refrain
　In purest rhythm flows.

And fairer than the fairest flower
　That decks thy dewy lea,
And richer than the gems that dower
　Thy billow-crested sea,
Are faith's uncounted blossoms bright,
　Whose sheen no blemish taints,—
Its gems that shed their fadeless light
　Around thee, Isle of Saints!

The great apostle's deathless fame
　Resplendent shineth there;
There lives thy fragrant lily name,
　O Virgin of Kildare!
Fair Erin's saints, a bright array,
　Fill paradise with bloom;
O'er heavenly meadows, "white with May,"
　They shed a sweet perfume.

By Celtic blood, my proudest boast,
　By Celtic faith, I claim
Sweet kinship to that countless host,
　Blest triumph in their fame;
And while I clasp, in fond caress,
　A mother's gentle hand,
My grateful heart shall fondly bless
　That mother's native land.

Sweet Innisfail! thou jewel set,
　Where sunlit billows glow,
For ever fairer, dearer yet,
　To me thy name shall grow!
And may my glance be turned to **thee,**
　If faith or courage faints,
To learn thy love and loyalty,
　O blessed Isle of Saints!

———

THE PURIFICATION.

JUDEA'S royal city wore
　The robes that suit a queen:
Auroral purple, studded o'er
　With gems of dewy sheen.
The mist-veil, from her brow unrolled,
　Above it lingered yet,
Still jealous of the sunlight's gold,
　Her morning coronet.
How fair, beneath that shining **crown,**
　Her stately towers gleamed!
How free, her palace walls adown,
　The flood of glory streamed!
Like radiance from Jehovah's throne,
　In prophet's vision caught,
Its smile upon her temple shone,
　With heaven's own gladness fraught.

On that fair city's queenly state,
  Exceeding psalmist's praise,
Two pilgrims, pausing at her gate,
  Fixed long, enraptured gaze ;
And fondly, on the temple's walls,
  That look ecstatic stayed,
As through its loved and sacred walls
  Their eager longings strayed.
But while they wandered, faint and lone,
  Along the wak'ning street,
A new and wondrous glory shone,
  Where passed their weary feet :
The shining temple of their God
  Waxed fairer as they came,
And while its outer court they trod,
  High leaped the altar-flame ;
The priest arrayed for holy rite,
  Awe-stricken, veiled his face,
For Sinai's flood of living light
  Filled all the holy place.
The pilgrims, meekly waiting, stand
  Before the sacred veil :
An aged man, with staff in hand,
  A maiden, faint and pale.
Yet on her brow, serenely fair,
  A matchless splendor shone,
As though all brightness lingered there,
  Upon its fitting throne.
Clasped by her arm, in fond embrace,
  A lovely infant smiled,—
The light that crowned the maiden's face
  With glory robed the child.

With visage rapt, and footstep slow,
  Forth came the priest of God,
And, dazzled by that mystic glow,
  The shining court he trod.
The maiden's doves, of stainless white,
  As in a dream, he took—
What radiant vision met his sight?
  What spell enchained his look?
Ah, favored sight! ah, wondrous scene!
  Jehovah's servant saw
The Mother-Maid, the sinless Queen,
  Fulfilling holy law.
The King of kings upon him smiled,
  His God before him lay,—
His hidden Lord, a seeming child,
  His Saviour, shrined in clay!
O royal virgin! spotless dove!
  The law was not for thee:
No gleam of seraph wing above
  Could match thy purity.
Yet be our model: foulest stains
  Bedim our drooping wings,
The serpent's slimy trace remains,
  The searing venom clings.
Teach thine obedience: bid us bring,
  Fulfilling heaven's law,
The contrite spirit's offering,
  Bowed low in grief and awe.
Be thou our dove of peace divine,
  Our messenger of grace,
And on the temple's holy shrine
  Our humble tributes place;

And, while its inner portal fair
  Is opened free and wide,
Its altar-flame of glory bear
  To spirits purified.

———

SAINT ROSE OF LIMA.

THOU hast rare and regal dower,
  O fair Peruvian land!
A boundless wealth of fruit and flower,
  From Nature's partial hand;
And thine is one transcendent gem—
  One pure and peerless rose,
The fairest crown of mortal stem,
  In thee its dwelling chose,—
Rare daughter of a radiant clime,
  Bright blossom of the West,
Glad starbeam of our gloomy time,
  Queen Rose of Lima blest.
Columbia's saint! her very own!
  The New World's favored child!
Our gem, enshrined beside the throne,
  " First flow'ret of the wild."
O wondrous life! O matchless bloom,
  From heaven's glory caught!
O ceaseless tribute of perfume,
  With pure aroma fraught!

The worship of a stainless heart,
  A fair, embellished shrine,
Grace-guarded, kept from earth apart,
  Fit home of love divine!
Meet votary of Sharon's Rose!
  To thee, pure flower, was given
Sweet semblance of each charm that glows
  In that bright Queen of Heaven.
A love unsullied bade thee bow
  At Mary's holy shrine,
And on her statue's shining brow
  Thy garden's gifts entwine.
Loved Rose of Lima! while we bend
  Before our Lady's throne,
To our frail, fading tributes lend
  The grace that decked thy own.
For lifted heart and humble head
  Win blessings from above,
And o'er our scentless off'rings shed
  The fragrance of thy love;
And so, each fair, immortal flower,
  Transplanted from the sod,
Shall bloom, with thee, in fadeless bower,
  The garden of our God.

"MY ROME IS IN YOUR HEARTS."

[These words occur in the address of the Holy Father, on the occasion
of the fiftieth anniversary of his ordination.]

RING, blessed words, that wake ecstatic thrill!
   O faithful hearts, behold your father's Rome,—
His city, throned on faith's eternal hills,
   And crowned by truth's illimitable dome!

Ay, loyal hearts, that own his gentle sway!
   Ye are the Rome wherein he deigns to dwell;
His towers, that rise o'er virtue's "Sacred Way,"
   His walls of strength, his rock-built citadel.

There glows his land of fadeless summer skies,
   A smiling Italy of grace divine;
There vast basilicas in splendor rise,
   And love illumes full many a garnished shrine.

Ay, there, perchance, the Pantheons of pride,
   The ancient homes of passion's gods of clay,
Their idols rent, their foulness purified,
   To conquering truth a ceaseless homage pay;

Or, sadly fair, in memory's moonlight glow,
   Of conflicts past the moss-grown ruins tell,—
Proud Coliseums of "the long ago,"
   Where martyred hopes on dread arenas fell.

Immortal Rome, fair realm of faithful souls!
  Eternal city! 'neath whose turrets tall
Time's Tiber-stream still mirrors, as it rolls,
  The fadeless cross that crowns thy living wall.

O world-wide kingdom! limitless domain!
  Love's mighty conquest, fettered, and yet free!
A willing captive, bound in blissful chain!
  A sovereign, robed in peerless majesty!

From Arctic snows to isles of tropic balm,
  From India, throned beneath her banyan's shade,
To Alpine vales, that smile in sunlit calm,
  'Neath sternest peaks, in icy mail arrayed;

Where myrtles gleam in fair Italian bowers,
  Where shamrocks weep on Erin's verdant breast,
Where proud Columbia weaves her robe of flowers,
  And woos the stars to gem her golden crest,—

Wherever throbs a loyal, loving heart,
  Wherever truth has decked a spirit-home,
There faith's bright realm must claim her royal part,
  There is our father's blest, eternal Rome.

O constant realm, in sunshine or in storm,
  Enrobed in bliss, or clad in clinging woes!
Your love shall shrine *one* patriarchal form,
  Your strength still be his refuge and repose.

Nor traitor's arts, nor fierce, barbaric swords,
  City of God! can bid that strength depart,
While o'er the ranks of wild, invading hordes
  Your watchword rings, " His Rome is in each
    heart."

THE BAPTISM OF OUR LORD.

O'ER all the fair Judean land
  A golden brightness lay,
And golden halos glorified
  The mountain's veil of gray;
So shone the feathery cedar spires
  On Lebanon's lofty brow;
Like fingers formed of living flame,
  Seemed every fragrant bough.
A deeper glow on Sharon's rose
  Showed in each velvet fold,
And e'en "the hyssop by the wall"
  Put on a crown of gold;
And Jordan's wavelets gayly flung
  Their wreaths of silver spray,
And danced, with soft and ceaseless tune,
  Along their shining way.
Why gathers now a silent throng
  By that bright river's side?
What hushes childhood's merry song,
  And manhood's voice of pride?
See'st thou that form so strangely clad,
  In robe of camel's skin?
That brow, unmarked by worldly care,
  Undimmed by shade of sin?
'Tis he, the "witness sent by God,"
  Precursor of the light,
Whose footsteps, on the mountain tops,
  Announce the end of night.

He speaks. To catch those magic tones
  The crowd, impatient, press;
Lo! this the " voice of one who cries
  Within the wilderness:"
" O Pharisee! who taught thy foot
  From heaven's wrath to flee?
The axe is gleaming at the root,
  Low lies the barren tree ;
Make straight the crooked paths! behold
  The kingdom is at hand!
The glory of its midday sun,
  Shall flood the darkened land.
The Monarch comes! bend, brows of pride!
  Before His searching eye,—
The Monarch comes, whose sandal shoon
  I dare not e'en untie."
As struck by Sinai's lightning flash,
  The trembling hearers fall,
And wond'ring awe and shrinking fear
  Hold ev'ry heart in thrall.
Slowly they lift the dazzled glance—
  Whose that new, kingly face,
That brow of regal majesty,
  That form of Godlike grace?
O favored waters! softly sing
  Your grateful gladness now,
Ye fall in blest baptismal-rain
  Upon a sinless brow ;
Ye mirror in your shining depths
  The op'ning heavens above,
From out whose glory gently floats
  The snowy-pinioned dove.

O sacred river! well art thou
    The poet's purest theme,
And well thy crystal waves may flow
    Through many a holy dream.
 O earth may boast of bolder streams,
    Of waters deep and vast,
Upon whose flood the haughty pomp
    Of victors proud hath passed;
But thou,—upon thy sacred banks
    The King of kings hath trod;
Thy waters laved, in tender tide,
    Thy Maker and thy God!

———

THE ANGELUS.

NIGHT sendeth her shadowy heralds
    Abroad over valley and hill,
And in the great heart of the city
    The pulses of labor are still.

And while o'er the toil-burdened spirit
    Peace broodeth, a heaven-sent dove,
Sweet, silvery voices are telling
    The mystical story of love;

And as the soft melody stealeth
    Afar through the tremulous air,
What visions seraphic are wakened
    By magical murmurs of prayer!

" The angel declared unto Mary "—
Joy, joy for the sin-tainted race!
A rose of the desert is worthy
 To bear the bright blossom of grace.

" Thy handmaid, O Lord, behold me!
 I bow to Thy word and Thy will: "
List, earth, to the answer submissive,
 That bids thee with ecstasy thrill.

" The Word was made flesh! " and among us
 The treasure of heaven lay hid ;
Love dwelt where the lily was blooming
 The thorns of the desert amid.

O mortals! when shadowy heralds
 Are gliding o'er valley and hill,
And in the vast heart of the city
 The panting pulsation is still;

When softly, o'er thoroughfares crowded,
 And through the lone forest-retreat,
The sweet silver tones of the belfry
 The message of mercy repeat,—

Bow down while the voice of the angel
 Is filling the peace-haunted air,
And waft the pure breath of thanksgiving
 In murmured and rapturous prayer.

" Hail! full of all grace! " among women
 The favored, the spotless, the blest!
Hail, star of the Eastern aurora!
 Hail, daybeam and light of the West!

Thus echo the greeting angelic,
  And bid the vast centuries ring
With praise of the meek Maiden-Mother,
  And joy for the birth of the King.

———

THE AMERICAN PILGRIMAGE.

PROUD fleets have swept o'er the sounding sea,
That echoed their pæans of victory,
And conquering legions have trod the vale,
With banners that streamed on the sportive gale;
And throngs yet bend in the minster's gloom,
At the royal grave and the stately tomb,
And countless votaries bow beside
The shrines of pleasure, and pomp, and pride;
But a ship speeds now o'er the sounding main,
With a goodlier freight than the victor train,
And a host shall march o'er a foreign land
In fairer pomp than the conquering band.
But they bring no gifts to a worldly shrine,
No voice of homage, no wreaths to twine
Where the mouldering relics of great ones hide
In the mausoleum of mocking pride.
The echoes that sound through the ocean caves,
And the strains that float o'er the crested waves,
And the sweet-toned hymn, and the pleading prayer
Of the pilgrim multitude gathered there,
In the bark that speeds on her sacred flight,
In the bark so hallowed by holy rite,

That beareth, over the sounding sea,
The tempest-Ruler of Galilee,—
And the hymn shall sound on the distant strand,
And the prayer arise in the stranger land,
When that host shall march on a peaceful way
To the founts that gleam in the desert gray :
To Paray-le-Monial, lone, apart,
The fitting home of the Sacred Heart;
To the fair Bethsaida, that floweth yet
In the wonderful grotto of Bernadette,
Where the penance-hour of France secured
The paradise-glory of lowly Lourdes.
Then onward! onward! to royal Rome,
To the sheltering arch of her sacred dome ;
To kneel in that glorious minster's gloom,
At the mitred fisherman's wondrous tomb.
To sink and to weep on the fruitful sod,
Where the crimson steps of the martyrs trod,
And the eager homage of love to bring
To the rock-built throne of the Pontiff-King.
To thrill at the glance of that beaming eye,
And to wish in the light of its look to die,
And to bear for ever the benison bland
Of Pio Nono's paternal hand.
And to feel that no fettering chains can fling
Their binding spell o'er the world-wide king;
That the " Vatican prisoner's" mystic reign,—
No tyranny checketh, no bonds restrain ;
And no strength can move, and no arm can cast
That form from its throne in the Rock made fast.
O beautiful path of the pilgrim band!
O march of triumph o'er wave and land!

O scenes of splendor for faith to see!
O worthiest shrines for the bended knee!
God speed ye, the favored, the true, the blest,
O'er the toilsome road and the billow's crest!
God hear your voices of pleading prayer!
May He send the doves of His peace so fair,
By your faithful hands, o'er the waters dark
That long have threatened His holy ark,
To tell that the deluge of wrong is o'er,
And the calm endureth for evermore.

THE BROWN SCAPULAR.

BLESSED badge of service sweet,
   Livery of a sov'reign fair,
Sign of fealty complete,
   Pledge of fond maternal care!
Dear to me thy fabric coarse,
   Fairer far thy hue of brown
Than the rays of rainbow source,
   Prisoned in a jewelled crown.
With the sacred scenes of yore
   Thou dost gift my spirit's view,—
Dreams of royal robes that bore
   E'en *thy* texture and *thy* hue.
Dreams of Nazareth,—Eden fair,
   Home wherein the holy three
Dwelt afar from worldly care,
   In a sweet obscurity;

There, beside her cottage door,
   Clad in woollen raiment dun,
Mary, spinning, pondered o'er
   Every saying of her Son.
Scapular of Carmel blest!
   Wakened by thy mystic name,
Visions rise of verdant crest,
   Crowned with ring of holy flame.
Carmel's Mount! whereon abode
   One whose pure, prophetic gaze
Saw, at midnight, skies that glowed
   With the wondrous morning blaze.
Now, to faith's illumined age
   Floats my soul in dreams adown,
And I see the saintly sage
   Clad in coarsest robe of brown,—
Holy Simon! 'Mid his prayer
   Shines a sweet, ecstatic scene:
Lo! the Maiden-Mother fair!
   Lo! the bright, celestial Queen!
See! within her shining hand,
   Carmel's scapular of brown!
Hark! she decks her sweet command
   With a blissful promise-crown:
" Give this pledge of peace divine
   To my subjects fond and true.
Bid them wear my service-sign,
   Coarse of texture, brown of hue,
For a matchless boon it bears,—
   'Tis my promise, made to thee,—
Who this badge devoutly wears,
   With the blest his lot shall be."

Sweetest promise! peerless boon!
  Let me read its meaning right;
Let me ne'er its truth impugn,
  Let me ne'er its treasure slight.
Of the badge of service blest
  Faithful bearer must I be,
On an ever-loyal breast
  Wearing that sweet livery.
Thus the promise shall not fail,
  Thus the treasure shall be mine,—
Crown of light that ne'er can pale,
  Royal robe of peace divine.

THE ROCK OF SAINT PETER.

THUS spake the builder, strong and wise:
" Upon this rock my Church shall rise,
And hellish might shall ne'er prevail,
Though all its demon hosts assail."
Swift, at His word, the temple rose
That still in primal splendor glows;
Age after age the tempest's shock
Assails that strong foundation-rock,
And billows rush, in wildest race,
Against its adamantine base;
But firmly, through the fiercest storm,
That Rock uprears its mighty form,
And backward e'er, with sullen sigh,
The baffled billows sink and die.

Those wondrous walls were guarded well
By many a mail-clad sentinel;
Throughout the warring ages long
They stood, a bright, undaunted throng.
As each was summoned from his post,
Then rose from faith's uncounted host
His swift successor, firm and brave,
To check the mad, besieging wave,
To scorn the tempest's mighty shock,
And hurl, from truth's eternal rock,
His arrow's sure, supernal blows
Against the fierce, invading foes,—
The demon hosts that madly dare
To crush the temple builded there.
So stands a watchful warder now,
With tranquil eye and dauntless brow:
Behold him on his rock-built throne,
Uncheered, unaided, and alone!
Yet wond'ring earth hath ne'er, I ween,
Beheld so proud, so grand a scene,
As that calm face and lofty form
Serenely throned amid the storm;
Unmoved, unharmed, though fierce the fight
Against his rock's cross-crested height.
O valiant Pius! thine shall be
A sure, supernal victory.
Again, as in the strifes of yore,
The baffled waves, with sullen roar,
Shall backward sink, and, murm'ring, die
Beneath thy throne secure and high.
Again the demon foe shall learn
How true the Builder's promise stern:

" That hellish might shall ne'er prevail,
Though all its countless hosts assail,
With flaming dart and tempest-shock,
His Church, enthroned on Peter's rock."

THE NEWLY BAPTIZED.

O EARTH hath still a shining store
    Of rare and lovely things,
Around whose peerlessness once more
    Sweet trace of Eden clings :

Fresh flowers, upon whose beauty lies
    Full many an emblem fair
Of graces dear to angel eyes,—
    Bright gifts for souls to wear ;

Rare gems that light the gloomy mine,
    And deck the lonely sea ;
Rich tints that in the sunset shine
    With heaven's own brilliancy ;

Gay birds, upon whose plumage gleams
    All wealth of rainbow dyes,
And countless stars, whose silv'ry beams
    Are set in clearest skies.

But fairer than the fairest flower
    That decks the sunlit lea,
And rarer than the gems that dower
    Dark mine and depthless sea ;

Richer than cloudland's hues of light,
　Brighter than birds' array,
Purer than beams that cheer the night,
　Or robe the summer's day,—

Ay, lovelier than all lovely things
　Is that unearthly grace
That shines, like gleam of angel wings,
　Upon an infant's face,

When the fair soul enshrined within,
　Heaven's own immortal flower,
Is cleansed from stain of primal sin
　By blest baptismal power.

O wondrous privilege to hold
　That flower in fond embrace,
And its new glory to behold
　Upon the tranquil face!

But holier duty 'tis to guard
　Its fair, transcendent ray,
And keep the ceaseless watch and ward
　About it, day by day.

Ay, Christian mother, dost thou know
　Thy holy task of love?
To own that living gem below
　Which angels guard above;

To treasure, with true tenderness,
　For thy dear Master's sake,
A lamb like those He deigned to bless,
　And in His arms to take;

To keep, with earnest, fondest care,
   That soul from stains that dim,
And safe, from worldly guile and snare,
   To lead it up to him.

———

OUR VILLAGE.

As a child, with soft hands folded,
   Closes, half, its azure eyes,
Droops a brow, divinely moulded,
   And in rosy slumber lies ;
So our village, lulled by humming
   Of the dull and drowsy mill,
Soothed with scents from flowers coming,
   Rests in dreams beside the hill.

Waked not by the brooklet's rhyming,
   Or the robin's matin song,
Only soothed by vesper chiming,
   Borne by echoing breeze along ;
Softly low the sleepy cattle,
   Bathing in the limpid stream—
E'en the merry infant's prattle
   Is as music in a dream.

Softly through the purple gloaming
   Floats the song of night's sweet bird,
While through forests, wildly roaming,
   Storms like far-off sighs are heard ;

Quietly the wheel is turning,
  Turning at the cottage door,
While the hearth-flame, dimly burning,
  Sheds its dream-light on the floor.

Thus a silence e'er is brooding
  O'er our village like a spell,
And the golden sunlight flooding
  Pleasant porch and mossy dell,
Only makes the stillness deeper,
  Deeper and more holy-seem,
As a smile on face of sleeper
  Tells but of a quiet dream.

Blessed hamlet! in thy shadow
  It is good for man to dwell,
Breathing fragrance from thy meadow,
  Music from thy vesper bell;
Leading, as in good times olden,
  Holy lives till life's sweet even,
Then, through flowers and sunlight golden,
  Passing calmly up to heaven.

THE ROYAL CATECHIST.*

GONE was the light of glory's day,
　And, from his throne of greatness hurled,
Within the gloom of exile lay
　The fallen master ôf a world.

This rash Prometheus, who stole
　Heaven's fire to light his visions vain,
Rock-fettered, felt within his soul
　The vulture-fangs of ceaseless pain ;

Yet blessed are the shafts that smite
　The daring souls that rashly soar,
For wisdom's radiance cheers the night,
　When glory's lurid day is o'er ;

And in its clear, unfading ray,
　How pales the tinsel glare of pride
That decked the gods of worthless clay,—
　The phantoms man hath deified !
　　*　　*　　*　　*　　*　　*　　*

---

*When Napoleon I was banished to St. Helena, the little daughter of one of his officers shared, with her father, the royal exile's captivity. "My child," said Napoleon to her, "you must begin to prepare for your first Communion. I will teach you your Catechism." Accordingly he devoted a portion of each day to the religious instruction of a simple child ; and when a priest was sent from Europe to give the last rites of the Church to the dying emperor, his youthful disciple received the Bread of Life, for the first time, from the same hand that administered the Sacred Viaticum to her royal instructor.

On lone Helena's desert soil
   The victor's noblest deed was done ;
His battle-tumult's ghastly toil
   Such conquest rare had never won.

On that bleak shore one flow'ret smiled,
   One golden sunbeam cheered its gloom,—
His faithful soldier's gentle child
   Adorned the captive's living tomb.

That royal captive, day by day,
   Watched the fair spirit's bloom unfold ;
He.turned its gaze on truth's bright ray,
   And showed religion's wealth untold.

He who had filled a world with awe,
   And ruled its realms with kingly rod,
Deigned to interpret heaven's law,
   And win a child's pure soul for God.

Heaven sent its peace, serene and fair,
   And his crushed spirit found a balm
When thus it decked a soul to share
   The nuptial-banquet of the Lamb.

And when religion sent her priest
   To soothe his parting spirit's strife,
His pupil shared her master's feast,—
   Her first, his last, pure Bread of Life.

DEATH OF TASSO.*

THE royal day is dawning,
  The regal prize is won,
Italia's grateful homage
  Awaits her gifted son ;
The laurel crown is woven,
  To deck his kingly brow—
Why stays the child of genius?
  Why waits the poet now?
This matchless morn of triumph,—
  Ah! long its magic gleam
Played o'er his dreary pathway,
  In many a fairy dream ;
And ceaselessly he followed
  Its false and fleeting light,
That danced, like mocking phantom,
  Before his longing sight.
The weary race is ended,
  The phantom flies no more,
And glory's noonday splendors
  Upon his spirit pour.
Fame's eager hand is ready
  To crown her vot'ry's brow—

---

* Tasso was invited to Rome to receive the laurel crown, but shortly
before his coronation he was seized with his last illness. He retired to
the monastery of Onofrio, to prepare for death. When one of the monks
sought to cheer him, by describing the triumph that awaited him at
the Capitol, he replied: "O vapor called glory! I feel too well to-day
that on earth all is vanity, but to love and serve God."

Why lingers favored Tasso?
  Why stays the poet now?
Too late his crown is woven,
  Too late the willing throng,
With loud applauses, hail him
  The sovereign of song.
Death weaves a crown of cypress
  To deck his noble brow,
Death's solemn mandate husheth
  Life's tardy homage now.
His sad and toilsome journey
  Hath reached its welcome close,
And in the peaceful cloister
  The pilgrim seeks repose.
To rouse his fainting spirit,
  They tell of vain renown,—
The morrow's matchless glory,
  Its fair triumphal-crown.
" Nay, cease thy tale of splendor,"
  The dying poet cried,
" Nor mock the parting spirit
  With worldly pomp and pride.
O vanity of glory!
  O phantoms that betray!
Too long my soul hath worshipped
  A god of worthless clay.
The festal robe for Tasso!
  He seeks the winding-sheet;
The poet's wreath he tramples
  Beneath his dying feet.
Whom would ye crown with laurel?
  The mould'ring prey of death?

The odor of the charnel-house
　Would mock your incense-breath.
Away with worldly greatness,
　The fleeting and the vain!
O earth! the love of heaven
　Alone is worth thy pain.
The worship of a Saviour,
　The service of His cross,—
This, this, is all of value
　Amid thy shining dross.
Sweet Faith! thy words of pardon,
　Thy potent voice of prayer,—
They are my car of triumph
　To heaven's kingdom fair!
To heaven's fadeless Capitol
　My parting soul they bear,
Bedecked, not as a poet,
　With crowns that time can taint,
But wreathed with light immortal,
　The chaplet of a saint."
He clasped redemption's symbol:
　"O Father! unto Thee
I give my trusting spirit"—
　The weary soul was free!
The royal day hath risen
　The regal prize is won,
No need of earthly glory
　To crown Italia's son;
Heaven's amaranthine garland
　Adorns his kingly brow—
In heaven's "Eternal City"
　The poet reigneth now.

THE MARTYRS OF SANDOMIR.

[A Legend of the Salve Regina.]

SALVE REGINA! sweetest words that Christian lips
    can sing!
For, clearer than the soaring birds, thy tender
    echoes ring,
Through all the past's pure atmosphere, to later
    ages down,
Recording, in each accent clear, a martyr's blest
    renown.
They tell of Sadoc's holy band, who came with
    footsteps fleet,
To bring unto the Polish land salvation's tidings
    sweet,
Who dwelt within their cloister calm, and craved
    no gift beside,
Save this, the martyr's mystic palm, and vesture
    crimson dyed.

   *   *   *   *   *   * . *   *   *

The first sweet day of smiling June was gliding to
    the West,
The warbling bird had ceased his tune, and sought
    his leafy nest,

And, gathered in their Eden-home, the monks gave
  willing ear
To one who read, from holy tome, the list of martyrs
  dear.
Why changed that clear and quiet voice to awesome
  murmur soon?
He read—O eager band, rejoice!—" The second day
  of June "
(At dawning of the morrow's sun, within that
  very year!)
The nine and forty martyrs won their crown at
  Sandomir,—
At Sandomir, 'twas their abode, and 'twas *their*
  record fair,
For never martyr's blood had flowed to bless the
  vineyard there.
" Tis heaven's message sent to us," the holy Sadoc
  said,
"An angel's hand hath written thus the warning
  thou hast read."
Submissive to that summons sweet, for combat to
  prepare,
They sought their hidden God's retreat, and knelt
  in vigil there;
And when the herald beams of light unbarred the
  golden East,
They decked the shrine for holy rite, and shared
  the nuptial feast.
And while the soft auroral sun stole through the
  arches dim,
The soldiers of the cross begun their ne'er omitted
  hymn:

"Salve Regina!" thus they sung, but, at its op'ning
strain,
What wild, discordant tumult rung, in mock'ry of
refrain?
Rejoice, ye soldiers of the Lamb! the glad release
is nigh,
And yours is now the martyr's palm, the robe of
royal dye.
In rushed the ruthless Tartar horde, with wild,
demoniac yell,
And calmly, 'neath the savage sword, those Chris-
tian heroes fell.
Nor ceased their holy *Salve* strain, for, as each voice
grew still,
Another rung the blest refrain, with glad, ecstatic
thrill;
And with the swiftly-flowing blood, the heaven-
ward-floating breath,
That music poured its pulsing flood úpon the place
of de th.
And when, save one, that martyr-throng had passed
the crimson sea,
One voice completed, clear and strong, the won-
drous melody :
It was the dauntless leader's tone that last and
longest rose,
That bore the sacred prayer, alone, unto its tender
close.
"O dulcis Virgo!" thus he sung, and, with that
latest breath,
His freed, exultant spirit sprung beyond the gates
of death.

" Salve Regina !" sweetest hymn that Christian lips
    can sing,
How grandly through the ages dim thy tender
    echoes ring !
How sweetly, gladly, waft they down, in tuneful
    numbers clear,
This golden legend of the crown bestowed at
    Sandomir !

LILIES AND MIGNONETTE.

BEHOLD the fair flower beloved by our Lord,
    More rich than the raiment of kings !
The balmiest dew in its chalice is poured,
    'Tis the hue of an angel's white wings.
The sweet, stainless lily ! deep, deep in her breast,
    Lies the type of a virtue as fair.
Ah, Purity ! when in a soul thou dost rest,
    Then heaven's best beauty is there.

And lovely, in truth, is the meek mignonette,
    Though low in the valley it lies ;
Though tiny its delicate petals, ah ! yet
    How sweetly its odors arise !
Humility thus all her graces would hide,
    But, deep in her heart though they lie,
There's a fragrance diffusing on every side,
    And ascending, like incense, on high.

O daughter of earth ! be this loveliness thine,
  In the day of life's beauty and bloom ;
Be thy heart's chalice filled with aroma divine,
  With piety's fadeless perfume !
So Israel's lily shone royally fair,
  Though hidden and lowly her place,
And o'er earth's drear desert of sin and of care
  She shed heaven's odor of grace.

Like hers be thy lot with the meek mignonette—
  'Tis maidenhood's loveliest part ;
And far from the worldlings' false glitter, ah ! yet
  Rare graces shall gleam in thy heart.
And bright with the hue of the angels' white wings,
  Thy life shall be gathered at even,
To bloom evermore where the tree of life flings
  Its luminous shadow o'er heaven.

SAINT FRANCIS BORGIA BEFORE THE REMAINS OF THE EMPRESS ISABELLA.*

Is this thy work, O death?
The regal mien, the fair majestic face,
The cheek's rich glow, the smile of matchless grace,
    Gone with the fleeting breath?

Ruler of kings art thou!
Stamped with thy seal, the marble turns to clay ;
At thy dread touch life's radiance fades away
    From lip, and eye, and brow.

And thou hast stricken down
The hand that late a royal sceptre bore,—
The queenly head that with such fitness wore
    Earth's proudest, brightest crown.

---

* The Saint, then Duke of Gandia, was deputed by Charles V, King
of Spain, to accompany the remains of the Empress to the royal burial-
place, in Granada. In accordance with a required ceremony, he was
obliged to identify the body, previous to its interment. On open-
ing the coffin, the remains were found to be greatly disfigured by
decomposition. St. Francis was struck with horror at the loathsome
and sudden change in the features, lately so beautiful, of this once cher-
ished sovereign. His reflections on the transitory nature of earthly
things, occasioned by this spectacle, led him to renounce all worldly
grandeur, and to serve an eternal and imperishable King, in the Society
of Jesus.

E'en as a dream, I see
A courtly throng, a stately palace-hall,
With floating banners, blazoned arms, and all
    The pomp of royalty;

And, brightly ruling there,
A gracious presence on a lofty throne,—
One peerless sov'reign 'mid that splendor shone
    Preëminently fair.

And princely heads were bowed,
The courtier fawned, the high-born haughty dame,
The valiant knight, the wily statesman, came,
    And endless fealty bowed.

The glittering dream is past.
That pageant proud, that grand and goodly show,—
Oh! was it false—a vain ephemeral glow,
    That would not, could not, last?

Ay, mortals, this is all—
A mass of clay, a cold and silent form:
Death's mould'ring prize, foul banquet for the worm,
    Beneath a sable pall.

Away, then, earthly state!
I vow new homage to a worthy King:
My tardy tribute to Thy throne I bring,
    O Monarch truly great!

Thy glory can not fade,
Thy reign is endless; on Thy kingly brow
The starry crown shall gleam, undimmed, as now,
    When earthly pomp is laid

Low in the dust; when all
This varied scene, this bright and busy world,
Back to its chaos by Thy mandate hurled,
In nothingness shall fall.

Let me *Thy* courtier be:
Thy faithful steward, while this life shall last;
A white-robed prince, when earthly toils are past,
Co-heir of heaven with Thee.

ADVENT.

O MOURNING earth, unveil thy brow!
Thine Eden joy befits thee now.
Hence, phantoms dark, and shadows drear!
Redemption's rosy dawn is near;
The beams of love, the dews of grace,
Shed gladness o'er each desert-place.
O happy month! thy snowy wing
The long-expected boon shall bring;
Thy skies reveal the golden gleam,
The light of blest, prophetic dream.
The strain whose far-off echo stole,
In rapture, o'er the Psalmist's soul,—
Its matchless melody shall thrill
Thy starry midnight, lone and still.
And humble hearts, entranced, shall hear
Celestial voices, glad and clear,—
Shall catch the gleam of pinions fair,
Adown the angels' shining stair,
And bow where seraphs watch above
The lowly hiding-place of Love;

And hail, illumed with heavenly ray,
A God enshrined in human clay !
O Christian hearts ! what rapture waits
At blest December's cloudy gates !
What halo-flame, what magic glow,
Transfigures wintry wastes of snow !
Yet pure and clear the glance must be
That would such Christmas glory see.
No blighting stain may dim the brow
That seeks beside Love's crib to bow,
And humble hearts alone can share
The peace that fills the Christmas air ;
Alone can deck a worthy shrine,
For benisons of grace divine,
The lustre of the wondrous gem
That shone in lowly Bethlehem.
A sinless mother watched His rest,
A "just man" was His guardian blest,
And blameless shepherds bent the knee
Before the Lord of purity.
Ah ! ye who would their treasure win,
Put off the purple robes of sin,
And, clad anew in nuptial white,
Receive the radiant Christmas light !
Let no discordant note destroy
The carol of your Christmas joy !
So shall responsive strains prolong
The music of the seraph song ;
So shall the promised peace be shed
On hearts by love to Bethlehem led,—
On hearts that breathe the bliss of earth,
The joy that hails a Saviour's birth.

AN OFFERING TO JESUS, MARY, AND JOSEPH.

WHAT shall I offer ye, glorious three?
Gold from the mountain, or pearls from the sea?
Jewels that rival the morning's glad beams,
Torn from earth's caverns, or won from her streams?
Spices of Araby, rarest perfume,
Wafted from islands of tropical bloom?
Poor are thy treasures, O earth! unto Him,
To the "light of whose glory the stars are dim;"
And faint is the breath of thy balmiest bowers
To the odors that rise from His amaranth flowers,—
The fragrance unfading of blossoms that grow
Where heaven's "still waters" unceasingly flow.
Rich were the offerings, borne from afar,
When, 'neath the light of the mystical star,
Kings from the jewelled and radiant East,
Came to the hovel ye shared with the beast,
Offered their treasures, and humbled the knee,
Low in your stable, O wonderful three!
Then were ye hidden in lowly disguise,
Then might earth give her ephemeral prize:
Now, to the riches of heaven, can she
Add from her baubles, all bright though they be?
What shall *I* offer ye? what can *I* bring,
Meet for the crown of my Saviour and King,
Fit for the brow of the heavenly Queen?
Worthy to rival the wonderful sheen

Of lilies that bloomed in his mystical rod
Who watched heaven's flowers, who guarded his
    God?
There *is* wealth, there *are* treasures, that mortals
    may bring
To the portals of pearl, to the throne of the King:
The jewels that fall from the penitent's eyes,
The sighs of contrition He will not despise;
The love like to that which anointed His feet
With fragrance all fitting, and unction most sweet;
The hope that had failed not, e'en under the rod,
The faith that e'er murmured, "My Lord and my
    God!"
Ah! these are the offerings worthy to be
Your wealth and your treasures, O heavenly three!
By the rivers of bliss amid infinite calm,
On garments washed white in the blood of the
    Lamb;
O'er the lyres of the seraphs, that joyously ring
When the sinner bows low at the feet of the King,—
Through all the "glad city" these tributes shall
    shine,
Crown-jewels resplendent, love's treasures divine.
The heart's lowly homage meet off'ring shall be
For the household of heaven—its glorious three!

THE PRAYER OF AFFECTION.

TO MIRIAM.

O A BEAUTIFUL dream thy life should be,
  If fate would list to the prayer of love,—
All fair as the face of a summer sea,
  All bright as the heavens that laugh above ;
And joy should waft, on his zephyr wings,
  The balmiest breath of the rose to thee,
And the sweetest carol the wild bird sings
  Should faintly symbol thy songs of glee.

But, alas for love and its fairy dream !
  Life's stormy billows will madly rise,
And clouds o'ershadow the golden gleam
  And the azure hue of the summer skies ;
The breath and the bloom of the rose will die—
  O woe for love, and its unheard prayer !—
And songs will change to the wailing cry,
  And the choking sob of a wild despair.

But I'll dream of the joys of earth no more,
  There's One will list to the prayer of love—
Look over life's sea to its peaceful shore —
  With the bow of His promise smiling above :
May its light illumine the darksome day,
  And span the gulf of the grave at even,
That the angels, over that shining way,
  May lead thy soul to its rest in heaven !

COLUMBUS AND ISABELLA.

O YE grand, heroic ages! O ye royal days of yore!
In your quaint, illumined pages shrining yet a
    golden store,
And from out those mines of glory yielding rich,
    abundant themes
For the scholar's lofty story, for the minstrel's
    glorious dreams,—
Lo! the misty veil is lifted, e'en from *my* untutored
    sight,
And the clouds are slowly shifted from that distant
    realm of light;
And amid the dreams Elysian, that from out its
    portal glide,
One, in sooth a matchless vision, shall for evermore
    abide:
On her throne of royal splendor sits the Sov'reign
    of Castile,
Worthy she of homage tender, worthy she of
    tribute leal;
'Mid the pomp that doth surround her, she hath
    kept a soul serene,
And a fitting fame hath crowned her as the good,
    the *Christian* Queen!

To the scorned Italian dreamer, who hath met but
    courtly sneer,
To the "visionary schemer," lends she now a
    gracious ear ;
And as she lists benignly to his strange, romantic
    dream,
Doth a vision, sent divinely, in her musing glances
    gleam ?
Ay, her spirit's gaze is gifted with a blest, prophetic
    power,
And the veil of doubt is lifted in that faith-illumined
    hour ;
And no motive base she feareth in Italia's dreamer
    now,
For a truth her soul revereth sits enthroned upon
    his brow.
And her gracious trust abideth, for, across the
    Western seas,
In the bark her gift provideth, sails the saintly
    Genoese ;
And, at last, his heart that panted for that wondrous
    Western land
Bows beside the cross he planted on its bright dis-
    covered strand.
O Columbia, starry-vested ! hail that dreamer ever-
    more,
Who, beyond the billows crested, sought thy darkly
    curtained shore,
And, bethink thee, he had striven to unfold his
    dream in vain,
Till the kindly aid was given in the sunny land of
    Spain ;

Till the prophet-glances gracious of the good, the
    Christian Queen
Saw thy realm, serene and spacious, o'er the waves
    that rolled between,
And in thy regal splendor, in the noonday of thy
    weal,
Give thy grateful tribute tender to that Sov'reign
    of Castile.

THE ROCK OF LOURDES.

THAT rugged rock in desert land,
Where, fainting, sunk the chosen band,
Before their leader's wand had brought
The fount with life and healing fraught,
Was not, I ween, a wilder spot
Than thy stern rocks, O favored grot!
Before the peasant maiden's hand,
Obedient to a blest command,
That fountain won, whose waters bear
Glad healing to the nations, there.
Nor did the Hebrew pilgrims bless
Their fount within the wilderness
With fervor more intense than theirs   •
Who hail the boon of answered prayers,
And rise, of direst evils cured,
From thy Bethsaida, blessed Lourdes!
But ah! that desert fountain's gleam,
When matched with thine, thou wondrous stream,

Was dim and darksome as the wave's
Within the gloom of ocean caves,
Compared with crests that sparkle free
Upon the bright, unshaded sea.
Ah! thou didst change, O Sov'reign fair!
That lonely desert, bleak and bare:
Thy mandate bade thy servant bring
From barren rock the healing spring,
When thou didst rise upon her view,
In snowy robe and stole of blue,—
Fit emblems of thy royal state,
Thy grace and truth, Immaculate!
And there thy sweet, consoling glance
Brought pardon to thy contrite France,
And gave, as pledge of peace secured,
The blest Siloam-fount of Lourdes.
Bright healer! from thy lofty throne
Descend on spirit-deserts lone,
And from each rock-encircled heart,
Ah! bid thy sweet Lourdes-fountain start:
There ceaseless wonders shall be wrought
By streams with grace and mercy fraught,
And gratitude shall rear her shrine,
As votive offering divine,
Upon that blest, transfigured ground,
Where once the rocky summits frowned.

THE BLESSING OF THE WINTER STORM.

"SWEET ARE THE USES OF ADVERSITY."

THE day-king reigned with all his tyrant power,
  His fierce midsummer wrath,
And singing stream and fragrant-breathing flower
  Were withered in his path ;
Earth glowed, I ween, with bright barbaric splendor,

  A golden-vestured queen—
But where, alas! her vernal freshness tender,
  Her dewy smile serene?
No fleecy cloud-wave on the " upper ocean,"
  To soothe its weary glow ;
Amid the boughs no softly-swaying motion,
  No zephyr's murmur low.
Soon spread the dust its sad " *memento mori*,"—
  Its penance-robe of gray,—
O'er verdant vales, that hide, in garments hoary,
  Their spring-tide's bright array.
No merry songs, no bird's sweet trill of gladness,
  Could pierce the dreary haze,—
The dusty veil, that wove its spells of sadness
  O'er long midsummer days ;
So, mute, benumbed, as 'neath the tyrant power
  Of dread magician foe,
Earth lay asleep, in strange, enchanted bower,
  Within that tropic glow.
          *   *   *   *   *   *   *   *

Down swept the storm, from cloudy caverns driven
  By wildest winter wrath,
And giant boughs, from moaning forests riven,
  Lay scattered in his path.
Earth woke, uncrowned, bereft of summer splendor,
  No more a jewelled queen,—
Her golden treasures summoned to surrender
  To one with awful mien,
Who sent the clouds in tempest gloom to hover
  Where shone the summer glow,—
Who sped the blast, and bade the fierce floods cover
  The dusty plains below.
    *   *   *   *   *   *   *   *
The storms are o'er; a voice of strength and sweet-
    ness
  Commandeth, " Peace ! be still ! "
And lo ! the tempest flies, on wings of fleetness,
  Beyond " the cloud-capt hill ; "
But,—glad result of winter's vandal-power,
  Sweet fruit of cloud and storm,—
Serene and smiling, in her bloomy bower,
  Lo ! spring-tide's fairy form !
A dewy freshness in the soft air lingers,
  Dream-odors freight the gale,
For gentle sprites still sow, with rosy fingers,
  Bright blossoms o'er the vale ;
Soft is the song of streamlets, swiftly gliding
  Through grassy meadows sweet,
Glad are the carols of the songsters, hiding
  In leafy-roofed retreat.
Won by the storm from dull, lethargic slumber,
  Where she so long had lain,

Cleansed from the dust that could so darkly cumber
   By wildest winter rain,
Earth rises now, serene, and crowned, and living
   In vernal freshness fair,
While warbled praise and songs of glad thanksgiving
   Fill all her spring-tide air.

   *   *   *   *   *   *   *   *

Behold thy type, in swiftly changing vision,
   Thy life, O human soul !
From blighting glow to vernal peace Elysian,
   From stern to sweet control.
Thy Summer smiled in long, unwaning splendor,
   Unclouded, still, and fair,
But ah ! no dewy freshness, soft and tender,
   Shed balmy influence there ;
Thy spirit-blossoms knew no fragrance holy
   Of kindly word and deed :
They bloomed, alas ! in selfish brightness solely,
   And served no gentle need.
And weary soon, with brightness all unbroken,
   And faint with changeless heat,
They lost each trace of beauty's tinted token,
   Each charm serenely sweet.
No birdlike note of gratitude, ascending,
   Rung blithely on the air,
No singing streams their joyous murmurs blending,
   Gushed forth in gladness there.
No cloud e'er crossed the skies so blue and smiling,
   No rain-drop softly fell,
And dreamy brightness wrought its charm beguil-
   ing,—
   Its soft and slumbrous spell ;

And naught of time's swift, changeful pinions know-
    ing
  Whereon the sweet days flee,
Soft sleep was thine, amid the summer glowing,
  Of bright prosperity.

    *   *   *   *   *   *   *   *

But swift and sudden came the tempest, sweeping
  From cloudy caverns drear;
And mighty floods, their guardian rocks o'erleap-
    ing,
  Wrought ruin, woe, and fear.
The blast swept on, now wildly, fiercely roaring,
  Now moaning as in pain,
While downward flowed, from depthless caverns
    pouring,
  The ceaseless winter rain;
But, sweet result of wintry devastation,
  Blest fruit of cloud and storm,
Crowned with the rainbow-pledge of glad duration,
  Lo! Spring's celestial form!
Sweet, star-eyed blossoms, 'neath her footsteps
    springing,
  Smile from the moistened sod,
Glad echoes rise of carols blithely ringing,
  To seek the ear of God.
Pure incense, borne on fragrant wings to heaven,
  Its sacred story bears
Of spirit-blooms washed free from earthly leaven,
  From dust of selfish cares;
Of sluggard-slumbers, now for ever broken,
  Of tempests sent in love,

Of blessed storms, that shrine the tender token
  Of mercy from above.
And learning thus the lesson, sweet and tender,
  That came through storm and pain,
Cease not, O heart! in spring-tide peace to rendér
  Thy thanks for winter rain.

———

SAINT MARY MAGDALEN.

"MANY SINS ARE FORGIVEN HER BECAUSE SHE HATH LOVED MUCH."

O WAND'RER homeward led!
  O prodigal restored!
I see thy humbled head
  Bowed low before thy Lord;

And o'er His sacred feet
  I see thee fondly pour
Thy ointment, rare and sweet,
  Thy tears,—a priceless store.

O recompense divine!
  "Thy love hath won thee grace:"
Well, well may rapture shine
  On thy transfigured face.

And now, O faithful saint!
  Thy love doth bid thee go
Where He, cross-burdened, faint,
  Toils o'er His way of woe,—

Ay, where the King of kings
  Hangs, throned in agony,
The mournful Mother clings,
  All desolate, to thee.

And scarce hath morning's hand
  Dispelled the shades of gloom,
When thou dost, weeping, stand
  Beside His empty tomb.

O sinner, clothed with grace,
  And crowned with heaven's light !
Thy risen Master's face
  Greets first thy favored sight.

The Lamb's triumphant song
  Thou, ransomed, joinest now,
And, 'mid the white-robed throng,
  Dost lift thy shining brow.

Thy halo-circled name
  Illumes our darkened earth,
The grateful Church doth claim
  Thy prayers of boundless worth.

O Mary, name of grace !
  Magdalen, saved by love !
Ah ! bid the Master trace
  Our names in light above.

Plead for the guilty soul,
  Guide home the steps that err,
And, 'neath thy blest control,
  O shield the wanderer !

And o'er her Saviour's feet,
  Ah! may each sinner pour
The balm of penance sweet
  With tears, a priceless store;

So shall her bonds be riven
  At mercy's hallowed touch,
And darkest sins forgiven,
  " Because she loveth much."

———

A SONG FOR THE MOSS.

SING for the moss, the clinging moss,
  High up in the abbey wall,
Weaving its network close across
  The turret gray and tall;
Fringing the ruined Gothic arch,
  As if it strove to hide
Each trace of Time's triumphal march
  O'er the works of human pride!

Bending down from the cottage eaves,
  Seeking, in love, to twine
With the glowing buds and dewy leaves
  Of the lattice-shading vine;
Creeping under the churchyard gate,
  Shrouding the unmarked bed,
Where the victim of a cruel fate
  Sleeps softly with the dead.

Shrinking down in a sheltered nook
  Of the dim and ancient wood,
Where the tiny waves of the crystal brook
  Dance on in their solitude;
Decking in pity the dusty breast
  Of the silent wayside stone,
Lying there, in its dreamless rest,
  By the busy road, alone.

Then sing for the moss, the loving moss!
  Long may it strive to hide
The brand of Time, as he sweeps across
  The works of human pride!
Long may it crown the turret high,
  And deck the ruined hall,
Long may it mingle lovingly
  With vines on the cottage wall!

Long may it shroud, with a quiet grace,
  The narrow graveyard bed,—
The last, the lonely resting-place
  Of the broken-hearted dead.
Ay, long may it dwell in the forest lone,
  The poet's loved retreat,
Long may it give, on the wayside stone,
  Rest to the wanderer's feet!

SAINT PATRICK'S PRAYER.

WITH his holy hands uplifted,
 And his glances raised on high,
While the clouds above him drifted
 Darkly o'er the midnight sky,
Prayed the saint, till dawn of day,
As a saint alone can pray.

When the morn, in sunny splendor,
 Journeyed to its golden prime,
When the twilight, soft and tender,
 Brought the sacred vesper-time,
Ever, on the trembling air,
Rose his *one* impassioned prayer.

For the land his zeal had gifted
 With the gems of faith and love,—
Thus, with holy hands uplifted,
 And with glances raised above,
Prayed the saint till dawn of day,
As a saint alone can pray.

Ah! what sought those echoes soaring
 Upward to the " great, white throne " ?
What the theme of fond imploring,
 Murmured in the midnight lone?
What the burden of that prayer
Rising on the morning air?

Sought he wealth of worldly glory
   For the land he loved so well?
Prayed he that, in song and story,
   Evermore her fame might dwell?
Conquest proud, and boundless power,—
Would he thus Hibernia dower?

No; a boon more richly freighted
   Would that voice for Erin gain,—
Saintly pleadings, unabated,
   Breath'd but one sublime refrain:
' May she, e'en though woes endure,
Keep Thy faith undimmed and pure."

To the potent voice that pleaded,
   Hath high heaven answered well?
Was that voice by Erin heeded?
   Let the tale historic tell.
Through the woes that long endure,
Has her faith been firm and pure?

Answer, dark, ensanguined pages!
   Answer, minstrel's wailing tones!
Sighs, that sound through weary ages,
   Mourner's sobs, and martyr's moans!
Winds, that wail where clinging vines
   Fondly clasp her ruined shrines!

Answer all,—want, desolation,
   Every grief that earth may know!
Answer, exiles' lamentation,
   Blent with Erin's wail of woe!
List! " Through woes that long endure,
Still her faith is firm and pure."

Thanks, O saintly voice uplifted!
　Thanks, O glances raised on high!
Through the clouds that long have drifted
　O'er the azure of her sky
Shines the ray those pleadings won,
Shines her faith's unfading sun.

Erin's pilgrim sons and daughters,
　Wanderers from your own fair isle!
Ye have borne, across the waters,
　Faith's undimmed and sunny smile;
Ye have blessed its guiding ray,—
Pillared flame by night and day.

Guard it still in joy or sadness,
　That across the sounding main
Ye may join, in tones of gladness,
　Erin's sweet, sublime refrain:
"Whatsoe'er our hearts endure,
Still our faith is firm and pure."

THE PAPAL VOLUNTEERS.

O BLESSINGS on that noble host
　　Who serve the Father's need!
Be theirs the triumph glad and sure,
　　Be theirs the victor's meed!
Beneath the standard of the cross
　　They battle for the right,
They shield the sacred shrine of truth
　　From fierce, despoiling might.
O God of armies! be their strength,
　　Arm thou each stalwart hand,
Let vict'ry light thy warrior's path,
　　And guide his gleaming brand!
Be Israel's arm of magic his,
　　To quell the lawless foe,
To check the ingrate Absalom,
　　And lay Goliath low;
To stand on Zion's sacred walls,
　　As warder firm and brave,
Undaunted, while the Gentile hosts
　　Beneath its ramparts rave;
To guard the ark of holy truth,
　　To shield the priest of God,
To free His chosen ones, who shrink
　　Beneath the tyrant's rod.
Go forth, then, soldiers of the cross!
　　Go forth, serene and strong,
And faint not, though the way be wild,
　　The battle tumult long;

For earnest hands uplifted are,
　　Until the fight be done,
·Till, with the potent aid of prayer,
　　Your triumph shall be won.
On, then, in Pio Nono's cause !
　　On, on, for truth's dear home,—
The sacred shrine, its gem divine,
　　The faith of holy Rome !
All blessings light your onward way
　　Who serve the Father's need !
Be yours the conquest glad and sure,
　　Be yours the victor's meed !

————

SONG OF THE ANGEL OF FIRE.

I RULE the shining element
　　That gilds the grateful earth,
And sheds its rich and rosy light
　　Around the cheerful hearth.
Ye see the flood of glory lie
　　On mount, and vale, and stream,—
And love ye not the gentle hand
　　That sends each golden gleam ?
And while in happy homes ye sit
　　And watch the ruddy blaze,
Will ye not bless the kindly power
　　That rules its genial rays ?
In classic days they worshipped me,
　　Ay, called my name divine,
And placed their costly gifts upon
　　My vestal-guarded shrine ;

They built the stately fane for me,
   And struck the sounding lyre,
And proudly, in their noblest hymns,
   They sung the praise of fire.
I do not crave such homage now,
   I only ask a smile
From eyes that beam with holy light,
   And lips that speak no guile ;
For I am but His messenger
   Whose fiat formed the light,
And bade its beams adorn the day,
   And cheer the gloom of night,—
Who, from the mystic bush of flame,
   In awful glory shone,
And gave His servant strength to stand
   Before the tyrant's throne ;
Whose fiery pillar shed its ray
   O'er Israel's desert path,
Who bade the sacred mountain shine
   With lightnings of His wrath;
Whose sunlight gilds the harvest field,
   And tints the regal flower,
Who forms the rainbow arch of peace
   From mingled gleam and shower.
I bow me to His mandate blest,
   Fond servant of His will,
I leave my place beside His throne,
   His bounty to fulfil ;
And o'er the glad and grateful earth
   I shed the golden glow,
And make the love-encircled hearth
   Heaven's fairest type below.

Lo! in my wealth of radiance,
   With warmth and gladness fraught,
I trace, in shining characters,
   Full many a holy thought,—
Bright emblem of the sacred flame
   Of fadeless love divine,
Of purity's own vestal ray,
   And mercy's beam benign.
The gleam of faith's uplifted eye,
   Hope's smile of radiant hue,—
All joy, all holiness, I bring
   Before the spirit's view.
O ye, on whose transfigured souls
   Redeeming love doth shine,
Who bask within its matchless beam,
   Its glow and warmth divine!
Leave not that smiling radiance,
   Guard well that sacred fire,
And bid its flame within your souls
   Burn brighter still, and higher,
Till, purified from earthly stain, .
   And freed from earthly leaven,
Your shining souls shall reach the source
   Of cloudless light in heaven.

MOTHER SETON.

Lo! the hosts of valiant women!
  Lo! the legions, brave and strong,
That have "come up from the desert"
  In a grand, immortal throng,—
That have fought, with hearts undaunted,
  'Gainst a fierce and hydra foe,
Till, within the dust degrading,
  They have brought his standard low!
But they seek no vain applauses,
  And they court no gazing crowd,
And they stand not in the forum,
  Lifting clamor shrill and loud.
No! the true strong-minded follow
  Where a calmer guidance leads,
And the lowly path of duty
  Is their field for lofty deeds. .
Ay, they tread, with steady footsteps,
  In *her* still, secluded way,
Who was stronger, in her meekness,
  Than a host in war array,—
Who, in Nazareth's cottage lowly,
  Bore her blest, yet hidden part,
While she kept her Saviour's sayings
  Fondly treasured in her heart.
And amid those silent toilers
  Is a wonder-working band,
Who have brought the boons of heaven,
  As they pass from land to land;

Who have braved the ocean tempest
  And the desert's burning ray,
From the Northland to the tropics,
  From Columbia to Cathay.
Noble daughters of Saint Vincent!
  Where the hosts to match with ye?
Legions of the Lord of pity!
  Valiant band of charity!
Who hath won your angel presence,
  Who hath brought your labors blest,
To the mighty land of freedom,
  To the empire of the West?
" In a sunny Southern valley
  Is an Eden, calm and sweet,
Where we gird our toiling armies
  For ' the burden and the heat ;'
And that vale of blest Saint Joseph
  Hath a dear and sacred trust,
For it shrineth *one* whose life-deeds
  Blossom, fragrant, in the dust.
O a rare and matchless treasure
  Is that angel-guarded grave,
Though no pompous tomb is o'er it,
  And no stately banners wave ;
For the mortal shrine reposing
  Till the resurrection there,
Held a stainless spirit-flower,
  In its casket, sweet and fair.
O our loved and saintly mother!
  O our foundress, true and brave!
Deathless are the links that bind us
  To thy dear and sacred grave.

And where'er our feet may wander,
  And whate'er our labors be,
While we serve our lowly Master,
  In His cause of charity;
While we keep our silent vigils
  By the weary couch of pain,
While we stanch the flowing life-stream
  On the ghastly battle-plain;
As we soothe the orphan's wailing,
  And assuage the mourner's woe,
As we turn the sinner's glances
  Where the beams of mercy glow,—
In the streets of crowded cities,
  On the wide and lonely sea,
Still we shrine our saintly foundress,
  In our tend'rest memory."
O ye hearts that bless the Sisters
  For the conquests they have wrought,
For the reaped and garnered harvest,
  With its rich abundance fraught!
Hail the noble hand that founded,
  That hath sown the magic seed,
That hath sought the earliest workers
  In the time of direst need.
Oh, on earth, sweet Mother Seton,
  Thou hast won a deathless name,
And the seraph hosts of heaven
  Shall for ever sing thy fame!

SAINT PATRICK CROSSING THE ATLANTIC.

HE hath heard the plaintive summons o'er the
    Western waters ringing,
      As it rung, O sacred Erin! from thy verdant isle
        of yore;
And he cometh swift and eager, to the land of sun-
    set bringing
      Blessed boons of grace and mercy in a rich,
        unfailing store.

Cometh he to far Columbia? Leaves he, then, the
    shining legions,
      That repose within the glory of the "great, eter-
        nal throne"?
From the blissful rest of heaven, from the fair,
    celestial regions,
      Doth he seek again the earthland serpent-
        blighted, chill and lone?

In the faith-illumined spirits of thy saintly sons and
    daughters,
      O thou loveliest island-jewel set within the shin-
        ing sea!
In *their* hearts the blest apostle beareth o'er the
    Western waters
    Purest altar-flames undying, that he kindled once
      in thee.

Ay, their souls, unstained and loyal, are the shrines
wherein he keepeth
Blessed balm of grace and mercy for the healing
of the West;
In *their* prayers *his* pleading rises, by their earnest
hands he reapeth
Boundless store from seeds they wafted o'er the
wild Atlantic's crest.

"LET US GO TO SWEETNESS." *

[A Legend of Nazareth.]

" All our happy sports are stayed,"
Wailed a childish chorus,
" By the tempest's threat'ning shade,
Looming darkly o'er us;
Mary's Child the sun will bring
In its bright completeness:
Let us seek the little King,
Let us go to Sweetness."

Trusting band of Nazareth!
When the cloud hath drifted
O'er our way with chilling breath,
Let *our* cry be lifted;
Mary's wondrous Child will bring
Joy's serene completeness:
Let us seek our infant King,
Let us go to Sweetness!

---

* This beautiful legend tells that, during the childhood of our Lord,
when rain threatened, or little quarrels rose, the children of Nazareth
would cry, "Let us seek Jesus, the little King! Let us go to Sweetness."

THE TRUE AND ETERNAL GLORY OF ROME.

"Rome! Rome! thou art no more
   As thou hast been:
On thy seven hills of yore,
   Thou satst a queen."—Mrs. HEMANS.

NAY, Rome! thou art far more
   Than thou hast been,
Greater than when " of yore
   Thou satst a queen ;"
The mystic " ring of flame "
   Gleams o'er thy brow—
A purer, loftier name
   Thou bearest now.

Rome! that imperial brow
   Higher shall rise,
Heaven's smile upon thee now
   Glows in thy skies ;
Ay, and thy gleaming sun
   From cross-crowned spire
A brighter gold hath won,—
   A holy fire.

A conquering train hath swept
　Thy streets along;
Thy echoing air hath kept
　Their lofty song.
Ah! not with pomp and pride
　The victors came,
Yet earth hath glorified
　Each hero-name.

Their song of triumph swelled
　When, with hushed breath,
The pagan throng beheld
　The Christian's death.
Each death of strife and pain
　Hath won for thee
Thy new, triumphant reign,—
　Heaven's royalty.

Out, out upon the dirge
　For glory past!
While Time's loud waves shall surge,
　Thy reign shall last.
Rome! Rome! exult thou must,
　Proud wealth is thine,—
Those martyrs' holy dust
　Thy tombs enshrine.

The wreath of victory
　They proudly wore,
Thy coronet shall be
　For evermore;

Thy royal robes were dyed
  In martyrs' blood,
Thy guilt-stains purified
  By that blest flood.

What, though the famed of old,
  Hero and sage,
Have passed—new names behold
  On history's page !
Pure victors, crowned with palm,
  Names without taint,—
The soldier of the Lamb,
  The white-robed saint.

And they who well may see
  Thy queenly brow,
Dare ask, in mockery,
  What thou hast now ?
Thou hast—O blissful thought !—
  The gifts He gave,—
The priceless boons He brought
  Who died to save.

A faith undimmed and pure,
  Shrines that shall last,
Temples that shall endure,—
  These, these thou hast !
Then, Rome, exult ! thou'rt more
  Than thou hast been !
Thy seven hills, as of yore,
  Still throne a queen !

THE EXILED SISTERS.

AGAIN we greet, as welcome guests,
  A persecuted band,
Again the holy exile rests,
  Within our favored land;
For He who guided Francis' sons
  To Francis' city fair,
Hath led again His chosen ones,
  His benisons to bear.

O cruel hearts! how could ye bid
  The sweet earth-angels flee?
Alas! ye know not what ye did,
  Nor what your meed shall be;
For thus upon your guilty heads
  Just heaven's wrath ye draw—
What woe awaiteth him who treads
  On mercy's sacred law!

Ah! holy handmaids of the Lord,
  Must this your guerdon be?
Was banishment the sole reward
  Of angel charity?
Unto the lonely orphan lamb
  A mother's care ye gave;
Your hands the fevered brow could calm,
  The erring wand'rer save.

Your tender ministrations soothed
  Each pang of mortal doom,
And for the fainting pilgrim smoothed
  His pathway to the tomb;
No shrinking fear, no thought of self,
  Love's laborers could deter,
Nor greed of fame or worldly pelf
  Was duty's daily spur.

Their motto was "the Master's will,"
  Their day-star was His law;
For love they wrought—His likeness still
  In suff'ring man they saw;
But scorn, earth's tribute to its Lord,
  Is theirs who bear His name:
Foul insult was their King's reward,—
  Their meed is still the same.

But we, to whom His spouses blest
  As precious gifts were sent,
Will bid each holy exile guest
  Forget her banishment;
For here their gentle sister band
  Have wrought their deeds of love;
· Their presence won for this fair land
  Rare blessings from above.

Our gratitude, ah! let us show
  By help in hour of need;
And thus, while gladly we bestow
  The generous gift and deed,
Again shall promise sweet be made:
  "All this ye do to Me;
In charity's dear band ye aid
  The Lord of charity!"

THE CENTENNIAL OF SAN FRANCISCO.

[Written for the Centennial Celebration of the Mission of San Francisco, founded, in 1776, by two Franciscan priests, Fathers Pallou and Cambon.]

'TIS well to ring the pealing bells
  And sing the joyous lay,
And make this glad centennial year
  One gleeful gala-day ;
For Freedom's sun, that floods the land
  With Summer's golden glow,
Dawned brightly on the night of gloom,
  One hundred years ago !

And, dwellers in this favored land
  Beside the Western Sea !
Be yours an added thrill of joy,
  A two-fold jubilee ; .
For—sweet and strange coincidence !—
  The bright, benignant glow
Of faith dispelled a deeper gloom,
  One hundred years ago !

All honor to our noble sires,
  The tried and true-souled band,
Whose valor loosed the Gordian knot
  That bound their native land ;
Who crushed the tyrant's haughty host,
  And laid his standard low,
And bade the starry banner wave,
  One hundred years ago !

All honor, too, and deathless fame
  Unto the brown-robed band,
Whose hands released from fetters dread
  Our glorious golden land;
Who gained a bloodless victory
  Against the demon foe,
And lifted high the cross of Faith,
  One hundred years ago!

The sons of Francis journeyed far
  From wave-washed Monterey,
To labor where his saintly name
  Had blessed our shining bay;
And well those holy toilers wrought
  To bid Faith's harvests glow,
And Truth's sweet vineyards ripen fair,
  One hundred years ago!

Nor San Francisco saw alone
  That fondly toiling band,—
Their missions blessed full many a spot
  Within our favored land;
And Peace divine, at their behest,
  Here arched her sacred bow,
From North to South, from East to West,
  One hundred years ago!

And not alone *one* chosen clime
  Obeyed their meek control,—
In earth's remotest realms they wrought
  To tame the savage soul;

From many a land that wondrous band
   Had chased the fiendish foe,
Long ere they won sweet conquest here,
   One hundred years ago!

How blest the children of the wild
   Beneath their gentle sway!
Not theirs the harsh command that bids
   The trembling slave obey;
Not theirs the stern, despotic tone,
   The tyrant's cruel blow:
By *love* the meek Franciscans ruled,
   One hundred years ago!

Ah! well the ransomed savage loved
   The kind paternal care
That with his simple joys could smile,
   And in his sorrows share,—
That could the blest baptism give,
   The Bread of Life bestow,
And cheer the darksome vale of death,
   One hundred years ago!

Within the rude adobé shrine
   What holy calmness dwelt!
How fervent was the savage throng
   That round its altar knelt!
How lowly bowed the dusky brows
   When, through the sunset glow,
Rung out the sweet-toned Angelus,
   One hundred years ago!

Pure, Eden-like simplicity,
　For ever passed away!
For, o'er the missions came, at last,
　A fierce, tyrannic sway;
And sacrilegious hands could dare
　To strike, with savage blow,
The band that brought salvation's boons,
　One hundred years ago!

But we, who know how rich the gift.
　That holy band bestowed
Upon the land where stranger hosts
　Since made their fair abode,—
Ay, we who hail the beams of faith
　In radiant noonday glow,
Will fondly bless the dawn that rose
　One hundred years ago!

O sovereign city of the West
　Enthroned in royal state,
Where bows the Bay his shining crest,
　Within thy Golden Gate!
Thou'lt ne'er forget, though o'er thy heart
　Vast living currents flow,
The herald-steps that trod thy soil,
　One hundred years ago!

And though the lofty steeples rise
　From many a sunlit hill,
Where, through the air, at dusk and dawn,
　The sweet bell-voices thrill,

Thou'lt fondly prize thy mission shrine,
  For, o'er its portal low,
First rose the cross, and rung the chime,
  One hundred years ago!

ADAM AND EVE AFTER THE FALL.

[Subject of Prof. Tojetti's picture.*]

A SCENE suggestive hath the artist traced:
The desert landscape of a dreary waste,
And earth accursed, that nurtures, even now,
The thorny garland for its Maker's brow!
From labor resting, on the lone rocks there—
Ah! dismal change from Eden-arbors fair!—
Sits the sad parent of our sinful race,
Deep desolation written on his face:
Around him strewn his implements of toil,
That win scant harvest from the rugged soil;
And meekly bowing at her consort's side,
The fallen queen, the prey of rebel pride!
Two fated children nestle at their feet:
Hate's guiltless victim, tender-eyed, and sweet,
And his dark slayer, in whose scowling mien
The brand's doom-shadow even now is seen—

---

* A gifted Italian artist, residing in San Francisco, has recently painted this beautiful picture.

E'en the dumb sharers of their sports full well
The symbol story of the future tell.
The pet of Abel is the figure calm
Of tranquil virtue, and the " Victim-Lamb;"
While Cain's companion, wild, uncouth, and rude,
Is virtue's foe, in dark similitude,—
Is that foul throng, that, on the fatal left,
At last shall stand, of ev'ry hope bereft.
Prophetic gaze to wretched Adam shows
The tragic future and its train of woes:
He sees his earth, through ghastly ages, rife
With tumult wild of fierce fraternal strife;
By brothers' hate are hapless Abels slain,
And oft on man descends the curse of Cain:
For, o'er and o'er, the brutal arm of Might
Is lifted still, to slay the victim, Right;
And guiltless blood, until the close of time,
For vengeance pleads against the hand of crime.
O dismal dream! O phantoms that appal!
O dark remembrance of that fatal fall!
Thus the dread knowledge of his offspring's doom
Wraps Adam's soul in deep, remorseful gloom.
In vain for aid he turns his weary eye,
From barren earth to tempest-clouded sky;
No sunny beam, no soothing, starlight ray,
Sheds faintest brightness o'er his desert way,
But from the clouds the angry lightnings dart,
Like serpent-fangs, that pierce his tortured heart.
Then woman's task of tenderness begins:
From dark despair the stricken soul she wins;

Through depths of gloom she bids the mourner's
    eye
Behold the bliss, to faith revealed on high.
On one fair spot, released from darkness drear,
Lo! dawning now, that revelation clear!
There clouds are rent, the tempest's rage hath
    ceased,
The "rose of dawn " is blooming in the East!
Eve's trusting glance, uplifted to the skies,
First finds the rapture of that glad surprise;
Her spouse, awakened from his mournful trance,
Obeys the summons of her upward glance.
O stricken soul! forget thy weary woe,
And hail the glory of the promise-glow,
For golden beams, in dazzling wreaths, entwine
The pictured prophecy of love divine :
A smiling Queen, the sinless Mother mild,
The infant God, the death-destroying Child,—
The Prince of Peace, whose bright, unfading
    reign
Shall dawn at last, to end the night of pain.
O exiled hearts! what pure, ecstatic joy!
What Eden-bliss, that time can ne'er destroy!
O banished monarch! from thy mortal line
A King shall rise, immortal and divine!
O'er the dark sky His kingly splendor streams,
And on the clouds, illumined by its beams,
Hope builds her arch, her bright, celestial bow,—
Her shining bridge, that spans the gulf of woe,
And heaven unites to smiling earth below!

O fallen queen! thy pitying God hath said,
" Thy blessed seed shall crush the serpent's head."
Lo! there the Victor! there the Sov'reign sweet,
That serpent trampling 'neath her sinless feet!
" Up from the desert," lo! she takes her way,
Fair as the moon, and bright as beams of day,
Mightier than armies, in their war array,—
The *one pure rose* that blooms from earthly sod—
Thy daughter fair! the Mother of thy God!

SUBSCRIBERS.

COPIES.

Sisters of Charity, Mission Street, San Francisco - - -	27
Sisters of Charity, St. Elizabeth's Academy, Madison. New Jersey	12
Sisters of Charity, St. Joseph's Academy, Emmettsburg -	10
Sisters of Charity, South San Francisco - - - - -	10
Sisters of Charity, Orphan Asylum, Madison Av., New York -	2
Sisters of Mercy, Grass Valley, California - - - - -	
Mother M. Austin Carroll, New Orleans - - - - -	4
Saint Rose's Academy, Santa Cruz - - - - - -	15
Sister M. Catherine, Petaluma - - - - - - -	2
Sister Frederica, Virginia City - - - - - - -	10
Madame Shannon, Convent of the Sacred Heart. St. Joseph, Mo.	6
Madame Moran, Convent of the Sacred Heart, Grand Coteau	1
Academy of the Sacred Heart, Salem, Oregon - - - -	2
Holy Rosary Academy, Louisville - - - - - -	1
Mother Emily, St. Clara Academy, Grant Co., Wis. - - -	1
Mother Ann Gertrude, Bethlehem Academy, Fairbault, Minn.	1
Christian Brothers, La Salle College, Philadelphia - - -	6
Christian Brothers, Manhattan College, New York - - -	6
Christian Brothers, Rock Hill College, Maryland - - -	5
Christian Brothers, Catholic Protectory, West Chester - -	6
Rev. J. M. J. Heany, St. Rose's, Kentucky - - - - -	5
Rev. J. McCloskey, President Mt. St. Mary's College, Emmettsburg - - - - - - - - - -	10
St. Peter's School, New York - - - - - - -	10
Rev. James Hanigan, Binghamton - - - - - -	1
J. B. Walker, Boston - - - - - - - - -	2
Joseph O'Connor, New York - - - - - - -	1
Rev. T. O'Callaghan, San Francisco - - - - - -	10
Rev. T. F. T. Hudson, Gilroy, California - - - -	5
B. O'Connell, Newark, New Jersey - - - - - -	2
Seminary of our Lady of Angels. Suspension Bridge - -	3
Very Rev. P. Melitus, St. Benedict's College, Newark - -	6
Rev. A. A. Lings, Yonkers - - - - - - -	5
Rev. P. Farrelly, Galena - - - - - - - -	1
Rev. J. M. Finotti, Omaha - - - - - - -	1
John Wensinger, Casey, Ohio - - - - - - -	1
Joseph Wensinger, Casey, Ohio - - - - - -	1
Mrs. John Wensinger, Minneapolis - - - - - -	1

From the Bishop of Savannah.

DEAR SIR:—I congratulate you on the appearance of your new Geography. A cursory glance over it shows me that it is well got up, and I wish it, most cordially, a great success.   ✠ W. H. GROSS,
Bishop of Savannah.

From Rt. Rev. Monsignor Seton.

Many thanks for the Geography which has been carefully examined, and found excellent in every respect.

From the Very Reverend Provincial of the Jesuit Fathers of the Baltimore Province.

DEAR SIR:— * * * I have found the book (Comprehensive Geography, No. 8,) excellent in every way—thoroughly but not obtrusively Catholic, accurate and sufficiently full in statement, admirable in its combination of history with geography—and, whilst I congratulate you on the intrinsic merit, and on the mechanical execution of your work, I must also express the wish that it may be duly appreciated by the Catholic Schools and Colleges of this country.   I remain yours, &c.,
JOS. P. KELLER, S. J.

LOYOLA COLLEGE,
Baltimore, Md., Dec. 14, 1876. }

DEAR SIR:—Your Geographies, Nos. 1 and 2, are a very good introduction to the study, and in their degree deserving of all the praise bestowed on No. 8.
Yours, &c.,
JOS. P. KELLER, S. J.

From Rev. P. Hennessy, St. Patrick's Church, Jersey City.

DEAR SIR:—I have received and carefully examined the Geography which you were so kind as to send me, and am happy to be able to say that I am highly pleased with the book, which I consider superior in every respect to any Geography with which I am acquainted, and which I am only too glad to introduce into our Schools and Academies to the exclusion of all others.

You are indeed to be complimented on the result of your labors in this particular line, since you have produced a Geography which cannot fail to make itself acceptable to the friends of Catholic Education throughout the United States.
Sincerely yours,   P. HENNESSY.

From the Provincial of the Christian Brothers.

MANHATTAN COLLEGE, New York City. }
Sept. 19, 1876. }

Mr. P. O'SHEA : Dear Sir—We have examined your Geographies and have noticed many important improvements. We have introduced them into all our schools in the East.   I am truly yours,   Bro. PAULIAN.

From the Ladies of the Sacred Heart, Manhattanville.

Mr. O'Shea: Dear Sir—We have examined your COMPREHENSIVE GEOGRAPHY, Nos. 2 and 3, and have much pleasure in giving the desired opinion. We consider that these books have been so carefully and judiciously prepared that they cannot fail to meet with a deserved success. Among many advantages peculiar to these books we would mention the brief historical notice accompanying the geography of each country; also, the taste and superior execution of the illustrations. We feel sure that these points will be generally appreciated.

ACADEMY OF THE SACRED HEART.

Manhattanville, Oct. 25, 1876.

From Rev. J. A. Boissonault, St. Johnsbury, Vermont.

DEAR SIR:—Your Geography is an excellent work. It is so admirably disposed, that I have no hesitation to adopt it for my school.

Truly yours,
J. A. BOISSONAULT, *Priest.*

From Rev. D. O'Donovan, Greencastle, Indiana.

I have examined the Comprehensive Geography No. 3, of Mr. O'Shea, and have found it to be an excellent production.

D. O'DONOVAN, Pastor of St. Paul's Church.

WYANDOTTE, KANSAS, March 9, 1877.

Mr. P. O'SHEA, NEW YORK.—Having had for fifteen years charge of schools, I felt always opposed to new books on account of the great expense and unnecessary trouble. If your Governor of New York complained about the perpetual change of books, how much more poor Catholic parents, or the priest who often has to provide from his scanty means one-third of his school with books. But in regard to your "Comprehensive Geography," I make cheerfully an exception. IT IS OF ALL THE BOOKS IN THAT LINE THE VERY BEST I HAVE EVER SEEN, and the very book that ought to be in every Catholic school; and for the sake of our holy Faith that has been trampled out of 18,000,000 ! ! ! in America I wish and pray, that your "Comprehensive Geography" may be introduced in all the Catholic schools of America at the next term, and may our 500,000 pupils increase to a round million before long, is the sincere wish of

Yours, respectfully, A. KUHLS,
Pastor of St. Mary's Church.

From the Sisters of Charity, St. Vincent's School, Whistler, Ala.

Your Geography is the most popular of any series, and we doubt not, as soon as its merits are a little better known, it will be introduced into every Catholic Institution.

EXTRACTS FROM NOTICES OF THE CATHOLIC PRESS.

From the New York Freeman's Journal.

After thus much of generalizations we must come to a special notice of Mr. O'Shea's Geography. It is not possible for us to deny it the merit of great skill, and indomitable industry.

The Letter-Press—that is, the Story of the Different Countries, is told with Intelligent Earnestness, and in a Sense more exactly according to Truth, than in any other Geography published in any Country, or in any Language.

We feel bound to say this, *on the merits*, and acknowledging that we have been no friend to its inception or its execution. The maps, so far as we have examined them, are greatly superior to those of any other school geographies we have seen. They are remarkable, not only for beauty and distinctness, but for typographical correctness—so far as school-maps can possess that character.

We feel bound to recommend the Superiors, and Masters, and Mistresses of Catholic Schools to get specimens of this Geography of Mr. O'Shea, and to judge for themselves. In our judgment, however, this Geography is a very remarkable work, and redounds very greatly to the honor of Mr. O'Shea.

Outside of its school use, we can recommend it as a very valuable book for family and personal entertainment and instruction—more interesting and instructive than all the Catholic novels and tales of fiction that have been published in the year past, or will be in a year to come.

From the American Catholic Quarterly Review.

* * * * We have no hesitation in saying that the whole series is one of rare excellence.

We have examined with special care the portions bearing upon Physical Geography and Historical Geography. It is not an easy task to combine these with topical, statistical, and political geography in one book without making it cumbrous in size, and sacrificing unity a . simplicity of method. Yet the author of the book before us seems to have done this quite successfully. The author has succeeded in imparting, in a manner easily comprehended and without breaking the continuity of topics, a large amount of valuable information in regard to the climates, the causes that determine them, and the vegetable productions of each country.

In separate chapters, in connection with the geography of each country, its history is given, briefly yet clearly. The author has been very successful in this—a work of no small difficulty.

The maps are clear in outline, accurate, and distinct. The illustrations deserve high commendation. They are well chosen as to subject, artistically well conceived, and beautifully executed. They are on the whole, we think, the finest we have seen in any school book.

From the Catholic Review.

"The workmanship on this book is in general admirable. We suspected at first that the copy sent us was an *edition de luxe*, so fine is the paper, so elegant is the type, and press work, and so beautifully colored are the maps. But we learn that the specimens are really inferior to the edition. As to the coloring of the maps, we feel bound to say, that such fine specimens of Xylographic work, as they seem to us to be, have seldom been surpassed in this country. The only Geography with which we can just now compare this portion of the work is from a leading New York school book house, and O'Shea's work in this department is immeasurably superior."

From the Catholic World.

We hope that this series will become popular, as it deserves to be in Catholic Schools.

From the Catholic Record.

This series of Geographies is one of great excellence.

In the arrangement and order of topics, simplicity of the same, clearness and fullness of treatment of them, in accuracy and other desiderata for school books, these Geographies are certainly deserving of high commendations. The maps are clear and distinct and the illustrations excellent, both as regards subjects and execution, some of which would grace an album or collection of prints for a parlor center table.

From the Irish American.

The want of a thoroughly genuine Catholic Geography has long been felt in the schools, but has, in our opinion, been at last supplied by Mr. O'Shea. The maps are models of clearness, and contain, owing to a novel plan of the compiler, more correct topographical information than any book of the kind we have ever seen. The map questions are skillfully arranged, and accompanying them is given all that is interesting and necessary of the physical and historical geography of each country. In short the whole work is one of unusual excellence: in fact it is the best of the kind we have ever seen, and Mr. O'Shea may well feel proud of the result of his labors.

From the Catholic Standard.

One of its great merits is its historical accounts of the countries and places which it describes. These have been prepared with excellent judgment. They are clear, simple in style, concise in language, sufficiently full of details to be interesting to the pupil, yet not so full as to weary his attention or overburden his memory.

These historical accounts, too, are written in a Catholic spirit, so that the pupil receives a correct and true impression from the study of them of the connection of the Catholic religion with the advance of mankind in government, art, science, literature, commerce and all that we comprehend in the word civilization.

The "Comprehensive Geography" has been well named "Comprehensive." It certainly comprehends an immense amount of statistical, physical, political and historical information, so well arranged that it can be acquired by any pupil of average industry and intelligence.

LIBERAL TERMS MADE FOR INTRODUCTION.

P. O'SHEA, Publisher,

37 BARCLAY STREET, NEW YORK.